PRAISE FOR BRENT ANTONSON

When travel writer Paul Theroux published his classic *The Great Railway Bazaar* back in 1975 to great acclaim, he started a resurgence of travel literature and especially train travel books. Brent Antonson continues Paul Theroux's tradition but with a comic twist: Can you enjoy five long train rides around the planet with your father and brother? The result is an easily read memoir with a sense of humor that Theroux himself never possessed. Well worth reading both for train aficionados and lovers of travel literature.

— MICHAEL MCCARTHY, AUTHOR OF *THE SNOW LEOPARD RETURNS: TRACKING PETER MATTHIESSEN TO CRYSTAL MOUNTAIN AND BEYOND*

TIES THAT BIND
CIRCUMNAVIGATING THE NORTHERN HEMISPHERE BY TRAIN

BRENT ANTONSON

PROUDLY PUBLISHED BY:

planksip®

Publisher: 0722401 BC Ltd dba. planksip® Publishing

Victoria, BC Canada

www.planksip.org

Library and Archives Canada Cataloguing in Publication

Versions

Hardcover: 978-1-77443-072-9

Electronic: 978-1-77443-071-2

Paperback: 978-1-77443-070-5

Cover

Gare Saint-Lazare, oil on canvas (1877) by Claude Monet. Design in collaboration with planksip®.

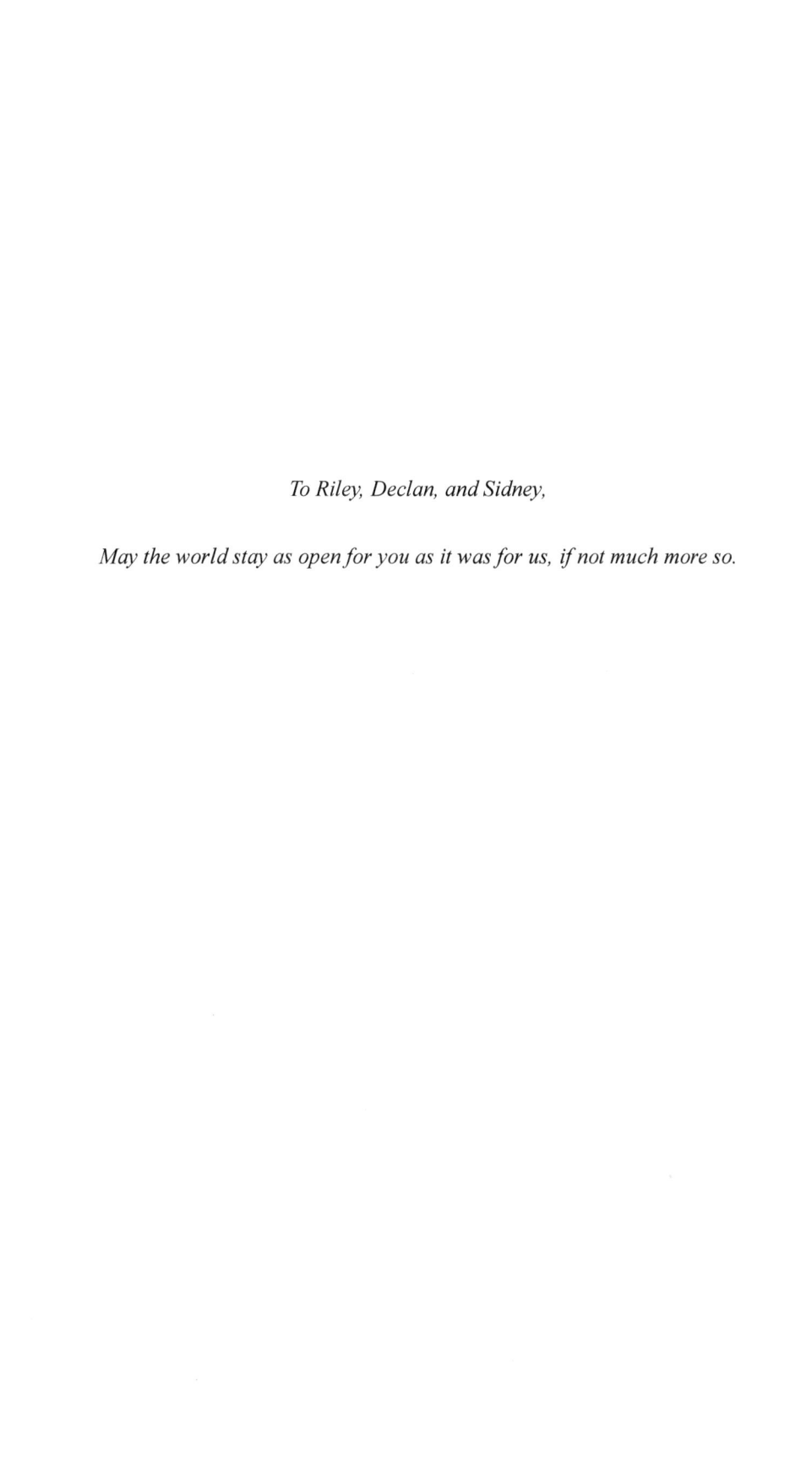

To Riley, Declan, and Sidney,

May the world stay as open for you as it was for us, if not much more so.

ALSO BY BRENT ANTONSON

OF RUSSIA: A YEAR INSIDE

OF RUSSIA
A YEAR INSIDE

BRENT ANTONSON

Author of *Ties That Bind;*
Circumnavigating the Northern Hemisphere by Train

REVISED EDITION WITH NEW AFTERWORD FROM THE AUTHOR

CONTENTS

Train Routes and Main Cities

Two brothers and their father took five train trips over a dozen years, riding on 16 trains in 13 countries, eventually circumnavigating the Northern Hemisphere's land mass by train. The trips as recounted by the author include:

- Moscow-Ulaan Bataar-Beijing
- Halifax-Toronto-Vancouver
- New York-Chicago-San Francisco
- Beijing-Pyongyang-Beijing
- Moscow-Minsk-Warsaw-Berlin-Paris-London

And so it began: Brent (author), Sean, and their father Rick.

PROLOGUE

You're about to ride along on train travels over 12 years, on 16 trains in 13 countries—as diverse as North Korea, Belarus and the United States of America. A father and his two sons took five railway trips over a dozen years and went around the world. They travelled on renowned and unknown railroads, including PKP Polskie Linie, Amtrak, and Russian Railways. They rode trains as varied as the Trans-Mongolian, the Ocean Limited and Ukraine's Д67. They ventured into unexpected and underappreciated lands, each with one eye on the horizon and the other looking over their shoulder. They navigated family woes and travel woes.

I am one of the sons. When we first departed, I had no idea how different I would be–indeed all three of us would be–after 15,000 miles on long-haul trains. As you climb aboard the first of those trains with my 27-year-old storyteller-self, here's a note from my journal at the time:

> *The Trans-Siberian's restaurant car was empty and the steam heat inescapable, providing a stark contrast to the snow-bound villages alongside the railway tracks. Van Halen screamed philosophy through my headset: "I went out, I bought some brand new shoes/Now I walk like someone else." I lit a cigarette. Then another. They burned fitfully in the ashtray aboard one of the world's most charming–if somewhat dilapidated–train sets.*

Smoking was vital to me but becoming a sickening task. Gasping for breath, I swore I would quit upon returning home. I hadn't used my tongue in weeks for anything but talking. Flavor was absent from every bite of food I'd taken–even the garlic borscht the babushkas prepared for lunch that day in a railway coach stuffed with men of a dozen nationalities and as many work trades, crime being among of them. Smoking masked my sense of smell; using deodorant had become my way of telling others I cared about them. With no showers on the Russian train and only a small basin of rust-tinted water with which to work, my personal grooming suffered setbacks. My baseball cap could not control a head of blazing hair. I'd seen myself in a reflection earlier that morning and wouldn't have trusted me with the time of day. Every now and then when I looked in a mirror, some-body else looked back. I bet he missed his senses, too.

That the final words about our five train journeys would be scrawled in my 39-year-old's journal a dozen years later, or that the storytelling of our interlinked trips would be completed in my 54-year-old's penmanship, was, at the time, unimaginable. As striking was that memories of Russia and my earliest dreams of riding *The Trans-Siberian* were rooted in childhood.

It started when...I was five years old the first time I went to Russia. It was 1974 and Mom and Dad won a trip to anywhere in the world. They chose Air Canada's farthest destination from our home in Vancouver, British Columbia. (On that flight I started collecting unused barf bags with airline logos. Today I have such a souvenir from 57 different airlines; not everything about me matured as I aged.) My role on that trip was to act as diversionary tactic whenever Mom and Dad were approached by anyone checking their papers were in order—the police, KGB, hotel staff, doorman, or anyone who could send people to places where people wouldn't live by choice. Think Siberia. My cuteness was to neutralize anyone with authority. I would wave my hand and say, "Mena zavoot Brent!" It worked every time.

While I was being dragged past the bottoms of portrait frames in Leningrad's Hermitage museum, my father struck up a life-shaping conversation with two British men who had just travelled *The Trans-Siberian Railway* from Peking, as Beijing was then known, to Moscow. Dad envisioned crossing the Soviet Union behind a chugging locomotive on the world's longest railway. He loved steam trains and *The Trans-Siberian* was the trophy of them all. He shared his hopes with the men and was told, "You'd be a fool not to do it once in your life. You'd be a bloody fool to do it twice." Dad imparted his love of trains, and his willingness to be a 'bloody fool,' to his sons.

Our grandfather's motto was "When your family doesn't have much money, you can either 'do' or you can 'have'." Our family forfeited "having" for "doing," and *doing* was travelling. Soon enough, my brother Sean–four years my junior–was old enough to cry through flights, upending toiletry bags and generally do whatever I dared him to do. We went to the Rockies, Western USA, the Caribbean and Europe. Luckily for Sean, and me our parents ascribed to a teacher-friend's advice: "Never let school interfere with your child's education." So Sean and I missed almost as much school as the kids who got mono.

Unluckily for us, Mom and Dad separated just as Sean and I entered young adulthood. In a close-knit family, Dad became the loose thread. Our parents retained a divorce-compatible friendship but the upshot was that Dad lost his veto power over Sean and me. We put him and fatherhood on probation. Dad's wisdom was officially suspect on all things. His honesty was in question. He had to earn back our trust, and travel would provide him the means.

During two European trips as brothers in our early 20s, Sean and I bonded. Temperaments aligned for a time, and then diverged. It came down to his calmness versus my irritability, his money savvy versus my willingness to live on the thin edge of nothing. Then, in 1994 at the age of 25, I found myself alone in Europe. The route to there broke my compass. It began when I fell in love. I did what any self-respecting, beta-male does when feeling raw sensations of wanderlust. I quit my job in Vancouver and took the object of my young love to Wyoming, hoping to build our dream cabin in the hills—admittedly, more my escape than hers. My penchant for space and irresponsibility flashed in contrast to her vision of stability. Not surprisingly, the endeavor failed. I did a 47-degree compass adjustment and ended up living on my own in the former Russian republic of Estonia, driving a Russian Orthodox Church bus by day and drinking cheap Russian beer by night— by the liter.

It had been three years since Estonia's independence and the Soviet smell was freshly stale. That stay, along with my childhood experience in the Soviet Union, nudged me toward their language and I became passably fluent in Russian–enough to get me into trouble but not always enough to get me out of it. A romantic-depressive, I fell off the romantic edge into a rut that flowed with substandard beer. Estonia reinforced my own quandaries because it, too, did not know where it was going. We were both in subtle chaos.

In 1997, Sean, Dad, and I tossed ourselves into a travel stew with all the ingredients for unpredictable incidents that–though we didn't see it at the time–would unfold over a dozen years. Take a huge dose of travel adventures, dollops of sarcasm, and a pinch of silliness. Season with respect. Stir vigorously and simmer for 12 years.

15,000 railway mileposts, and nearly as many personal ones would measure our journeys. It started with a tourism conference that my father attended every year. Beijing was set to host the 1997 event. Give me credit for suggesting, "Let's take *The Trans-Siberian Railway* from Moscow, through Mongolia and into China, arriving in time for the conference," The three of us–otherwise alone in our worlds–slammed together for the escapade.

I was a slender 27-year-old whose tousled-hair James Dean look came from my mother's genes (an advantage over Dad's), along with inheriting her spontaneity. My impatience and impudence were all my own doing. Sean was 23, with that age's broadening of shoulders and chest. A writer, looking not unlike the intrepid Tintin character and with alert eyes tucked behind John Lennon glasses, he was the intelligence we needed along, his having been gifted mom's nonchalance that each day would be a good one. It was the year Sean had his first short story published, in an anthology. Plus Dad, 47, had a couple inches of height on both of us. Cresting six feet, he had career-hazard chubbiness and moved like a lynx in a leg clamp. (The math is correct; he'd been 20 when I was born.)

Could I endure nine days on trains with them? Could they endure those nights with me? Could we bring ourselves to protect the pack? Could we embrace this journey of journeys, suspend our pre-judgments and pretend we were compatible– all for a shared ride on *the* train of trains?

One question overrode the others: would our Dad be a caricature "dad"? If so, we'd leave him in Omsk with a map of Tomsk. Anticipating such difficulties, Sean and I laid down the rules to him: respect of our personal zones; unrestricted freedom to utter pejoratives that Dad couldn't make us take back; and acceptance of frictions that he would have to know were purely "ours" – injustices we felt without needing Dad to chime in with "I once felt the same way but matured." We stipulated it was "not on" for Dad to act as the trip's authority figure. If he tried to, we'd demand turns being the elder; one day it would be Dad as dad; next would be Sean as dad 2.0, then my turn. The mere threat of this tamed Dad's predispositions.

On another front, I was pushing my affair with alcohol toward a landscape of crevasses, but I was immune to criticism, examples–and any truth-based epiphanies.

We hashed through these challenges at Neighbors Restaurant, a character-riddled establishment in our hometown. In the pre-trip era, the three of us met regularly for lasagna and a few glasses of wine with the restaurant's owner, George, a Greek mariner of worldly euphemisms. One of his prophecies would prove most true. After listening to our planned route across Siberia, Mongolia and China, George cocked his head, smirked as much as smiled, and claimed it was the Greeks not Confucius who first observed, "Those who return from a journey are not the same as those who left." In response we threw impossibilities, dangers, and rivalries across the table just to clutter it and our lives. George, listening to our consternation, looked into each set of eyes, one person at a time, then said, "Family. Never take it for granted. You're fortunate to share dreams." What he said next came to us this way: "Family. Trains. Tracks. The ties that bind." So it was, we travelled with love and some misgivings.

With George as our witness, we shook hands on a one-off train trip of 4,753 miles (7,621 kilometers): from Moscow to Lake Baikal where we'd take another train into Mongolia, and, eventually, catch a train to Beijing. Our travel plans were loose, our sense of direction even looser and our attention to detail all but lost. This wasn't the Internet age. Our travel agent had an elderly fax machine. Confirmations for travel details arrived at my home after we'd departed on a plane.

This one trip led to another, and that to a third, eventually unfolding into five expeditions. Unplanned, we circumnavigated the Northern Hemisphere's landmass by train, in a manner of speaking: 14,924 miles (24,018 kilometers). By that time, twelve years later, we would not be the same three men who left George at Neighbor's Restaurant on the eve of our first journey.

FIRST JOURNEY ~ Moscow-Ulaan Bataar-Beijing
THE TRANS-SIBERIAN RAILWAY

T he signature starting point of our train journey across Russia, Mongolia and China would be at Moscow's Yaroslavl Station in a few days time. Getting there, however, took circuitous routes for Dad, Sean, and me. It began at London's massive airport.

"Don't leave luggage unattended or we'll blow it up" announcements ricocheted off the high ceilings of Heathrow's Terminal 3 that April afternoon. Sean and I were there to rendezvous with Dad, who was flying in from a business trip in Thailand. The Arrivals doorway split open and glassy-eyed passengers bled into the foyer, scrutinized by the waiting crowds. Scruffy-looking Sean and a not-bathed me had arrived from Belgium that morning and were reliving our previous week's seduction by the German Autobahn's unlimited speed. Their roads were powerful, the drivers intelligent. We'd hit 120 miles (200 kilometers) per hour in a five-speed bin of tin, built for recycling or funerals, narrowly avoiding collisions. Now we were parked and antsy waiting for our travel partner.

The doors pulled back and there stood Dad. Fresh, clean-shaven and smartly dressed in a vest–no eyes-at-half-mast hangover and nowhere near the point where one's underwear feels like a tight corner on the Formula One circuit, as did mine. Sean and I were bearded, vagrant-scented and steaming sweat. The three of us traded savage hugs and raised proposals about where to spend the night, all before the doors closed behind Dad.

"If you hug me any longer," I told him, "I'll have to charge you my hourly rate."

Dad broke away and asked where a washroom was. Sean said the nearest bathroom was in an expensive steak restaurant hoping Dad might spring a meal for his hungry lads. Dad took the bait. Relieved of the pressures of the long flight, a few minutes later he was pulling out a toner-scorched fax showing our itinerary–an updated that list I hadn't been finalized until the day before.

"Moscow–two nights," he skimmed. "On the train for four nights, then stop in Irkutsk two nights, then on a different train to Mongolia, three nights in the capital Ulaan Baatar, another night on the train across the Gobi Desert, and then through the back end of China, staying for a week."

We bumped fists before it was popular.

A taxi brought us to a London hotel I'd overheard someone mention in the restaurant, and we gambled they'd have rooms. Dad smiled at the decent rate and said he'd cover it. Dad's suite was three stairways up from the storage room set aside for Sean and me. We found a 24-hour Tesco and bought basic food for our excursion should we face mystery meat on the train–whether domesticated, rural payment for a favor, strays, or track-kill. We packed a smorgasbord of fresh fruit, water, soups, and cheeses—anything we'd been warned would not be found "on the other side" in the folklore of Russian cuisine—into a duffle bag, creating our seventh pack.

The next morning our Aeroflot crept down the taxiway. The engines' twin fury chucked us skyward, with the security of Western soil falling away.

Dad opened his writing scribbler and faded into unreachable mode. Sean was replacing his Walkman batteries, which kept popping out and rolling away from him. I walked to the rear of the plane and planted myself in a fog of smoking Russians. Aleksey, on my right, introduced himself as an oil industry executive living in Siberia. I detailed our travel plans, which included Irkutsk.

He smiled with pride. "The Paris of Siberia."

I hadn't expected such a slogan.

"It earned that reputation at the turn of the century, when it was the administrative center of Siberia and home of the gold rush. It is beautiful place," he said, his voice trailing off.

"Beautiful in a Parisian sense, or a Russian one?" I asked.

"A personal one."

Hours later the plane's landing gear grumbled out. I leaned over the laps of the passengers seated between the window and me and scoured the view. The sky was an unjustly Russian grey; dark clouds spit off in the airliner's wake. Rain dribbled down the windows, blurring the discolored hangars and limp windsocks of Moscow's Sheremetyevo airport.

The aircraft vacated with a diuretic swiftness that carried us into a cavernous area for customs inspection, captive with little personal space. Anticipation kept us eager and content. Then sweat dripped off our faces. We had dressed for cold Arctic fronts. This was not one of them. I removed my jacket as we triumphantly took a step forward. An hour later, and not much further ahead, our sense of antici-pation was draining away. "Line-ups are a national pastime in Russia," Aleksey said, appearing over my shoulder. "And you're not even *in* the country yet. Do you know we have line-ups for line-ups?"

"I can only move and sit," I said. "I don't do standing."

"I think we are queuing like the British, not Russians," Dad said after yet another man cut in front of us.

"I think I'm right," Sean said as he put his foot in front of a Russian and segued the three of us forward.

Dad asked whether we'd gotten all our medical shots.

"I upgraded at the clinic," I said. "I could swim in Third World hospital waste."

Those in the crowd who understood English took a step back.

"I'm tired of pretending I'm awake," I said.

"Just think of the freedom beyond the kiosks," Sean said.

Hours later we were the last three people to reach the only open inspection booth. Abiding by Western etiquette wasn't going to work with Russian conduct.

An official stamped our visas and we found our bags circling the carousel alone. We labored past happy hour at the security desk to be greeted by a deter-mined woman in a unisex skirt: "I am Plocha, your Intourist hostess." She folded up a placard marked "Antonson," threw it in a bin and motioned for us to follow her. She was gone with a velocity suggesting she had other plans that may not involve us.

Dad was quick to exchange our home currency for a fistful of heavily devalued rubles. That hour the exchange rate was 5,700 rubles to the American dollar. Less than ten years earlier, you could have been a member of the bourgeoisie flashing bills of that caliber–but now it was a month's wages. With a brush of her hand, Plocha escorted us to the cold drizzle of a taxi zone and disappeared.

An aged taxi driver, the kind of old you hate to see lifting your luggage, hoisted all seven bags into the trunk of his sorely aged Mercedes. The trunk refused the seventh bag so the old man attacked it, slamming it with his buttocks first.

"There go the crackers," Sean sighed.

The highway and roadsides slumbered beneath the residue of winter sandings. Fat slabs of concrete apartment blocks squatted among acres of barren land. Pockets of hardened snow lay about with the same dim "blah." Rows of trees, planted in ruler-edged lines, were black and leafless. The sky was the texture of dirty bath water.

Groups of residential blocks with views of other residential blocks, rolled by my window's muddy residue. Entering Moscow, we passed a majestic Soviet "high-rise," steepled like a wedding cake. The driver's bony finger trailed it while he muttered in Russian, "This is one of the 'seven sisters' of architectural marvels —Vysotki skyscrapers constructed under Stalin's orders to commemorate the Soviet Union's victory over Nazi Germany." He didn't mention Stalin's tall-building envy began after his visit to New York.

Locals bundled in furs and hid behind scarves against Moscow's late-winter chill. Many wore the traditional fur hat with earflaps. We felt on safari, watching the *Homo Sovieticus* in their habitat. Buildings ate the sidewalks' width, making drivers and pedestrians appear insignificant and shadowed. Some people hurried, walking like scissors. They maneuvered around one another, stepping off cracked sidewalks then dodging a slushy puddle. There were no lines, no lanes and no discernible method of movement for the traffic madness. Tails of wet snow arched from the backs of vehicles as they deviated around potholes. Feeble mopeds fought to wend their way. Trolley busses, slow behemoths, forced other vehicles to weave into oncoming traffic. Horns shrilled, engines whined, and bald rubber screeched. We pulled into the Hotel Belgrade driveway, carrying Plocha's vouchers for our three nights' accommodations. We counted the bags off, our attempt at security, to ensure that our 300 pounds of possessions remained our own.

"I'm two."

"I'm three."

"Two."

"Seven, then," said Dad as though we needed his mathematical prowess.

There were no computers in sight at the check-in counter. Robotic clerks armed with pencils and rulers were copying out the particulars of our stay in one ledger book after another. Passports were removed from our possession for the duration of our stay. They gave us directions to the few amenities that survived since the hotel's brochure had been printed. Our signatures graced the final column of a ledger book fat enough to possibly record the number of soaps unused during Fidel Castro's last visit.

The clerk announced, "You have two rooms." Dad thought Sean and I were chain-smoking, boisterous hooligans with a propensity for loud music, slam dancing, prank phone calls, tagging gang signs, beer pong, and staying up so late it was early. Thus we should have a room to ourselves. Dad–docile, forgiving and pragmatic, jealous of his privacy and quiet–wanted none of our festivities and took the other.

The small elevator, with the humming palpitations of a washing machine's spin cycle, rose to the 13th floor—Soviet atheism, Russian Orthodox witch-burners, and a general superstitious population notwithstanding. The doors opened to a large-bosomed floor attendant who looked like she was still pissed off that no one had asked her to the Soviet prom. She spoke quickly and made indecipherable gestures. Intimidated, we chose not to ask about ice buckets and fire exits. She took our key cards and threw open the adjacent doors.

"*Spacibo*," I intoned, handing her a maple-leaf pin and receiving a semi-satisfied grin in return. There was a flirting in her eyes so I made my gaze say, "That's not going to happen." Or at least certainly not in daylight.

Anxious as we were to board our train, we wanted first to trudge around Moscow for a day. We quickly returned to the lobby to cash travellers' checks with a young woman who stood behind a barred enclosure. It was probably her youthful beauty that kept her out of the union of "floor lady" babushkas. For now. She counted and recounted our rubles, fanned them for our approval and then pushed three stacks of colorful rubles through the grill with the skill of a blackjack dealer who counts her own cards. Russians speak fluently with their eyes so it took just one prolonged look to confirm the transaction.

Outside to our left, Smolenskaya Avenue rose towards an intersection, cold-showering us in frigid gusts of wind. To our right, the road sloped several blocks to the Moskva River and an eight-lane suicide crosswalk. To stay warm we needed to keep moving. The Borodinsky Bridge, with its evening traffic of Ladas and Volgas, was an option. The river made wind-driven waves on the river's stone bank. The sidewalk ended without warning. We did short full-torso turns, crossed the road, then that sidewalk fell away.

"Hey, this is it," Sean announced. "This is the Arbat."

The pedestrian thoroughfare was a maze of souvenir stands, organ grinders, small arms dealers, face painting, and jugglers, and men with menu boards. Sean and I lit cigarettes. Dad, who on principle didn't like our smoking, took to a pipe. Though hypocritical and often wrong in his theories about the lives of others, and each of our personal evolutions, he admitted he was learning from us–albeit at a pace that would take a lifetime. Under the flashing bulbs of bars and restaurants, Dad tugged a bowlful of tobacco from his pouch, lit his pipe and wandered along, free of concern.

The tobacco's sherry-tinged cloud wafted on the breeze. A memory of my childhood arose, of winter nights learning chess in our den at home–the room filled with a thousand books and the fugues of Bach. Dad, armed with a snifter of warm brandy, would surrender his pen, turn his chair towards my pajama'd body and say, "Rook to F-4, and don't even think of pushing my buttons with that bishop or I'll drop you into insolvency, which means no allowance." Given that style of rearing, how did I get bent on smoking cheap tobacco, guzzling third-rate beer, and always wanting to be somewhere else than where I was?

Eastern European countries provide large stores for one item and kiosks for everything else. One may find a store that carries a thousand pairs of size-eight leather shoes and, next door, a counter displaying surgical tools, used gauze, tangled necklaces, and a litter of Shih Tzus. Approaching a department store, we anticipated seeing *real* Russian products–calendars, nesting dolls, and arc welders. We spread out and attempted purchases. We each pointed across a counter (bottle, artifact, sandwich): "That one, please" and, in return, were handed a slip of paper. "It shows the price," the clerk told Sean, or so it sounded. Sean took it to the end of the longest queue to await a confrontation with the cashier. When the payment had been slid into the register, she gave him a receipt and a twitch indicating that the transaction was over. Sean returned to the line-up in front of the original clerk to show his proof of purchase. All this queue-causing hassle was to buy a bottle of water–a process that had to be repeated to get a pencil and, separately again, a writing pad.

While perusing pocket watches (time being the failed end of Russian technology), I heard a commotion in the next aisle. A stern *don't-fuckski-with-me* voice was saying in Russian, "No smoking immigrant." I rounded the counter. Dad stood there, crowned with a wreath of pipe smoke, staring blankly at the two babushkas yelling "*Nye Koureet!*" at him. He could make nothing of their charades. He just pulled on his pipe and coolly observed them. Other shoppers appeared at the ends of the aisle.

"Dad," I yelled. "You can't smoke in here."

My thought-arrow struck his normally large mental target, somehow slimmed in the moment. He jammed his fist, still holding the pipe, into his pocket. I was embarrassed for my family and country. "Germans," I yelled to the assembled gawkers and hustled Dad into the canned-goods aisle. Smoke rose from his pocket. "We're Germans. We're on earth just to piss you off."

Morning arrived with jet lag on its breath. A fist thumped the solid door of our hotel room. Roused, I put on one shoe and groped to the bathroom as Dad's knocking persisted. I woke Sean, showered and suited up for whatever the elements could heave at me. We retraced our steps to the charm and merriment of Arbat proper–the pedestrian corridor–until we found a Cyrillic McDonald's sign hanging from a building of eastern European character.

In this cobbled street, we could hear far-off church bells belt out a melody of faith. For seven decades, Sunday after Sunday, year after year, Russians had to answer the call of God in silent prayer for fear of being punished for believing in their preferred deity that would save one from the wrath of an imposed deity, the Politburo.

Low buildings guided our stroll through gentle bends and turns. Kiosks were being set up, accompanied by huffed profanities from within. In the Russian sense of the word, kiosks are shopping centers confined to the space of a large phone booth. At one, a clerk balanced on crates of illegally pirated music tapes, seated like a prisoner behind a breadbox-sized window–the only means of contact with the outside world. It can take a while to look through the sun-faded inventory, for any one kiosk can be the factory outlet for computer software, underwear, newspapers, license plates, key chains, squirt guns, nail clippers, a toothy comb collection, aquarium filters, vodka, broken watches, spoons, jewelry, running shoes, grotesque ceramic figurines, and the left taillight from a Ford F150 pickup. These kiosks are a joy because you never know what you'll find and might still not know after you purchase it.

The Arbat ended when grey buildings pulled back like stage curtains to reveal the crenulated walls of the Kremlin. A fortress of unimaginable strength stood before us.

The Kremlin is a triangular fortress dating to the 12th Century and is the point from which all of Moscow radiates. It is also the domain of the former Soviet government and the stage on which the tyrants Vladimir Lenin, Ivan the Terrible and Josef Stalin played their parts in the theater of the past. The Kremlin is the voltage of Russia. Standing at the Manezhnaya pedestrian crossing, Dad, Sean, and I stared at the Kremlin's intimidating walls. High guard towers rose against the sky as if a brick god had built a brick heaven. Arsenal turrets interrupted the solid red wall, which rippled and bowed over two miles around 68 acres that–at times– encompassed the power center for much of the world and held aspirations to do so again. At the ticket wicket of the Kutafya tower, we followed the wide ramp under Trinity Gate.

Inside the Kremlin, among buildings 800 years old, we fell quiet. History stood still. These were palaces from trenches in time, churches and armories cloaked in secrecy. We rested near Cathedral Square. Golden, onion-shaped domes topped with crosses rose above us, survivors of a time without God. Soviet-era state buildings faded to match the yellow of vitamin-enriched urine, harmonized with the dead grass and leafless trees. The trees stood strong and stern, fronted by guards posted far apart from one another, acting as a public guidance system.

Mom was of frequent reference in our conversations, particularly when we walked where she and Dad, with me as a smiling prop, were captured in photographs of the Kremlin. I wondered: if she and Dad were still living together, would four of us be travelling on the *Trans-Siberian* train?

ｉｉｉｉｉｉｉｉｉｉｉｉｉ

St. Basil's Cathedral is Russia's Eiffel Tower, Taj Mahal and Statue of Liberty all in one. Officially recognized as the Cathedral of Vasily the Blessed–or, alternatively, as the Cathedral of the Intercession of the Virgin by the Moat–St. Basil's is *the* postcard from Russia. Erected in the 16th Century as a prototype for Russian churches, St. Basil's rises with multi-colored domes swirling from stonework towers. It looks edible. The fairytale design was the work of a genius instructed by Ivan the Terrible to create a monument commemorating victory in the feudal Zagon state. Legend has it that when the cathedral was completed, Ivan was so taken by its splendor that he asked the architect if he would be able to duplicate such a creation. The response was "Yes." Ivan had the designer's eyeballs gouged to prevent him from replicating the feat. That may help explain the construction of all the cold, grey buildings that proliferated across the republics afterward.

Inside St. Basil's, all three of us passed off our driver's licenses as student cards, setting a habit I would adopt for life. Given the large number of people shuffling about, the basilica was eerily quiet. The walls could echo your thoughts. Damp breath projected my inner self outward. The prevalence of icons, bloodied Christs hanging agonized on crosses, paintings of a cloaked Mary flat and haloed, and frescoes of saints was overpowering–and far from representing the God that my grandfather thought saved him parking spots.

A long queue wove out from a room and into the common area but we filed out in silence, emerging to find Red Square alive with sightseers wandering under a broken sky. Lenin's tomb, still an object of pilgrimage for Russians, was closed. I'd read that a team of embalmers topped up Lenin's fluids and changed his boxers every year. This seemed to be that occasion. The tomb is morbidly odd and sits before the Kremlin wall where Lenin made speeches. His mausoleum is fine Russian architecture. Built from dark red granite and black laborite, it is smug and silent, insensitive and durable. I followed the bright red zigzag, expecting to see a McXpress or a Subway or a subway station, but instead found a revolution's necropolis. Buried in two mass graves, there lay 300 soldiers. Tombstones of Soviet leaders and heroes rose beyond them. Immured in the Kremlin wall were numerous urns containing the remains of prominent scientists, war veterans and the likes of Gorky, Lenin's wife, Nadezhda Krupskaya, and Josef Stalin. I tried hard to be moved by the tomb yet found it devoid of sentiment, just like the Soviets who lay there.

To the right of the square was the GUM department store, the most recent development in the square, having been started in the 1890s. The complex was intended as an experience for the Russian elite. Nearly 200 elegant shops graced the mall's bright marble corridor. Iron catwalks traversed planters and sculptured fountains, as decorative placards and banners praised the 850th year of Moscow's founding. The prices of the goods suggested that entire residential blocks of citizens could not afford to fart in these stores. This was a tourist's Rodeo Drive with a Marxist-Leninist stained-glass ceiling.

When my parents brought me to the USSR in 1974, we'd been put up in Moscow's Hotel Metropol, one of Russia's finest hotels. My memories include vomiting after a good pull on a water fountain and a smiley-faced woman feeding me porridge.

Now, 22 years later, as Dad, Sean, and I stood outside the Metropol, I again felt queasy. Dad splayed his arms and announced he would treat us to Chicken Kiev to commemorate a meal he, mom and I had shared there long ago. I was quick to note that since Chernobyl's reactor number four forced an unprecedented tonnage of "really, really bad shit" into the air, Chicken Kiev had taken on a new meaning. It had a half-life.

The hotel was still a five-star establishment. We sat in high-backed chairs positioned around a solid oak counter the size of a snooker table. A five-star waiter, complete with a five-star smile, placed a triplet of beers, one per 300-thread-count doily, in front of us.

"Nine bucks American a beer? Nine bucks," Sean murmured.

"Yeah…," Dad grunted.

"There's a kiosk outside selling a bottle of beer for 40 cents," I noted.

"Well," Dad replied, getting testy, "enjoy this one like it was your last."

Until now, "Critical Dad" had been silent. Perhaps being here took him back to a place and time long ago when most of his life was ahead of him unlike now when it was possibly behind him, and that might have been a factor.

After our Chicken Kiev was devoured, Sean and Dad wrote postcards as they sipped more tall pints. They acclimatized. I did not. The dining room overflowed with elegance behind French doors; its interior was checker-boarded with white cloths draped across tables, cloth napkins in pewter rings and cutlery hierarchies. No puddles ringing the glasses of water, and no washroom key chained to something so heavy that you'd be sure to return it. I didn't know this five-star world, didn't speak the five-star dialect, and didn't look the five-star type. And I didn't feel like pretending I did. With this feeling of inferiority rapidly developing into a complex, I took a final two-dollar chug of my beer. I strolled off alone past the lobby's car-sized chandeliers and hotel staff who–for a price–would tuck you in and read you passages of Turgenev. I needed to get back to the beat-up world where I belonged.

As if on cue, a battered Lada Niva 4x4 mounted the curb in front of me and died at my feet. The driver, a surly bearded man, got out and slammed the door. He cursed the vehicle as though it had left him for another full-bellied man. He bounced his fist hard off the hood, repeatedly yelling a Russian phrase, which roughly goes *"You stupid bitch. Aaah. Faltering to old age. Huh! I scorn you for this lack of courage. Huh! Start! Start you stupid bitch!"*

Summoned by the force of Russian inclusion, smoky old men emerged from nearby shops to engage in screaming. Fingers pointed, hands raised. "Hey, hey! What are you going to do, hit me?" and "How could you not check the oil?" One man stood behind them, nipping from a flask, appearing concerned. Soon, greasy fingers probed at the vehicle's heart. Parts were withdrawn and balanced on the curb. A few of them made it back beneath the hood. The driver got in and kicked the engine over. It belched blue donuts of exhaust. The Niva honked its way back into traffic.

When Dad and Sean arrived outside an hour later, we plodded towards "the House of the Government of the Russian Federation." Curiously to Westerners, it is known in Russia as "the White House." In 1991, it was here that the hardline old guard came to take a stand against the Soviet leader, Mikhail Gorbachev. Gorbachev had opened the Soviet Pandora's box by embracing two prerogatives that shook the core of Soviet political values. *Glasnost* and *perestroika*–economic/political restructuring and openness, respectively–were boundless and limitless. The Soviet Union was bankrupt. Gorbachev was held hostage at his summer home and began changing the letterhead. Russian president Boris Yeltsin welcomed a weakened USSR as it would give his country more power within the Soviet federation. In a striking photo-op, he climbed onto a tank and defiantly urged patriotic Russians to surround the White House and block the approach of rebellious Soviet troops. Yeltsin even managed to sway the troops: when their generals ordered them to attack, they refused. Public opinion veered across the threshold of democracy. Gorbachev resigned. Yeltsin was installed in the Kremlin and immediately banned the Communist Party.

Two years later, with a new parliament of Russian nationalists festering Communist support, Yeltsin disbanded it. He was one-man democracy in action. The power structure of the Kremlin (aka Yeltsin) versus Russia's elected White House went head to head. Yeltsin ordered the White House encircled by the very troops he'd converted just 24 months prior. He demanded the occupants to leave. Pro-parliament demonstrators clashed with the military. Riots left 62 dead. The next day, tanks and machine guns attacked the White House and troops were sent inside to ferret out dissidents. Seventy more people lost their lives as a result.

Those decisive days in history brought me, Dad and Sean to the black iron gates now in front of us. The White House had been built in the 1970s; as a result, architecturally, this House of Soviets was sterile, blanched and simply "there." I mustered up a throaty "Hmm." I could imagine the staff gathered at the water cooler, discussing how much they loathed their day. We pulled ourselves along the gates to the back, where we happened upon old wooden crosses and fresh flowers propped in a circle of dirty trees–colorful tributes to those who helped change the grey world.

The front of the edifice was a children's park, muddy enough to conceal small muddy children. Sinkholes ate at my heels. The only refuge was a pinnacle of turf that slid into a hill of more mud. Were it not for the bloody encounters and its political importance, this building was merely another box on the skyline.

Across the Kalinin Bridge, opposite the White House gates, sat another Gothicmotivated 'high-rise," the Ukraine Hotel. I settled on the steps and lit an American cigarette while Dad and Sean carried on inside. As I scouted the building's rim for gargoyles and jumpers, a queue of taxis huddled up to me–like pigeons landing at the foot of someone on a park bench, hoping for crumbs. Sean came out and said, "The hotel is like a museum without art."

A small grocery store lay around the corner, typified by its shallow doorway and lack of signs. Old women shuffled like cattle through the aisles. As we entered, Dad delegated: "Sean, get baguettes, lots. Brent, cheese. See if you can taste a hunk first. Hey, we're in Moscow. I'm off for drinks. Two Pepsi and a Pepsi Light?'

I found the cheese between severed pigs' heads and eight-per-carton eggs. The attractive woman I faced wiped her bloody hands on a towel and flung it into a bloody basin. Russian women's eyes often convey, "*You're* interrupting me." She was beautiful and the bloodletting added a romantic angle.

"Ya hotchoo kopeet… ya bwi xotel seer," I stumbled.

"*Kakoi?*"

I looked among blocks of white cheeses, each with a different price, and pointed to the one I guessed least likely to be lard.

"*Skolka*?" she asked–how much? I put my elbows on the counter and did a shadow puppet on the wall. It was better than tickling. She laughed loud enough for the shuffling babushkas to turn their heads. Whatever went between us was neither Russian nor English, but we liked it.

She handed me a slip that I knew was to be handed to the cashier as the next step in this high-employment purchase process. The cashier looked as though she'd eaten her way back up her family tree and chased the others off. The nose guards on her eyeglasses splayed out. She stamped my receipt hard enough to dent it. I decided not to count my change. I returned to the cheese girl, who knifed off a large block of "God-please-let-this-cheddar-looking-cheese-be-from-cow's-milk."

"*Ezveni*," I whispered, excusing myself. She smiled smoothly, as if she were awaiting a punch line. I motioned the chopping up of the cheese, rolling my eyes humbly to convey that I needed the cheese in slices. Though there was likely another department for this task, she sliced the cheese and gave me a forbidden smile with a "*Pajaloust.*" Dad and Sean were outside holding armloads of a cheap lunch. We ate on a bench in the middle of an attempted park. The Pepsis were labeled in Cyrillic, the bread doughy and the cheese agreeably aged.

Flustered people walked by; the fabric of their clothing rubbed smooth with speed. An old man, dressed like a lonely derelict, prodded forward with his cane, his dignity intact. Children laughed and giggled behind our bench. The topic of my personal finances and non-existent retirement savings entertained us because Dad had just paid someone to explain it all to him. He was passing on the advice for free. We slurped our pops and traded fistfuls of bread for more cheese.

Our picnic over, we moseyed on. A knifing wind played at our jackets and unwrapped our scarves, which trailed down to the sidewalk. We neared a blue circular sign with a capital M emblazoned on it.

"Metro?" I asked.

"Mafia," Sean said. "It's the Russian underground."

"I meant 'should we Metro?' Like a verb."

We paid a pittance for three newsprint tickets and stepped onto the descending escalator. The railing moved twice as fast as the stairs. The steps clanked as if one of them might slip out of sync and chuck hapless riders into their gears. We sank inside a dark and hollow throat. My ears popped. Then we hit bottom.

The Metro stations had been commissioned by Stalin as "an architectural ensemble of monumental installations." To show that the coming Communist era would harmonize with the people, Stalin stipulated that each of the 158 stations be both stunning and different. Designers wove in statues, frescoes, mosaics and stained-glass ceilings to promote culture, comfort and wellbeing. These subterranean stations made you feel cozy under only 276 feet (84 meters) of bedrock entertaining gravity. More than 9,000 trains carried nine million people a day over nearly 186 miles (300 kilometers) of track. With three billion passengers a year, that made Moscow the world's busiest subway system. Each station did double duty as a bomb shelter, providing the bomb wasn't in the shelter.

The chandelier crystals above us jiggled as the train neared. Thousands of people packed the platform, sandwiched between two electrified tracks. A train pulled up and spread its doors. Even if you love claustrophobia, there's something unsettling about being pinched between tracks running with 800 volts that could seriously mess with your day. Shoving, and pushing hats down over the eyes of those in our way, the three of us fit into the coach's vestibule so tightly that we couldn't have fallen down if we tried. The doors closed. Someone screamed. Everyone leaned in unison towards the rear as we sped off to the next station.

We were delivered into the Baroque trappings of Oktoberskaya station and carried along by the human exodus onto the escalator. I tried to gauge the distance. There were 40 bumpy lights spaced a little over two lengths of Brent (let's call it six feet in cowboy boots), making the steep ascent 500 feet of diagonal climb or a fifty-eighth of Everest's height. There are, on occasion, breakdowns and the resulting pandemonium rates a probable 10 in that event class. A forced air exchange takes place three times an hour at every station.

From the underbelly of Moscow, we emerged confused about our direction. We were flung almost immediately into a crowd of kiosks, each of which demanded attention. To our backs stood a statue of Lenin. Vladimir towered three storeys above the traffic. I stood humbled, looking into the gaze of a legacy he lived to see only a glimpse of. The power it represented was sufficient to honor: the people who believed in him, the principles that guided his rule, those who saw him a political prophet of biblical force. Respect for the revolution doesn't make me a Leninist any more than respect for Lamborghinis makes me a Lamborghini owner, but it fascinates me that mankind has tried to govern people in so many ways. Lenin served history, primarily the philosophies of Marx and Engels, but history didn't serve him well, except for Stalin proffering everyone an icon of Lenin as a post-mortem figure to hang in their living room. Then Stalin insisted his own portrait be placed beside Lenin's.

Sean led us away on a route with the least incline. The late afternoon sun found us at the gates of Gorky Park. April's weather made it look like the post-retreat German front: bleak and sickly, muddy snow with windswept swirls of littered Styrofoam that crinkled under our feet and blew past us only to get stuck fast in mud. An amusement park loomed behind a chain-link fence and a passerby would periodically waddle alongside us. If Gorky Park was considered a place for picnicking and badminton, I could understand the national proliferation of alcohol abuse. This was depression made tangible.

In the Moscovian twilight, we again found the Arbat. Restaurants cast fiery light onto the stony walk. Dad sparked up his pipe. We picked up the sound of a stringed instrument accompanied by a low voice singing a soft Russian ballad. A crowd bundled in a horseshoe around a man with a banjo-like lute. Dad has a lone but keen musical ear, and an appreciation for banjo music. Mercifully, neither was passed on to his progeny. A woman stood beside the musician, hands clasped and head swooning as she sang the long, full notes. The duo warmed us like a flame from the inside. Time stopped. A spark lifted off Dad's pipe and hovered like a fairy, only to be carried by a light breeze. Dad left. Sean followed. The ember floated above the crowd until–judging from the abrupt change in pitch–it settled on the singer's skin.

Morning woke with enthusiasm. The Intourist folks at the Belgrade Hotel handed back our passports, train tickets and boarding passes. Trains have an uncanny fascination with strict time references. Often, there is but a fraction of a second that separates a platform calmness and receding wagon lights. Our chant: 'I don't have a watch, do you have a watch? No, I don't have a watch....' Not a travel clock among us.

There is a bit of history to this matter, on our 1974 journey to the USSR, our departure was inadvertently delayed by a week. Upon our eventual arrival in Moscow to make the rescheduled connection to Leningrad, we were told "Good thing you weren't on this flight last week. It crashed." Our frustrations and disappointment with the "delay" evaporated. Dad, being an armchair philosopher, rationalized that our preoccupation with time was stupid. He decided never to wear a watch again and, ever since, had never been on time for anything. Seconds and minutes are the currency of life. And now we'd be losing time zones nearly every day, without a chronometer to track it.

A battered yellow Mercedes with a "Taxi" sign flashing erratically pulled up to our tiny section of icy sidewalk in front of the hotel. I opened the front seat's passenger door and out rolled a bottle of vodka, minus a third. It clinked on the asphalt and rolled under the front wheels into a halting crevasse of muck. "Nyet," cried the driver, as if he'd just driven over a child. He managed to rescue his liquid friend and place it on the front passenger seat as the three of us squeezed into the back. We lurched off, leaving the muddy figure of an ampersand. The vodka rolled around the front seat, quivering like a stormy lake. The taxi slid into a chiropractic U-turn and rode up onto the curb in front of Yaroslavl Station.

Around us, babushkas dragged large, expandable plastic cubes of clothes and toiletries. Young men stood in groups, keenly watching for a hole in the defense system of a foreigner. A dancing placard read 'Джон 3:16.' Row upon row of tracks stretched into a web of horizons. The sun slipped down its wall of light. Above the commotion of *ushanka* fur hats and tight scarves scrolled the destinations of Minsk, St. Petersburg and Omsk. Intercity *electrichka* destined for Tver, Vladimir and Bryansk awaited the nightly rush of rumps. Passengers for Minsk, St. Petersburg and Omsk dragged their lives behind them along the platform, or pulled themselves onto carriage decks. I was becoming romantically involved with Russia. We were "in." The dimness of the cavernous train station overtook us.

For the first time in Russia, I saw Asiatic Russians from that side of the country –and in their clusters, stacked crates and cubes of wrapped clothing separated them from one another. In an empty corner, we fashioned a pyramid from our belongings. Dad and Sean set off to use the Telephone Bank while I squatted defensively beside our bags. Two babushkas leaned into each other arguing with fervor. Children played tag around their family's trunks, screaming cheerfully. A child stood silently, one arm wrapped tight around his mother's calf. His entire other hand was used as a pacifier.

Rising from the longest wall, in phosphorescent red-pinned lettering, hung that travellers' beacon: the departures and arrivals board. It announced the location of every train bound in or out, from and to everywhere. The letters spun a fuzzy transformation, throwing up a new destination: Peking. Our first train to what would be our journey's end was scheduled to leave in 45 minutes. *Rossiya*, the name given to the *Trans-Siberian*–famed trekker of the Motherland–was due to show at the tracks anytime. My stomach ached with anticipation. I re-counted our baggage to kill time. Seven. I did it again. Seven. The paranoid traveller courts confidence in the oddest ways.

My brother and father emerged from the crowd, Sean mumbling "First country to put a man in space and they can't even get you a telephone line out of their country."

I suddenly noticed *Rossiya* berthed at the station. The realization that it could depart while we argued about Russian technology hit me like an electric current. We swooped up our bags and took them into a crowd-stopping funnel of traffic at the turnstiles.

"*Bilyeta*," said an old porter, smaller than all but two of our bags.

"He wants our tickets," I said.

"What for?" Dad asked.

"Dunno.... *Pachemoo*?' I enjoined the porter's knotted eyes.

"*Poez-duh*," the porter enunciated, with an emphasis on *duh*. "Vagon?"

"What wagon are we in," Sean interrupted, thinking he was helping.

"*Da! Shtoy vagon?*" The porter waved a mittened fist at all of us, though I took it personally.

His mitt ran a thick finger over the ticket, humming as though a secret number was encrypted. In Russia in the late 20th Century, someone was still writing out all travel documents by hand.

"*Vosyem.*" Eight.

He pushed the cart ahead of us hollering to the platform full of people to mind their bodies. Trudging past 18 carriages, we were captivated by the Cyrillic signs stenciled "Moskva–Peking" black on white. A chugging idle hummed from beneath the carriage. Two Chinese officials in heavy, decorated coats sized us up. We had reserved three beds in a four-person berth to Irkutsk, four days away. We were intrigued by who might occupy the fourth bed and our remaining breathing space in the coach.

A young Russian man, inebriated enough to stagger, joined our group, hollering a good lungful of vodka-laced air with an arrogant confidence offered by his consumption. I could not translate the slur and guessed he was our roommate. The shorter of the two Chinese men spoke in a forceful tone, to which the drunk produced a crumpled ticket. An official arm pointed far down to the last cars. To our relief, the drunk stumbled off.

The Chinese officials finally smiled and shook Dad's hand. "Preese, wekom." We hoisted our luggage inside the coach's vestibule. Our compartment was at the far end of eight rooms. One official slid open the door of our temporary tenement to Siberia. Spacious enough for one, close for two, tight for three, and something like prisoner-of-war conditions for four. Dad and Sean fought ahead of me to load the cabin and claim bunk rights. The Chinese man rubbed his cheek and slid open the door to the next free berth–encouraging me in with "Preese, wekom."

I set out to make *my* room look as inhospitable as possible to any passersby contemplating cohabitation. I opened every zipper, placed perishables bruised-side-up on the table, crushed a brand-name cola can on the floor, unscrewed a light bulb, and disrobed. I put my ear to the thin wall to hear Dad and Sean fighting for space.

Sean's face–loaded with suspicion–appeared in my doorway. "Dad, come take a look at this," he called out. I dumped my backpack's contents as a barricade should either relative attempt entry, and adjusted my underwear.

Dad's face appeared above Sean's. "What are you doing, son?"

"The Chinese guy gave it to me."

"A whole cabin?"

"I prefer Couchette B3. The B is for bling. Or Brent. But yes, the whole thing."

They looked at each other. Dad gave a shrug and left.

"He snores, you know," Sean said to me, watching Dad amble back.

I pulled a quick ploy from my files. "Primogeniture."

"What?"

"It means first born, right to inheritance, the crowned allegory, et cetera et al. As in born, birth, first, one, me, my berth." I smiled the tug-of-lip smirk of someone who'd breezed into Mensa.

"If I was a monkey, I'd throw feces at you," said Sean. "You're greedy and selfish."

"You are a prop in my movie."

In the train's corridor, we opened a heavy window halfway and looked onto the platform. Retreating flares of sunlight drew long shadows alongside the train. The track clock nudged toward the departure time of 19:50. The Chinese official shed his overcoat, pulled up the stairs with an iron-levered clunk and closed the outer door, sealing us off from Moscow. Then, the first whisper of motion. It was one of the proudest experiences of our lives. The platform inched past. As the train quickened, the commotion and the station fell away behind us.

"This is our *moment*," Dad yelled, as much to the Moscovian night as to Sean and me. We held onto those few seconds, as one would cradle an Oscar.

The train sped along the tracks, through double-slips and crossovers. The wheel assemblies' hard surfaces glanced over the rails. The ties that bind the rails rocked the wagon side-to-side and, just as surely, rocked and bound the three of us together as our Greek restaurateur/philosopher friend George foreshadowed. Our train trip sung into being. My heart belonged to Russia. We screamed joyous expletives to the sea of tracks as they danced to our applause. Our coach official had lost his hat, rolled up his sleeves, and was now walking towards us with clanking bottles of beer, looking less and less official.

"Beijing beer," he announced, passing one to each of us. He jammed a palm towards Dad. "*Khan.*"

"*Rick*. Pleased to meet you, Khan."

"*Sean*. Nice meeting you," Sean said with an air of speculation.

"Khan," he repeated, turning to me.

"*Brent*," I said, taking both his hand and the bottle opener.

"You are so calm," he enunciated, as if he'd invested a lot of brain matter into memorizing this specific observation.

"Thank you. I'm not," I said. "Medicated for anxiety though. But you're making me question my panic."

"So calm." He gurgled a throatful of beer. Instantly, he departed for the other end of the coach. We figured this was to let us enjoy leaving on a journey that had taken much effort to arrange. Moscow's urban landscape receded into a silhouetted skyline of antennae-populated rooftops. A quarter moon hung like a white sickle in the darkening sky. The *Rossiya's* speed furthered the euphoria, fueled our excitement and created a sharp gust of air in the corridor. Sean noticed it first and quieted us. Something was amiss. The three of us stared down the carriage's corridor. No one emerged from any of the compartments; all the roomette doors were closed and silent–this on one of the world's notoriously boisterous trains. We had figured the entire train would be crawling with strangers and that we'd be taking shifts to guard our baggage.

I ventured along the corridor for a visual inspection of why we were alone in a coach on such a crowded train. The final room housed Khan, who sat with his feet up. He was smoking something that smelled obnoxious. I asked for one. His disheveled torso leaned forward to light it. Half an hour earlier, he'd been dressed as someone who might shoot you for spite. Now he looked cozy as if, with all due respect, he was into his fourth quart of Beijing beer.

"Brent." He stood, bowing slightly, and smiled like we were old friends.

"Hey, Khan. I'm sort of curious. Are we alone? I mean, are we alone until Irkutsk–or is this thing gonna stop in five minutes and pick up a xenophobic mafia biker gang?"

"You are so calm" Khan said, confirming the language barrier was much bigger than I'd thought. *Calm*? What was he expecting? I moved back along the coach and told Dad and Sean that we were alone, that Khan was our Chinese *provodnik*, Russian for a male coach attendant (*provodnitsa* is a female coach custodian). Khan, I added, was on the other side of being reachable with any of our known forms of communication.

I caught sight of a violet sky outside the window. In the clickity-clackity echo, evening drifted into night and dazzling constellations emerged from the blackness.

Dad brushed his nose. Dad clucked his cheeks, raised a closed fist and extended a finger: "One. Watch your hip pack. Secondly," another parental finger appeared, "Don't trust anyone." I waited. Dad always comes in threes. "And thirdly –Brent, I want you to hear me–never drink with strangers. Would you mind looking at me while I'm talking to you?"

"I am," I said, looking away. "It's Peripheral Vision Day in Armenia. I'm honoring that."

"Repeat them back to me," he said.

"*Dad.*"

I felt for my wallet as Khan staggered up with another round of beers and a rosy glow on his amber cheeks. Sean came around from the nearest washroom looking like he'd just found out the truth about Santa Claus. He was shifting his eyes quickly; it was evident something had spooked him.

"What happened to you in there?" I asked.

"Nothing... You'll see... No, nothing." He glared awareness. "OK. It's Unspeakable. Dire conditions."

Khan waved us to come along as he wandered back to his cabin. Dad stopped us. "You know I can't stand the smoking. So, Sean, here's the deal. We allocate Brent's temporary living quarters as the smoking place."

Khan broke into song far off in his tiny room. Sean nodded to Dad, as did I. Khan sang in a crushing-of-tin falsetto, waving his arms in a Tai Chi fashion as Sean and I shadowed his door. A transistor radio was tuned to one of those stations that cling to the end of the dial. Khan stopped as he saw our eyes survey his compartment. We were ushered in, urged to sit and drink another bottle of beer. For long minutes nothing was understood. "Access denied," his face seemed to compute. We sipped our beers and stared at his Chinese calendar pinup. Khan raised his lower bunk and withdrew a small stack of stapled papers. He wrapped his lips around printed English phrases. They included attendant-focused, closed-end statements that had prepared him for encountering English-speaking passengers.

"Herro."

"Hello," Sean replied.

"Goo-od evenering," he tried, rolling excitedly on his posterior quadrant.

"Good evening," I said.

"You are so calm."

At this, I pulled the bottle away from my face and shimmied over to see what Khan was trying to get at. He had his finger stuck tight on the sentence.

"Kind. You are so *kind,*" I yelled.

"Calm," he corrected me.

I said, "Kind!" He looked confused but appeared to be homing in on the error.

We bade Khan goodnight.

Sean threw back his compartment door and there, seated comfortably with his writing binder propped between his knees and pipe clenched between his guilty lips, was our father. His eyes widened as his brain registered his guilt. He was smoking in the panic room.

"Political Science 101, Dad. Ye who make the law will break the law."

Returning to my compartment, I fumbled for the light switch–intent on reading–but found myself groping empty walls. I lay on the bunk. Shadows flit with passing lights. The distant clanging of a road-and-rail crossings rose in pitch and then fell. The train's fluid motion clicked over the links of rail like chattering teeth. We were in the hinterland of villages one can only find in a Russian atlas. I fell asleep to the cradle-rocking hum of the *Trans-Siberian.*

Hours later I awoke and stayed perfectly still, taking time to place myself. I sighed contentedly and drew back the thick cotton curtains. Sunlight shot through my pupils and burned away memories, passwords and the entire week of my first crush. Tearing, I stood back as sunshine thwacked the roomette with a brilliance you see when replacing a light bulb while power's still on. Unthreatening clouds cluttered the sky. A forest edged the tracks, whipping by without interruption. Consulting my mile-by-mile guide of indispensable information, I placed our whereabouts somewhere east of the Volga River. The mighty Mother Volga itself had passed underneath a train bridge in the darkness.

I was keen to find something politically sensitive–aka officially forbidden–to photograph. An aerodrome or military installation, maybe a rusty missile silo, would do. The Soviets had a reputation for confiscating film, taking away photos and being quite suspicious of recording technology. However, I had an honorable photographic ambition: I thought a picture of a muddy family in a muddy town of muddy streets and no running water would speak more to the world than Moscow's Arrivals terminal. I didn't need to take a picture; I just wanted to know that I could.

The guidebook listed the rail stations along the way, including the expected length of each stop. Hence, the entire rail journey was notched with many five-, 10- and 15-minute pauses, during which passengers could accost the local station's kiosks and stretch their limbs. I put away the guidebook and turned to gaze at an endless birch forest.

The *Trans-Siberian* travels its entire route while remaining on Moscow Time, which is Greenwich Mean plus three hours. It does so in its own little ego-orbit. For example, the night had passed with the introduction of a new time zone, Moscow + 1, without anyone aboard changing the time on their clocks. The result of this curiosity is that a trip to the eastern seaboard in China has passengers arrive in the time zone of Moscow + 7. Since there were no watches among Dad, Sean, and me to reset, this transition hadn't affected us. Yet the time changes might excite my circadian rhythm, tossing me into a cycle of restless catnaps. Dad slid back the door without knocking and handed me a steaming plastic cup of instant coffee.

"Hey, kid. Do you know where we are?"

"Morning, Dad. I put us somewhere between Svetcha and Kotelnich. I'm just waiting till we cross the Vyatka to confirm...."

"We're on the *Trans-Siberian*," he stated gleefully, his inflection italicizing the name. "Whatcha up to?"

"Counting trees."

"Yeah, it's been like this since dawn." He leaned into the doorframe. "Looks like this train thing's gonna be a good place to get some writing done." Dad had lately taken to writing his long-awaited novel, though he was the only one who had long awaited it.

"It might be nice if you made an appearance next door in our den of opposing philosophies." He looked around carefully. "How did your room get to looking like you have more people in it than we do?"

"I do not know," I said truthfully.

He left the door ajar. It lazily opened and closed with the train's speed and bends. I sipped the hot water, propping my journal between my knees to the pages full of trip sketches. I could see into the past, all of it. It felt like I'd been gone a year, even though it had only been two weeks. I strapped on my hip pack and nodded into Dad and Sean's room.

"Thanks for the coffee. Though I'd like to request that, from now on, my instant coffees get stirred. I'm too awake now to lounge in my quarters. I'm taking my journal for a walk to find the restaurant car."

I cracked the big handle to open the heavy door between the wagons and crossed the rubber-encased path, the dancing steel plates rubbing and sliding across each other, suffering every bump and turn. I passed into a coach overrun with families and crying children. Each of the four cars on my route to the dining car was crowded with people pressing into the smudgy windows or stepping back into their cabins to allow my passage. Children's screams rang from behind partially pulled drapes. People were stacked like baggage, sandwiched between cubed plastic boxes.

It was then I realized the three of us were travelling in a Chinese-operated coach off the corresponding, and Chinese owned, Beijing to Moscow service. We were the coach's only occupants, and with our own Chinese custodian, Khan. Russians ran every other coach on this train, and they were crammed to the gills with people, often six to a room.

Finally, a door spilled me into the restaurant car, the middle wagon of the train. A whiff told me the Russians operated it. It smelled like a pallet of cabbage. Three Englishmen sat at a table behind where I landed. They were arguing about the European Union. They took a rolling-eyeball look at me and carried on. We—and they—were feeling out fellow travellers.

I left the dining coach to inspect the remainder of the train. Mongolian and Chinese passengers were everywhere resigned to laying among the Russians, isolated by language, for days on end. I passed through to the next car and found more of the same. Luggage spilled out of compartments into the common area through which everyone had to pass. Laughter erupted from a cabin where a group of men were playing cards. Yells and cries in foreign languages rose above the din. I crossed into another wagon. Then another. The coaches were essentially Russian-made human transports with no barriers to keep out the sounds of the squealing wheels. The bluish-green walls looked sickly. The train consist was chipped with age and the thin carpet had holes the size of footprints. Cool drafts flowed in every direction. The reason for the quality contrast with our car? Ours had been produced in West Germany.

Eventually, tracks could be seen receding from the last window of the last carriage. Here, three men were arguing loudly in Russian, breaking into a laugh every now and then. I was tapped on the shoulder. I swiveled quickly and covered my hip pack with my forearm.

"Americanski?" asked a tall, thin Russian with a cratered complexion.

"Uh, *nyet. Ya Canadyets*."

"*Ah. Vwee goveryety pa-ruski*," he exclaimed, pleased that I spoke Russian. I located my junior grasp of the language.

"*Tolka choot-choot*," I replied. Only a bit. I lost control of the next question and answered *"Tolka choot-choot,"* again. They stared. The key phrase I'd mastered was "*Esli vree goverytye miedlina, ya paneemyoo*," meaning, "I'll understand if you speak slowly."

"*Sergei*," the pimpled one introduced himself.

"*Brent*."

"Brant? *Eta Pavel*," he said about the heavy-set man loaded with weight-bearing Asian features standing to his right.

"*Ee Vladimir*." Sergei pointed to a man of average everything–height, weight and handshake. Vladimir rifled off in a blaze of unintelligible verbiage. His eyes seemed kind but they darted around, calculating. I did my own math.

Their cigarettes burned loosely, churning lumps of carcinogenic exhaust into the compartment. The three of them were going to Vladivostok and then to Khabarovsk, on the volcanic rim of the Pacific. Vladimir, the first Kazakh I'd met, was an airline mechanic. His broad nose swept back across his wide cheeks while his ink-black hair hung limply across his forehead. Pavel and Sergei claimed to be something, and then burst out laughing. "Unemployable," I said about myself, trying to fit in.

They insisted I return to their couchette for a drink. Warning signs flagged through my mind. I refused. But they wouldn't hear of me turning down their invitation. I thought perhaps they'd never had the opportunity to rob a North American and this could be a novelty for them. I resisted further. Under the circumstances, it was futile, unwelcome and–above all else–un-Russian. I sensed it. Nine wagons away, Dad was naïvely happy we were all safe and abiding by his "law of threes."

We shuffled to their room. I sat on a bed and found myself sandwiched between Sergei and Vladimir. Pavel returned with a large, quiet friend and a lawn chair, which he placed to bar the doorway. He slid the door shut with a solid thunk. Beers were pulled from a tired knapsack and passed to each of us.

"*Nostrovia*," we toasted, using the Russian cliché to our health. Sergei plucked a well-worn deck of playing cards, split it in two, and flipped the piles in front of us. Dog-eared and torn, the cards led me to conclude that–in time–familiarity with the cards' backside crinkles would reveal a complete knowledge of the deck. I chugged beer with the intent of playing their game and picked up my hand of cards. If it was hearts, I was good. If it was blackjack, I'd be lost. If it was poker, I was stable. It was none of them. When my turn came, Sergei would peer over and scan my hand and pluck the appropriate card. Someone must have won, for eventually the cards were rounded up, shuffled and set aside.

Pavel flipped back the knapsack flap and pulled out a long bottle by its neck. Stale rye bread, cheese and a cucumber were diced into hors d'oeuvres as the bottle bowed before three shot glasses. Perhaps it was my status as a foreigner that made them wait and watch my peer-pressured arm lift the glass to my lips. I emptied it and heard cheers during my shaking off the distillate's impurities. I tipped back against the wall. Another ounce was poured. Food was offered. Here I was at an early morning hour, fully buzzed, and trespassing Dad's warning-of-all-warnings aboard a Russian train: "Never drink with local strangers." My father's ghost appeared rippling in the room's corner, haunting me with a shaking finger. There I sat, my hip pack loaded with every piece of identification I owned plus my entire stash of travellers cheques, my passport and enough cash to be bloodied senseless for. All I could do was sit with a smile on my face and watch Sergei pull the cards from my atrophied hand. Visions of being thrown from the train surfaced: me, scrambling to the tracks in my boxers and socks to watch the back end of the train fade.

As I thought of beating my way out of the room and into the hall, everyone suddenly stood up. Sergei slid open the door. We ambled to the end compartment. While they chatted casually, I listened for familiar Russian words for context. Sergei invited me for another round of cards, more vodka and petrifying fear, but I declined and told them they could find me in the restaurant car if the need arose. After goodbyes and *do svydania*s–words I never thought I'd hear–I was left alone. I smiled. I'd survived all three of Dad's taboos.

I fled to my quarters, euphoric, and entered the wrong one in the wrong coach. The occupants were preoccupied so I moved along to mine undetected.

Dad came around the corner. "Are you drunk?"

"I will never ever play Russian Roulette with a gun again … promise." I turned my face into my pillow. "NEVER!"

"Brent, son," Dad said calmly.

"Well, that's all there is on this train. Strangers."

"You –."

"I didn't have a choice in the matter. But it was voluntary."

I was the only patron in the restaurant car later that afternoon. Looking through the dusty film on the window in front of a display, my right eye fixed on a large bottle of beer sitting helplessly in a sinister heat bath. A card table laden with chocolate bars, potato chips, juice, beer, vodka and menus displayed the train's sundries. My left eye wandered about the car in search of something interesting but defaulted back to the bottle. I moved across the vinyl bench and rose to grab it. Then I cornered to face the kitchen to pay.

The Russian cook was quick-tongued. "*Southpaw sits atop bunny droppings. Bunny droppings.*" That is what I made of it. Whatever his Russian banter, it could not be translated by my Berlitz guide.

I withdrew and opened the bottle enroute to my base camp table in the dining car, which now sat in the angled sun, indicating we'd altered course ever so slightly. My dehydrating was masked by the Russian beer; Black Bull 12%.

I opened my journal and found an entry Sean had written in black felt pen on the title page. "*This book has been modified to fit your intellect.*" Creasing open a new set of pages, I attempted to catch what had passed since I last spoke intelligently with my family. The gentle tossing of the train car and sun-warmed stillness encouraged a cozy feeling that everything would, forever and a day, be all right. Hordes of dancing, prancing visions were hit point blank by the cupid of another room temperature Black Bull.

My headphones found their way to my ears. Bruce Dickinson growled, "*My grandfather taught me how to fight/Old fashion stuff like wrong and right.*" I thought about one of my own grandfathers. He died the month before we left for

Russia. He and I were close and remarkably similar. His values, morals and genteel sophistication were qualities that seemed to be declining with the death of each gene-bearer. He was a man who would help his enemy. Who wouldn't go to a doctor unless he had nine wounds. I gave a small salute, toasted his spirit, and felt him gently squeeze my knee.

A young woman entered the dining car, followed by a man roughly her age. She was dressed in a tight bright dinner dress and high heels, not really suited to a long railway journey unless you were renting out your body. They sat across from my booth and I clumsily reorganized my position so as to better my view of her. They spoke Russian in breathy voices, indicating some level of professional courting. The woman drew a long cigarette from a pouch, while her companion slid his cuff-linked arm across the table, sparking a lighter that produced no flame. There she was, not two feet from me, this white Russian witch with her painted lips wrapped around her thin cigarette, making the international motions for a match. I froze like I'd stumbled upon a fawn in a clearing, careful not to frighten her away. Slowly I slid my lighter from my pocket.

We established our nationalities, marital status and reasons for being on the train. Her name was Tsveta Krasavistya. She spoke English with a worldly accented pride. Misha, the gentleman, who she confessed to having met only an hour before, saluted me and moved to my booth. Tsveta slid next to him.

Misha knew three words in English; unfortunately, they weren't ones I recognized. Tsveta translated the exchange, considerably lengthening our discussion. Misha had the angry expression of someone who had done and seen a lot more than he wished he had. His dark hair was shaved close to his head and, at 22 years of age, his Russian features were as harsh as his experiences. Tsveta interpreted his history for me, pausing frequently to challenge him with questions of her own. At times, she was visibly shocked, though I was not privy to those little eddies of conversation. Misha, we learned, had just defected from the Mafia in Moscow after six years of ruthless activities that had sculpted his face, given him physical and mental scars, and affected the privileged way he carried himself. He was returning to Krasnoyarsk, to his family, whom he'd not seen since running away from them and their Siberian lives. He'd been propelled by a young man's dreams of the big city. In Misha's case, that city was Moscow. The years of extortion, violence, murder, drugs, and the resulting lifestyle had given him a dose of remorse that made him want to go home. His mother was a high-ranking officer in the Russian army– "an establishment as corrupt and dangerous as the Mafia, so they have a lot in common".

"Did I just say that out loud?" I asked.

Tsveta nodded. They were silent. I took a swig of beer and pondered why some seconds are so long when others are so short. One should be able to control that. Misha got up to get potato chips.

"What about you, Tsveta?" I asked, leaning my elbows on the tabletop.

She smiled, a little embarrassed, and toyed with her curls. Her name in Russian meant, "color." Her brown shoulder-length hair, marbled with dewy highlights, rounded her cherubic face. From her innocent demeanor, I gauged that she was an untarnished child living in a well-developed woman's body. She held her innocence well. Tsveta was a stripper, though she preferred the term dancer. I said "Tomahto-tomayto." She had plied her trade in Irkutsk, the city she called "hometown." However, a developing interest in kitchen cabinet remodeling had lured her to Finland, where she'd been working for two years. But that ended in a way she didn't want to talk about. She smiled when saying that the train was taking her back to Irkutsk. She was hard. She was soft. Ironically, her icy Prussian eyes held the warmth of a nativity scene.

"Vat aboutch you, Brrrant?" She rolled the second letter of my name around her throat.

"I worked in the cablevision industry but I wasn't a news anchor or the guy who makes weather maps. I deliver TV to TV-addicted families. But I'd really like to write. I think I hear my heart saying that. Or my soul… whichever one is saying 'Get us down from this fucking telephone pole.' Yeah, I like to write. My whole family does."

"Have you been published," she said, a lock of hair falling over her icy right eye.

"Not even photocopied. Writers don't judge themselves by getting published. Only other people do." I took a swig of beer while trying to convince myself of this. "Sean's got a short story done. My Dad has been published. I'm next. I've written really good classified ads that have seen print. And I can do a red-carpet obituary. So if you ever die, look me up."

She asked to be excused and left to change.

Misha stood as if to go with her but returned with a Black Bull smile and a bottle for each of us. He and I watched Tsveta leave, and then composed uncomfortably to face one another. The language barrier was like a muddy trench. I would ask a question and get an answer 10 times longer and more incoherent than the one I was prepared for. Misha sensed this and pulled a deck of cards from his vest. He shuffled.

Tsveta returned, sumptuously decorated in a tight-fitting dress that pressed her breasts together like gears. I noticed that Misha noticed. I resented he hadn't suddenly taken ill and left the two of us–me and Tsveta–alone. Instead, he dealt card hands and initiated the game Sergei had attempted to teach me earlier.

"I lost my virginity in a card game," I offered.

"Do you do magic tricks?" she asked.

"No. But once I disappeared for three days."

"This is new game to you. It is called Russian Stupid." Tsveta smiled without self-injury.

The rules seemed to change every time I came close to understanding them. I pilfered the occasional face card in a game I called Me Not So Stupid. I tucked the stolen cards into the seat beside me, out of sight. Soon there was roughly half a deck left. Misha spoke to Tsveta with his head cocked coercively. She turned to me. "Would you like to see Misha's gun?"

It crossed my mind that he wasn't playing with a full deck.

"I don't know if that would be wise," I said, but Misha was already bouncing it uncomfortably off my knee below the table. I guessed he was prone to pointing weaponry directly at people. Reaching under the table, I rotated the gun away from my vital organs and weighted it in my palm.

".357?" I queried with a look I hoped conveyed I was informed about weapons. It wasn't a shotgun and this was the only available term I knew.

"Da," he replied with a gloating pride. I sewed my eyebrows together and looked it over as I held it against the seat. I nodded approval and passed it back– barrel toward Misha–beneath the table.

"You have Russian Roulette in Canada?" she asked.

"Uh, we draw straws." I said.

"In Russia we say: Punch me. I think I'm dreaming." she pronounced.

"It's *pinch me*, I think I'm dreaming." I started to explain, "Forget it. I don't want to mess with natural selection."

As another round of warm Bull beers grazed the table, compliments of Misha, my brother walked in and immediately dropped himself beside Tsveta, thereby decreasing the odds Misha and I had silently acknowledged between us. 1:2 became 1:3. Sean answered a battery of questions launched by Tsveta. Her dream was to go to America, the "U-YES of A," she said, as if she had pompoms. Canadians, by default, attempt to dissuade anyone who harbors feelings that America is the world and instead offer our serenity, apologies, and kindness. I gave it my best try.

My short dissertation was not well received. Though the popularity of Canada is largely due to our national *modus operandi*, we fall short of egos, Hollywood, Disneyland and the superlatives of everything you would lust, kill or die for. I said this apologetically, even adding, that we had a political leader who had probably, if rarely, slept only with his wife. And then I ran out of ideas. I retreated and tended to my Black Bull.

Sean entered the conversation armed. "*Americans* and *Canadians* live off the same buffet of television and music. We share most of the same fast foods, the same franchise outlets and gas stations. Illegally, we even fish the same waters. But you can spot the differences. It doesn't take a brain surgeon to notice that some neurons don't fire in the Americans. And thank God some of ours don't spark like theirs. They have 10 times the population; ergo, 10 times most everything else. Except hand-carved bears made out of tree stumps, maple syrup, loads of wide-open-spaces and the lucrative part of the North Pole."

I was on his side–even though Russia had much of the North Pole, lumber that sped by as we spoke, and the idea of "wide open spaces," wasn't something you could sell to people who live in Siberia. But he didn't need to know I agreed with him. "Did you really just say *ergo*?" I winced at him.

At the sun's critical last attempt at light, it thrust sharp yellow daggers at the sky. Then it was gone. Tsveta got up and left to change again. I caught Sean trying to wink, a social custom he's always done simultaneously with both eyes. Then he and Misha got up to score a bottle of vodka. Soon my intolerance for drink would shine through.

The first few shots sank into me like an attacked battleship. I started listing to my starboard side. I recall the train's dinner crowd arriving and leaving. I watched darkness lurk beyond the light thrown into the woods by the restaurant car. I drew a second wind. I remember referring to myself as an *objet d'art*, trying to teach line-dancing to the kitchen staff, and whispering, "I'm not yelling."

The dark hours of early morning were filled with a bitter restlessness. Though eerily quiet, with nothing but blackness filling the window, substantial events were taking place "out there" beyond the tracks. We traversed the Ural Mountains, the spine of Russia. Another time zone swept over the train. More importantly, the white stone obelisk that breaks apart continental Europe and Asia was out there. We wound down from the mountains into a dark plain of emptiness. Finally, I was jarred fully awake with the deceleration into Ekaterinburg, a place I'd hoped to visit and–were it not for the timetable getting us in at three in the morning–I might have.

Ekaterinburg (or *Sverdlovsk*) represents a powerful migraine for Russia. Tsar Nicholas and his family had been exiled here and here they were murdered in 1918. Their bullet-riddled and bayoneted bodies were dismembered with axes, bathed in acid and deposited in a mineshaft. It was long believed that Nicholas' youngest daughter, Anastasia, survived the slaughter. However, Anastasia died alongside her family on that fateful July evening in 1918. Ekaterinburg also houses the remains of the American U2 spy plane shot down by the Soviets in 1960. Gary Powers, the pilot, parachuted safely into the arms of the Russians who used the incident as leverage in the Cold War. The city is also the birthplace of Boris Yeltsin.

We were on the Siberian Plain. The first signs of dawn appeared. The forest, still thick with its zebra pattern of birch and verdant needles, faded to reveal grassy fields of golden taiga. A black line of surface soil nipped at the rail bed of gravel like the shallow surf on a lake's shore. Suddenly, we felt the train brake– screeching with the moans of stressed metal. A train cannot "slam" on its brakes, as the wheels will warp. The decrease in speed, an urgent and staggered affair, pitched me from the bunk to the floor. The grinding noises rivaled the chord range of a violin coming unstrung.

We gawked out the window and there, directly ahead of the engine–which bowed into our view with the track's curve–raged a wall of forest fire. Tinder-fed flames leapt, stretching over acres of scrub forest fuel now charcoaled black. The untamed fire fanned itself up and over the tracks.

I headed through the crowded halls of several wagons, Sean at my heels. As we neared the engine, the fire was a mesmerizing force of hunger, its arms flickering wildly to engulf fresh trees. We crashed against the door into the closed coach door one back from the engine. Two men armed with machine guns threw open the door. They stood among boxes, wooden crates, and large cloth bags of mail. One guard was on the train's phone system speaking, I deduced, to the engineer. The other shoved us back into the vestibule and slammed the door shut. It occurred to me that the only guys with machine guns on the train didn't have windows in their carriage, so they could not see the fire happening.

The cavern of searing flame was high on both sides of the track, creeping up on us. Curiously, the smoke was blown low through the forest. The fire wouldn't have been seen above the treetops until it was nearly too late to stop the train. The train was without a public address system, hence no announcement; it was all guesswork. The attendants could not have known any more than did the passengers.

The engineer decided to gamble. The engines jumped to speed. The fire's heat was pressing through the windows. Sean and I ran through the carriage corridors, heading to find Dad. The fire raged alongside our tracks for the length of the train. People choked and covered their faces.

Our engine, mail car, dining car and eight coaches rolled precariously forward. Danger licked the windowsills from the outside. Once the train exited the threat of fire, the acrid smell stuck with us for days and nights to come.

A dirty suburb of Omsk came upon us after our train's crossing a branch of the mighty Ob River, whose ink-black waters contrasted sharply with its large, flat shards of ice. Clouds grew into a dark canopy as the tracks multiplied, criss-crossing the rail yard. Displayed atop the stationhouse doors, as if refusing to leave, clung the iconic hammer and sickle. Passengers mingled with peddlers selling homemade debris on the platform. Multinational traders hawked their inventory from the Rossiya's windows and steps. The common language was currency, and mitsful of rubles earned the citizens of Omsk a variety of essential items. Blue jeans, leather jackets and footwear were bartered for with a fluency that befell all the long-haul trains pausing at this junction.

Upon disembarking, Sean and I took photographs of stray dogs and stray people. We edged up to the front of the platform, admired the engine's combination of lights and identification: ChC2-643. We exchanged polite words with the two engineers who invited us to mount the metal stairs and enter their cavern of command. The gauges, buttons, knobs and levers offered a rare view into the complexity of their task.

Sean and I went our separate ways. I leaned on a stack of corroded track fish-plates, lit my pipe, and surveyed the yard. An iron catwalk rose ahead of me and over the tracks, landing on a central platform where a squealing freight train eased eastbound. A group of dust-covered women armed with shovels were transferring coal from a wooden cart into slots on the wagons that made up our train. The coal would be burned for warmth as well as for heating the *samovar*, the tank at the rear of each coach from which passengers drew water for washing and tea. I watched a stammering brigade of freight cars marshalling off to the lace of tracks, meticu-lously reversing up a hump of track and disconnecting its cars–one by one–onto a split of lanes. A man stood off to the side switching the tracks this way and that way to divide them, piece by piece and car by car, to build three new trains. As this action shunted back and forth, the engine plumed columns of diesel exhaust.

Although I was confined to the borders of the bustling rail yard, I was never-theless pleased to be in Omsk. This is the place where Fyodor Dostoevsky spent his hard-labor years in a workers' camp. To be present in Omsk was to bear witness to a bleak and color-deficient canvas of Russian life–an opaque financial entity born of necessity and consequence, not philanthropy or entrepreneurialism. I felt at home and at ease among the platform traders, the pervasive hard-boiled egg and bottled borscht vendors, and the station officials, all with their functional clothes of autumn browns and drab greys.

I was jolted out of my musings when a pair of tracks switched without warning to slide an incoming commuter train onto a siding. Cobweb strands of electrified wire, suspended from bracket arms, sizzled life into the idling locomotives. The engines moved like whales, shuffling their positions and tracks in a mix of back-ward and forward throttles to connect with the carriages of cargo–whether passenger or freight. A load of prefabricated track lengths secured on concrete sleepers awaited attention. Everything looked as though it were waiting for a toe to be stubbed on it. The aesthetic illustrated Russia's taste for cold.

The atlas I brought with me to the dining car showed we were passing 40° of latitude above India and Sri Lanka. I scanned upper Europe and found that there were two Brests, one in each of the erogenous countries of France and Belarus.

Beyond the red plastic tablecloth, a sign on the far wall read: "*NYE KOURIT*".' a serious upper-case Cyrillic 'NO SMOKING.' The haze in the coach indicated no one had been complying. Three male kitchen staff exited their hovel of hissing steam and clanging pans for a cigarette. One of them, a weathered sandy-haired man, between 20 and 45 years old, sat with his legs stretched and crossed, right over left. His left arm slumped over the end of the booth, where he would tug at strands from the conveniently ripped fabric of upholstery. The three men seldom spoke. Sometimes I heard rough Russian grunts escape their lips. I translated those grunts into:

"Nice birch passing us today, Maxim. I much love this."

"*Da*, almost as good as Thursday's. Except today there is less snow."

"*Da*. Maybe less, then again it may snow tonight. That would mean more. Maybe much, much more. Anatoliev, what do you think? Snow tonight?"

"*Da,* Victor. Maybe… just maybe. Oh, I much love birch in snow."

Perhaps, they were conversing about the quality of the potatoes they'd just picked up in Zavitaya. Or, about the platform attendant in Izvyestkovaya, who the week before had given them each a bucket of coal for their homes in exchange for a hot meal. On occasion, they would break into a lazy game of cards. Their wheezes of conversation ran like saliva from a newborn. At times, I like to paint the world with a big brush. Things just seem to make more sense to me that way.

Russia continued to slip by, rail by rail. *Just out there.*

I kept reminding myself. If people visit a place often enough, there are eventually no surprises. But that was not true here in Siberia. Though Russia has a large tourist enterprise, few tourists visit beyond Moscow or St. Petersburg. Yet it is only once you leave those city limits that the *real* Russia emerges. Making friends with people who live where few outsiders know reveals the shocking culture, the recollections of what was and what it became, and why Russians are so… Russian. Sadly, given enough time, this train might cart German tours across Russia as if 1942 never happened.

We were soon heading into Moscow + 4. Small shantytowns bent around the tracks. Tiny one-room wood cabins or *dachas*, firewood grafted to their sides, sat romantically in the woods outside our window. Smoke plumed out of rocky, unco-ordinated chimneys. The mossy thatched roofs, carved shutters, brightly painted doors, worn axe handles, well-kept gardens and windowpane crosshairs pulled at my heartstrings. Muddy roads, carved into ruts by horse-drawn carriages, were the paths these isolated souls trod to get to school, passing branch fences and puddles that never drained.

The tight chronology of the travel-by-rail itinerary means that villages beside the tracks could set their clocks to be within a few minutes of Coordinated Universal Time. *Why would they?* I asked myself. The lure of this backwoods backward backcountry is precisely its imprecision. These pocketed places, sheltered from invasive technology and free of the initial impact of the Kremlin's decisions, were represented by thousands of stipples on the Russian map. In many, I learned that communism was preserved like Lenin himself. They knew of no other way. Their past, present and future were dictated by the same laws of classical physics: predictable, immutable and unalterable.

We witnessed this more than once when the tracks swelled to allow an intercity train to slow and halt in towns with no platforms, no stations. Passengers would climb aboard from a rocky slope, tossing on old leather packs or army-issued rucksacks to allow them to gain a grip on the carriage pole. If the engine was patient, the passengers would get on. If not, they ran along a waist-high *verst* (acre) only to lag behind as the train stammered to speed.

I was gazing out the window when an older, bearded man in a suit entered the restaurant car and began collecting various snack packages from the display table. I recognized him as one of the Englishmen who'd been talking politics earlier.

"Excuse me," I said. "I couldn't help but overhear you earlier. You're English, correct?"

"Scottish," he said, throwing me a sideways glance before returning to his food collecting.

"I heard your accent as I passed by. London, South London, Crawley? No. Brighton, is it?" I'd always wanted to say that to someone.

"Scotland. Edinburgh."

"I think you and your group are the only other English-speaking people on the train. I thought we should meet."

"I'm terribly sorry," he said, turning to me, "but we've gotten off to a rather nasty start."

"No bother. Let's try again. I'm Brent."

"Sorry, I meant *my* group has gotten off to a bad start. I'm Quinn. At the journey's start, just outside Moscow, in a brief instant, my colleague rested her hip-pouch down and it was taken," he said in an irritated voice. "All of her documents–passport, travellers cheques, everything–taken. Her husband's as well."

"That's a shitty break," I sympathized.

"They had to get off in Yaroslavl to return to Moscow only two hours after departing Moscow," he grunted, adjusting his tie. "There were six of us. We're all working in Bahrain for an oil company. This was to be our only vacation. We spent months preparing for this journey, only to have this incident occur soon after it started. Another went along with them to provide security for the first two, leaving myself and two other gentlemen to continue." He sighed. "Well, an extreme guilt has set in and we are going to fly back from Irkutsk to meet the others. I figured I'd grab snacks for the flight back."

I was scared, for them and because of them. We were fortunate enough to have our own coach. Dad was spending most of his time in the room writing and window gazing, doubling as bag security guy so Sean and I could wander. Quinn's trip had been ruined in the blink of an eye by the "rampant thievery" we'd been warned about and against which he had taken precautions. He paid the kitchen for an armload of chips and chocolate bars, and nodded sadly at me before leaving. It would be the only criminal activity on the train that I would hear about.

The Krasnoyarsk railway station slid past and the train anchored to a halt soon after dragging the last Russian wagon in front of its platform. Misha was well dressed for the occasion. I could not read his mind but I empathized with whatever thoughts it held. The look on his face told me he was ready to kill something, but it had looked like that when he was having fun. He and Tsveta descended from the train to the platform, where his mother materialized in all the splendor I had envisioned. She was a pre-babushka, wore army boots (honest) and unflattering tight canvass pants, and boasted military-grade breasts. His sister–whom I took to be no more than 14–ran at him clumsily in stiff attempts to control her center of gravity over high heels. Thick makeup exaggerated her every feature.

The mercury at the station hovered around 75° Fahrenheit (25 Celsius). The scarves and thermal jackets we'd worn to face polar conditions were cast aside in favor of T-shirts. I found men dressed in orange coveralls encircling the steel wheels of our restaurant carriage. A short man in red coveralls, revealing the colorful hierarchy, jumped from the platform and pried off a wheel hub. The others rubbed it, seemingly for texture or wheel shavings, and one man smelled it. They replaced the hub and shrugged their shoulders. Such silent problems keep trains intact.

Once our family and Tsveta boarded, the train shunted and departed. I spent the rest of the day in the restaurant car with Sean and Tsveta, who confided her younger brother had not been exposed to anything more technically advanced than rural farm machinery and, once, to a rotary dial phone. Sergei and Pavel entered the dining coach looking like they'd been lynched; such were their drawn faces. They sat down a few tables away with a shifty-eyed bounce of acknowledgement.

We lurched our way into the Moscow + 5 time zone, crossing the halfway mark to Beijing. Tayshet, a five-minute stop, had been the junction for the northern line to Bratsk and the start of the Baikal Amur Magistral Railway, known as BAM. The route had been plagued with problems and was still not entirely functional, despite its sixty-odd years of development. The BAM line runs east, crossing the Lake Baikal region in the north before arching through the mineral-rich districts of northern Siberia and terminating on the Pacific coast.

Tsveta wanted, with all her heart, to go to America. The crowning jewel of her anticipated American experience? Visiting Disneyland.

"Disneyland?" I asked. 'Don't you wait in enough line-ups here?"

Khan banged on the door to my roomette, loudly manipulated several ill-fitting keys and pulled it open. We were approaching Irkutsk. I pointed out to Khan that it was still night, waving him off to bed. The next time I opened my eyes, the panorama of blackness faded to a sooty view of a valley. Tiny bulbs of life gently passed. I flew into manic mode. We were scheduled to get off the train. Now.

A baseball hat was pasted atop my long and unruly red mane. My backpack bulged as the final zipper rounded through the last row of teeth. With six inches to close, the contents disgorged from within and hung out the sides. The pack said, "Go on without me. Leave me here to rot."

"No. I wouldn't have gotten this far without you, Pack," I whimpered, pounding the bag's gut.

"Oof, oof," it choked anthropomorphically.

Khan stood 20 paces away, sternly scouting the situation. Although the sky fired a flaming sunrise for our arrival, Irkutsk itself was draped by low rolling fog. The train pulled alongside the silver Angara River, grumbling to a halt in the rail yard. Khan descended, pursing his lips as he pulled down on the large handle that leveled the stairs to the platform.

"*Well*," he seemed to say with the sharp crinkle in his brow, "*I guess this is it*." We traded handshakes and I slipped him enough flag pins to puncture the lapels of his entire family.

"There you are, Misters Antonsons," announced a thick voice coming our way. A tall man introduced himself as Fyodor, a representative of the local Intourist/Baikal office. Intourist was, in the Russian fashion of security, to deliver us to our hotel. Fyodor was thick built with thick hair, thick neck, thick moustache and thick, thick hands. His eyebrows could have stopped a bullet. He piled our luggage into the bright yellow Ford van labeled with an artistic Intourist/Baikal logo. Fyodor crouched behind the wheel. Hotel Irkutsk was an instant away on the opposing riverbank; it was only a matter of crossing the Angara by a low iron bridge.

Fyodor posed forward sounding questions about our intentions. "Of course you will go to Baikal, how *vloepye* of me to ask. That would be as going to Bratsk and not seeing the dam, or Norilsk and not seeing the smelter."

The van circled the hotel lot and stopped. At the front desk, Fyodor received keys for us. We were in our rooms quickly enough to see–from the sixth-floor window–our beloved train chug away from the station, bound for Vladivostok. The tracks it travelled underlined the hills of concrete tenements and radio towers on the city's west bank.

The elevator dropped us to the lobby. The Angara's bank lurked just beyond the hotel doors, drifting in a sweet breeze. The riverside path was alive with racy neon clothed joggers, arm-locked couples and leashed pets. Trees were trying to overthrow winter and push up the occasional flower. The Angara stretched out smooth, dark and still. Upriver, out of the flow, an enclave harbored ice. Hundreds of fishermen perched atop it, minding their ice holes and yanking fish. Some sat on wooden stools a foot from the ice-free current, next to their fresh catches. It looked as if any minute a crack would give independence to a hundred small bergs and shoot up the town's vacancy rate. I watched as the "ice people" population swelled in minutes. Children skated, a couple erected a tent and a car eased down from the shore onto the ice and parked. The Russian brain tolerated long, cold winters for only so long before willing itself to violate common sense.

Upon our returning to the Hotel Irkutsk, a woman wearing a large grin approached us, her hands cupping one another as though she were carrying an insect. Vera, a distinguished hostess with warm Irkutsky blood, would accompany us on a tour of Irkutsk now, and Lake Baikal later. I gathered she was perpetually just over the edge of 50. Her English was sufficiently fluent to pepper her syntax. Though small in size, she was flamboyant with her vibrant blue overcoat and a mustard-colored scarf. Sweeping her arm in a motion to follow, she led us out to the idling yellow van with Fyodor at the helm.

Irkutsk has the novelty of surviving much of the Soviet era intact. It seemed alive and well, typified as Russian by the grey blocks of housing and bleak facades of government buildings.

However, beneath the shadows of those structures, survive ghosts amidst a wealth of Siberian cabins, the traditional log chalets that were home to many an exile, particularly the famed Decembrists who attempted the 1825 coup in Saint Petersburg. A group of military officers had opposed the crowning of Tsar Nicholas I and rallied in support of Constantine, the natural heir to Alexander I. Their demonstration brought about their demise–exile for those who hadn't been executed. Nicholas was installed and the Decembrists were doomed to live out their lives in Irkutsk. Their handsomely decorated quarters, later flanked by install-ments of low-level buildings, endured not only the Communist period but the Great Fire of 1879, which claimed three-quarters of Irkutsk. The fire came at a time when the city was a convivial point from which all roads radiated. Tea merchants arrived from China, exiles trekked from west of the Urals, fur traders travelled from the north, and gold prospectors came from all over. Convicts, cara-vans and pioneers converged here in the center of Siberia, 3,100 miles (5,000 kilo-meters) from Moscow.

Vera coaxed us out of Fyodor's van, which had stopped in front of the time-eaten, wooden church of Christ the Savior. The protective enclosure of the city wall had started here but failed to meet fire safety standards and eventually fell to the Great Fire. A few paces ahead, the street spread out to a large square–of the district's war memorial. In Russia, what Westerners call the Second World War is known as the Great Patriotic War. Strewn about the great granite slabs etched with name after name were fresh wreaths and floral arrangements choked with blood-red ribbons. Four guards–no older than 18–shouldered rifles and stood motionless at the compass points. In the center, blowing with the convections of a campfire, burned the Eternal Flame. I was temporarily lost in the purpose, overwhelmed by the display of nationalism. Sean and I neared the sparking blaze to take a photo when the guards suddenly spun their rifles and yelled short commands in unison. The guards rotated to the west, goose-stepped off to the side, clicking and clacking their black boots and marched promptly out of the square.

"Fifteen-minute shifts," said Vera. Sure enough, the replacements–two of whom were young women–stepped into position and resumed the watch.

Fyodor drove us past the Decembrists Museum to the riverside. The ice-people were still tempting fate with heavy machinery, waving their families onto the shelf with them. On shore, a large obelisk rose from the embankment's square, dedicated to the explorers of old Russia. Tsar Nicholas dedicated the monument to those who had opened up the country, such as Vitus Bering, the Dutch/Russian sea navigator who lent his name to the body of water Russia shares with Alaska. We rested on the riverbank railing as Vera told us we'd missed a solar eclipse of the region by one month.

"Enough. Now we go to Baikal," she announced and we boarded the van.

The bucolic sheds of a placid, rural neighborhood ended with an arresting army of birch trees enforcing the "nature only" apartheid rule. Fifty miles of Russian forest and many low hills later, Fyodor made a turn, following a winding, rustic switchback. Vera rolled her head back with a wide smile of anticipation. The trees fell below, exposing an extension of Heaven, and the glory of Lake Baikal spread before us like an intense, eye-penetrating sheet of lightning. Vera held her smile, positioning her oversized sunglasses on her face.

On a map, Lake Baikal bows in the shape of a fattened feather, remote and isolated from any similar-sized body of water. Baikal is a composite of superlatives in virtually every way. She holds a fifth of the world's fresh water, enough in her nearly 5,000 cubic miles (20,000 cubic kilometers) of volume to supply current global demand for 40 years. She is the world's deepest lake, with depths of more than one and a third of a mile. Formed nearly 50 million years ago, she is also the oldest of lakes. More than 100 species of fish and wildlife are unique to this lake and its shore area. Vera told us, "Three hundred and thirty-six rivers and streams feed into the lake, but only one–the Angara–flows out."

Fyodor pulled the van's brake, ushering us into the presence of the Hotel

Baikal. Paces away from the entrance stretched a wooden-railed lookout. Vera went indoors to arrange lunch while Sean wound through a roll of film. It was not obvious to us then that the sheer brightness of the view would overwhelm our cameras, burning away most of the evidence that we'd been there. Fortunately, for posterity I added my name and the date to the railing, carving and chipping, as had many others before me.

Inside the hotel were framed photographs profiling a 1989 visit by Russian President Boris Yeltsin and German Chancellor Helmut Kohl. The fact that Mr. Yeltsin is not exactly photogenic seems to have gone unnoticed. Tiny Russian captions beneath each picture tracked the president's actions. I tried improv to interpret them for Dad and Sean. "Yeltsin knocks back flask in foyer of Hotel Baikal;" "Yeltsin visits men's room of Restaurant Baikal;" "Russian president (in towel) discusses plumbing quality of Hotel Baikal."

In the main restaurant hall, we took seats with a stupendous view of the lake. The sun held at noon. A multi-course meal of local culinary fare arrived plate by plate, by plate. A waiter presented beer, bathed in a tub of lake ice. Soup including every local ingredient, led to a plate of various Baikal fish, baked, fried, poached or grilled.

Having been raised on North America's West Coast, where fish and diet are synonymous, it is odd I've never developed a taste for seafood. It may be that a hamburger doesn't scream cow, nor does bacon speak of pig. However, when eyeballs, gills and fins hollers "I'm a fish, full of slippery entrails, and here's my proof leaking into your salad," I was all too aware that the dish in front of me had once been a living creature. Being that it was too late to set the fish free, I chose to push its silver body around the plate instead. When Vera became suspicious, I stabbed the beast with my fork. That drew an oozing juice that curdled my blood. The eyeball stared back at me, and I decided then on an all-malt lunch. Vera watched me. "Are you allergic to anything?" she asked warily.

"Frankincense and myrrh. But I'm not fond of fish."

'Hmm. I've never met anyone who didn't like fish,' she said. It wasn't the fish that was being judged.

Winding down the road from the hotel, Fyodor ensured we entered the lakeside village of Lystvyanka. Secure amidst the sharp drop of the surrounding mountains, wooden houses–faded, aged, and leaning precariously toward collapse–laced the dirt road. Strands of fish netting, bleached buoys and upturned boats festooned the rocky shore. The shoreline was stenciled with all manner of debris–beam supports, oars, and rusted rigging gear. When the road ended, Fyodor parked the van. An agile Vera beat us to the lake's ice line and gazed out with pride.

"Can we walk on the ice?" Sean asked.

"You could drive tank on it," Vera grinned, as if articles didn't have a choice in her English.

That was all the confirmation I needed. I ran out, chuckling until the ice broke and my leg shot through the frozen lake. I shrieked the cry of someone coming down the wrong side of a ladder. Sean doubled over in laughter. Dad's pipe fell from his lips. Vera tipped back on her pelvis to scrutinize a developing cloudbank. Fear of the magnitude I felt rarely makes it back to the ears of the living. Vera pointed a gloved hand to the ice hole drilled by local fishermen into which I'd stepped.

"If one washes in Baikal," Vera said, imparting a piece of local superstition aimed at easing my embarrassment, "it will add five years to his life."

Baikal owed me at least five years after nearly taking all thirty I had lived. Dad, Sean, and I washed our faces with Baikal's life force and crunched back to shore, my pant leg hardening in the freeze. Dancing scarves of storm dove from the ridges; Lystvyanka quickly grew dark.

We drove ahead of the approaching storm, the road dappled with a renaissance palette. I told Vera about a television show on the American Public Broadcasting Service. "The show documented the *Trans-Siberian Railway*. On the journey, the camera crew detoured to interview a skilled sculptor who lived somewhere near Baikal. Do you know of him?" Vera instructed Fyodor to do a wheel-searing 180-degree turn that launched us onto a rutted muddy path. Weathered houses, enclosed in perimeters of birch-twig fences, appeared beside the rocking van. The single-lane roads crossing our path were bare of townsfolk, quite possibly because they had swallowed entire families. There was no one, except for the occasional stalagmite of a resident leaning on his fence. The van crept over the spitting puddles at the grassy sides until we stopped with a sharp jerk. This, Vera offered, "Is this the home of the sculptor Yuri Andryevich Panov." His tiny residence, devoid of any colors save for the spectrum of aging wood, stood stout amid a clutter of carvings.

From sticks and driftwood to the full rooted trees just off his veranda, nothing had escaped Yuri's creative hands. Faces, life-sized and remarkably full of expression, had been whittled into the wood. Famous faces seemed to grow from the bark: Russian poets and writers–Dostoevsky, Pushkin, Tolstoy–cowering demons, the wincing stares of Stalin, Hitler, Marx. A screaming ghoul clutched moaning souls in its talons; its tortured eyes spilled wooden tears. *Yuri's head was clearly not a neat place to be in*, I thought.

Vera knocked hard once on the door. Impatiently, she followed this with a set of swift knocks. A clinically short woman rounded the shed and spoke with Vera. She looked us over with gentle eyes, hobbled up a step and went inside. A short while later, Yuri appeared on the front steps. His wife stood at the doorway looking on. As he shook our hands, I noticed his knuckles were like walnuts–his pads coarse and his grip crushing. Yuri was 85 though looked 20 years younger, a fact he attributed to Baikal's longevity waters. His curly hair, grey as steel wool, fell into a beard lacking any hint of a moustache.

Yuri led us around his yard pointing out his legacy as Vera interpreted. As a fit young man, he'd been raised during the growing pains of the new Soviet government in the 1920s. His means of conveying the then-current struggle was to annotate his thoughts onto the nature that surrounded him. Nothing in his yard avoided becoming an expression of his soul. It was an amazing example of what one could reveal to the world. It was an invigoratingly personal exhibit hidden away in Siberia for few to see.

Yuri invited us in for tea his wife had already brewed. He'd sculpted the inside of his home, too. Antlers from various beasts, given immortality by his blade, were laced with landscapes and fishing scenes. Yuri and Dad withdrew into a discussion of their own. For a sizeable sum, Yuri was prepared to part with framed birch-bark paintings of a cabin on the Angara. Dad purchased three and dealt them to Sean, Vera and me. We thanked Yuri and his wife for their kindness and for signing the artworks. As we loaded into the van, the wind picked up and lifted Yuri's hair and beard. Hard pats of rain lashed Fyodor's windshield. A storm billowed in, fiercely enveloping the village around us.

Back in Irkutsk, the weather was calm, as we'd left it. Baikal's storm-brewing abilities were confined to her reach in the smaller villages. We praised Vera for her

courtesies and the events she had created for us, and then retired to our rooms. The sun fired the smog at an evening angle.

The following morning we arrived to board the *Trans-Mongolian* train, Irkutsk's railway depot displayed a squalor normally attributed to urinals. Or at least that's how it seemed through my lens of insufficient sleep and no coffee service. Dad, Sean, and I were the only people in the large room aside from two sleeping drunks and a triad of Asian traders. Dad bought a Fanta from a vacant table by leaving change where the bottle had been; it felt warm, perhaps already opened. For half an hour we stared at the large Arrivals and Departures board, hoping to see our train number or destination. Wandering wasn't an option. An isolation of sorts was built into the scheme, so all that was available to us were the features of the board and the drunks.

Finally, letters on the board scrambled to spell out our hoped for locomotive: *Trans-Mongolian*. The train would be our home until we reached Ulaan Bataar. We funneled our bags to the corridor. Our tickets seemed to have been printed with the intention to keep the cabin number a secret. When we boarded, every roomette's door was locked. Being attached to the idea of lying down, I went to find the *provodnitsa*, the all-important custodian of the coach.

At the far end, in their own roomette, two large women were speaking in high-pitched tones, their faces inches apart. They made it clear I was interrupting them. The one who saw fit to rise looked like the choice recruit of militia groups. As to how she wound up as custodial staff on the traveller-prone train, I can only speculate: nepotism or community hours. I understood why Americans feared Russians. She chuckled, tickled by my request as she fingered through the keys and approached our new quarters. With no mercy, she dealt three heavy blows onto the door, and then drew the panel back to reveal a freshly awoken Mongolian woman lying on one of the four beds. The *provodnitsa,* whom I monikered "Bayonette," clapped her hands and, with no regard for the sole occupant, recessed the top two beds. I could hear her thinking, "God, this is *sooo* beneath me."

Ooayaoouai, our unwilling cabin companion, shuffled her belongings into a pile on her horizontal seat where she'd been sleeping. Introducing myself and travel companions, I learned she was returning to the Mongolian frontier via the

Trans-Manchurian train, another transiberian-route. She planned to disembark there at "Ulan-Ude" which she pronounced with a drawl. In response I said her lovely name several times, perhaps to her entertainment, perhaps to her annoyance. "Ooayaoouai. Ooayaoouai." She did her best to feign sleep atop the bulking items propped about her bed. The addition of our packs in the 60 cubic feet space left barely enough room for keeping one's thoughts to oneself.

I was set to appreciate the railway's accomplishment as each mile unfolded beside me. The Circum-Baikal railroad over this stretch might seem a bit confusing with its three versions. The *Trans-Siberian's* best-known route goes along here and onward to Vladivostok. The *Trans-Manchurian* also passes over these tracks on its alternate routing, heading to Beijing. At this point we were technically riding the latter train until we reached the Mongolian border where our route would take us on the *Trans-Mongolian* southward into its namesake country, and eventually to Beijing. The sky blazed denim blue that barely hid the stars. A cloud like billows of bed sheet bulged into the shape of every continent until high winds tugged it away in ribbons.

Beside our tracks, Lake Baikal glared at me, as victors often do to their victims. In front of distant, darting hills decked in the greenery of spring, she was a vast frozen plain of light. An hour passed, and the lake was still sparring for attention with the landmass encasing it.

The engine's horn blew, signally a slowing train. I put down my journal. A forest sidelined us, then gave way to a few wooden buildings and a partially eroded station platform. The faces of elderly Russians squinted, eyeing the train's wagons. The train slowed to idle, revealing babushkas standing over their wares: bottles of beer and jars of homemade pickles, pickled eggs, goulash and borscht. Their mouths, carved into their faces, hung open. Their hands pocketed in thick-knit sweaters. Some wore large muddy boots. Others squeezed into ancient slippers, their boots behind them on the platform's deteriorated concrete. Each wore a weathered scarf covering her head.

Mothers bounced babies on boisterous chests, old men with fur hats grimaced at our arrival, seemingly happy and insulted that we had arrived. Young girls showed off dyed hair and (to me) unflattering lipstick while young men sporting equally slick hair ogled them with a Russian seriousness that ran the length of their bodies. The men stoically smoked cigarettes as though they were soon to face a firing squad–then recklessly shot the butts into the wheels of the train. This was a town without a name. It wasn't on my map and we didn't stop long enough to get off and join the locals. The train picked up speed and the forest regained its ubiquity. A yawn erupted in our roomette, and sleep overtook me.

Dad's action woke me as I dreamed about polar ice caps blocking my attempt to drive across the Bering Strait.

"Were you folding my bed against the wall?" I asked.

"I was wrestling with the food bag. Can I make you a soup?"

"French onion, with real cheese," I ordered.

"Sorry. Your choices are dehydrated beef, chicken or pork." He displayed three crushed packages of noodles.

"Beef, please."

He poured the packs into two mugs and went to the samovar for boiling water. Ooayaoouai snored in the bunk below me, her leg twitching with Mongolian myoclonic jerks. I looked over at Sean, asleep and wearing a loose smile on the bottom-most bunk.

"Hey stranger," I whispered. "New in town? Looking to party?"

His lips parted as if to reply. I would have continued had Dad not returned with the steaming mugs.

"Have you been writing the whole day?" I asked.

Dad had been attacking the same book project for years. His work life rarely gave him the opportunity to gather his thoughts and apply them to his avocation. He'd often lift his head from his binder, look around as if someone had called him and tap his pen on his lips before diving back into the text. "Yeah," he replied. The pages were a battlefield of colored ink, crossed lines and highlights. Discarded crumpled sheets littered the floor. Sean turned on his side with a grunt. Dad picked up his writing and softly tried out a few passages on me, pausing every so often to scribble notes. Finally, he took in the roomette, the train and the moment. "Every time I look up, I still find it unbelievable that we're here."

"This," I told him, "has already been the best trip of my life."

"This is a father's ultimate dream," he said.

I could feel what he meant. His sons were with him on a voyage he'd dreamed of making since he met those two Brits in Leningrad 25 years before.

"We should hit Ulan-Ude pretty soon," I said, seeing paved road out the window. "*Ulan-Ude,*" I thought, as I do about cities I've only imagined, "*what will you look like?*"

The city had eaten its way up most of the surrounding hills, securing in its girdle enough discolored infrastructure, spindly radio towers and vortices of garbage to suck away any thought of ever returning to an attractive enclave. This city munched on a diet of rotten concrete. Despite the disregard for esthetics, Ulan-Ude was a monumental stop. For it was here that the aforementioned *Trans-Siberian* and *Trans-Manchurian* (with Ooayaoouai on board) continued to stretch eastward where they would eventually split from one another in the junction town of Tarskaya. Our train, now the *Trans-Mongolian*, left them here, and we steered south behind a new locomotive and with a new dining coach and additional coaches.

The platform filled with crowds whose sole purpose was greeting our train's arrival. Sean pulled down the window. Peering along the length of our wagons, we could see the onboard traders dangling their cargo for public inspection even before we'd completely stopped. The haggling and bartering exchanged fistfuls of currency, deft swapping of goods and the lessons of rural economics dominated the ten-minute stop. Even as motion crept back into the train's wheels, the selling continued until our speed hampered transactions. Only then were the offered leather jackets, button-fly jeans, and gowns drawn back into the coaches.

Although the station yard had a number of locomotives–both diesel and electric–preserved on display for interested individuals to inspect, Ulan-Ude did not wish travellers to stay. With little time to appreciate whatever else was saved from the past in this sad city, the diminishing downtown core was soon behind us. A hinterland of urban hardship lingered. Thousands of concrete auto sheds slid by, roofed in rusted metal sheets, sun-bleached shades of fiberglass and rotted plywood. Muddy tire ruts in the churned earth snaked towards more civilized asphalt streets. Graffiti, spills of black and red paint, was rampant. "Kolya Dubrovinik loves Melonhedic Loshinski;" "For a good time call 27-63-91-05-92-14-67-2 and ask for Marina Shytesoetskovritch;" "God Bless Atheism;" "Dmitri Yanosominovitch was here May 21/91."

Sean and I were admiring the swift recess of it all from the open window in our corridor, enjoying the breeze when Sean yelled *Duck!* and threw up the window-pane. Three young boys were throwing bottles at the passing train. Two of the boys knelt on an auto-shed roof, re-arming from the bowling-pin configuration of bottles in front of them. The third executed his pitch, expertly tipping forward with the follow-through. His brown, quart-sized bottle shattered on the metal bar between our windows. Compare this pastime to spending time glued to a PlayStation and one could not help but conclude that idle time belonged to the devil. Dropping 60 bucks on a computer game may be a form of crime prevention.

When the hillsides reappeared, the train rolled through the pitted crux of a graded crevasse. Flashes of light in the topsoil stunned my eyes, like an array of flashbulbs.

"Thank you… thank you, please sit," I said, announcing to the others that I was heading to the restaurant car. Dad found a hundred thousand rubles in his laundry and passed them off to us. In hours they would be worthless on our travels, as well as illegal to carry across the Mongolian border. He asked that I empty the garbage of his crumpled notebook pages, empty noodle packages and dead fruit. Sean plugged a bookmark into the spine of *The Big Red Train Ride*, Eric Newby's account of his railway journey in Russia decades before and decided to follow me.

At the end of the corridor, the provodnitsa had just finished folding the hallway's cloth floor mat, halving its surface. (I would see her later in the evening, unfolding it, free of footprints and pleated, ready for inspection by her supervisors at the upcoming station stop. This saved her whisking a broom over it and scouring the unavoidable dirt and mud.) She grumbled at the sight of my heavy dustbin, taking it from my grip without comment. She opened a metal lid in the end vestibule, which I had thought was a convenient seat, to expose a square throat open to the bare tracks below. She upended the can swiftly into the hole. As it digested the contents, we heard the breaking of bottles and 'per-twangs' of aluminum cans hitting the tracks. She handed back the empty dustbin and left. Few things are more harmful to the railway's reputation than what I had just witnessed. This was a source of the glittering rubble flowing out of Ulan-Ude. I decided this did make sense–but only in the Russian sense.

No stretch of corridor was without bulky packages and opaque passengers. Neither yielded willingly to passersby. A naked baby ran screaming from his mother's clutch, tripping every few steps. Choking sounds seeped from a cabin where an old Chinese man sucked on a long, skinny pipe. In another, a Russian couple stared out at the necklace of sparkling debris.

The grisly smell of boiling cabbage grew sharper as I approached the restaurant car. Draping shower curtains and imitation floral arrangements in dumpy vases created a sad contrast to the previous train's coziness. No matter, said my eye for detail, it's probably the way I would decorate it.

Sometime later, Sean left and I was alone in the car pondering imponderables and tinkering with infinity. An old man in a weathered trench coat and a face sporting a few days' growth of beard came in from the Russian end of the train, purchased a bottle of vodka, and seated himself a few booths away. I read in his face the description of Job: "Old and full of years." He poured himself a shot glass, which his lips suckled quickly. He replaced the bottle's lid and stared at me. He had the pensive look of an irritated drunk with a history of resentment distilled through a 180-proof past. His eyes spoke of a trapped soul. Breaking his stare, he stroked his chin as though he'd found a way out.

I thought about what Russia had shown me. With our arrival in Asia long past and the border with Mongolia approaching, I had to get hold of where I was before the memory faded. Russia has a thrilling history, spanning all ages. travelling through it was like watching a movie unfold. The brutalities of Russia's past were black and white scenes shot from different camera angles; my role was to watch the movie, then purchase the action figures and ask for posters at the local video store. To buy into it. Of all the countries I've seen, Russia was most like me; it was the place that mirrored me best.

After the better part of an hour, I passed by the washroom in our carriage three wagons back. There, leaning in the corner, were two thin, four-foot metal signs reading "Moskva-Ulaan Bataar" in bold Cyrillic font. I recognized these as the metal sheets that hung off the wagon's sides. "Hmm...." I could see myself hauling them off to my room. But that's as far as my imagination got because I could also foresee the provodnitsa's fury. No, I decided, trying to smuggle them home across the two countries we were about to travel through, one of which had Martial Law 1989 on the wine list, was not conceivable. But when have I ever been constrained by other people's interpretation of "inconceivable"? This I knew: everything has a price in Russia. I approached the provodnitsa and offered 10 dollars and a roll of rubles. Her expression showed that now, with money exchanged between us, we were on the same level. She soaped the signs down and helped me carry them back to the cabin. I could overhear Dad talking to Sean.

"You didn't get braces because, if you remember, we all agreed to get cable TV instead...."

"Dad, Sean. Check *me* out," I interrupted. "Travel bling!"

They were impressed. Train travel allows for embellished stories so I prattled on about the smallest details of my negotiations. We wrapped the signs into the tight cocoon of a sleeping bag to camouflage them from customs officials, trying to not make them not look like a body.

Five hours after leaving Ulan-Ude, the last of the Russian frontier closed in. We eased through the border town of Nash, after which the train slowed into a setting of grassland and a station. The sun teetered toward the last of afternoon, still warming the air as we disembarked after handing over our travel documents to an official. The station—nothing but a room, really—was barren, save for lacquer-deficient benches in the foyer and a few dozing bodies. An aroma sliced the air with the scent of stale potato juice.

Outside the stationhouse, a few hundred people were milling around in an open-air market, cordoned off by a peeling green fence, through which we ventured. Every conceivable animal by-product was being sold. Tendon, thigh, paw, liver, hoof, brain, tongue. Pickled, dried or in the freshness spectrum of bone-white, blood red and pink. Cubed, stewed, slabbed, and minced. Abacuses snapped out totals. Rubles and products changed hands. We carried on with slow strides to the platform, resting against the large trees that guarded the station's static entranceway. The inanimate scene looked eager for movement.

The engine had been uncoupled and sent to the locomotive yard for companionship. I'd read this was also to prevent anyone from commandeering it and wildly running the border. I'm not sure what would possess someone to see that as a viable option. It's not as if you could hide a locomotive in a desert and elude the search party. I pulled out the guidebook to skim over the Nash particulars. Waits of up to six hours were not uncommon, and 10 hours was not unheard of. I read it aloud twice, so as to not be the only passenger suffering from this knowledge.

Silhouetted outlines of buildings and people stretched until they melted into the onset of dusk. Dad hovered a match above his pipe bowl, then strolled off until he was no longer in sight. Stars filled the gap of sky while Hale-Bopp, the badminton comet, emerged. One by one, families, groups and lone travellers returned to their coaches and cabins. Everyone's land legs had returned and they wanted back into their cramped spaces. An oddity of rail travel, I suppose.

We eased into our couchette. My fluid consumption needed to be relieved. A search of three wagons proved every restroom to be locked, a measure that prevented people from locking themselves away during customs. "Prevents more than that," I said. At the decking plates between the cars, in the envelope of the rubber cave, I looked to the gaps and tracks below, checked for possible intrusions, and conducted my business efficiently. Suddenly a voice from below hollered. Someone moved over gravel; a face peered up at me through the crack, screaming angrily, his flashlight igniting the darkness below. Constrained by the speed of light, I sought refuge at the back of my top bunk, hiding under a book. "I just pissed on a guard," I said.

"WHAT," yelled Dad, his tone suggesting that at any moment we'd hear a heavy pounding on our door before being marched off to the gulag.

"Forget I said that, just forget it. Now you are accomplices. Forget it."

As the four-hour-wait mark neared, the provodnitsa returned our documentation. The patience required to sit on an idle train faded. It wasn't the freedom restrictions and impending scrutiny/search that made me antsy and unpleasant; it was the immobility. I missed the motion of the train. It's like when the masseuse stops to answer the phone.

There was a sharp crack at the window. The sound of stone on glass. Sean jumped and cupped his hands to see beyond the reflection.

"It's a Russian guard!"

Under my breath I prayed "Not the one I pissed on."

Dad and I peered out. Not five feet away, standing with official erectness, a guard brought a quick hand to his mouth and shot it down. The three of us looked at each other, shrugged and looked out again. Dressed in formal polished boots, a heavy below-the-knee overcoat and high-fronted, sickle-brimmed hat, the guard repeated the motion.

"What the hell's he doing?" I asked.

"I think he wants a cigarette," Sean said.

"He could walk in here and confiscate himself a carton if he wanted to," I said. I produced a package of Marlboros and held them quizzically to the windowpane.

"He gave the thumbs up. Give him one," Dad said, a bit excited that we were doing something risky but not quite understanding why.

The three of us labored to open the window but to no avail. I pointed my arm across the car to the corridor windows, indicating to the guard that he go around to the other side of the train. In a quick sidestep and topple, he slipped beneath the carriage and emerged on the other side with a cuff sopped in grease.

Sean encouraged me. "Throw it. He'll get it! Can't you see he doesn't want to get caught?"

I tossed a cigarette through the window. In a fashion not unlike practiced pigeons or chipmunks, the guard eyed the perimeter and purposefully strode towards the prize. In that split second of reclamation, an authoritative voice bellowed. The guard froze, then paced off towards the direction of the holler.

"Shit, we got him in trouble," Sean exclaimed and broke away into the cabin.

"Well, I'll be,' I thought aloud. "That guy is my Russian self. I would have done everything he did. That's why I don't have a Lamborghini."

Minutes later, a stone bounced off the windowpane, and the procedure was repeated.

"Spacibo," he exhaled.

Another guard marched to his side. The first happily held out the gifted cigarette, pointing at Sean and me hanging our arms limply over the window ledge. Three-quarters of a pack and half their comrades later, the train inched to a crawl. The Russian guards nodded a friendly farewell as we entered Mongolia.

Mongolia! Our elation of arriving in this particular country was the result of much anticipation; it was as if our entire world had changed. No sooner had we hugged and shared handshakes all 'round than the train stopped.

We were still on the cusp of competing authorities. A group of Russian soldiers entered and lifted the long panels of corridor floor. I could see the undercarriage. Flashlights bounced around, crossing with the beams of other guards below. Stowaways? Drugs? Contraband? Waldo? We were not privy to information about the search and were ushered into our cabin unceremoniously with words to the effect of "Zare eez noting to see here, people. Now move along, move along." If someone were stowed beneath the train, somewhere under the grime and sediment, he'd be the farthest person from excitement in the entire world. This investigation of the flooring ate up much of the next hour as subsequent cars were searched. The hour was late, approaching a new day.

A full quarter of the moon rose above the horizon, climbing into the Hale-Bopp comet. Movement at last! Good reason to cheer. As the train nudged along, beer was opened, passed about. Other passengers converged in the corridor, no doubt with their steel bladders begging for relief.

The train stopped.

It was time for the Mongolian guards to do their part in receiving us. Suche

Bator, the fringe township, similarly took away our engine for security against its theft–perhaps to avoid a dash *back* across the border, which by this time looked appealing. The process of giving up our passports, identifying our bags, and declaring the amount of money we carried was not a rigorous affair. The further two hours of waiting was. Yet to our relief, no one questioned the train coach signs wrapped in the sleeping bag. At long last, we felt the belting reversal of the reattaching engine. The sharp motion jarred the train, knocking my subconscious off the shelf of monotony and causing my travel-ego to stir. We were in Mongolia. As the train rhythm soothed us, one by one we drifted into sleep.

Sean hollered for us to wake up. The room was black. Disorientation reigned. Ahead of the skidding engine burned another wildfire. The metal wheels screamed in bursts; a full-out locking would have shaved them flat. And that's an even worse scenario, as flattened train wheels need to be replaced before the train can move down the tracks. Flames leapt and danced, enabled and encouraged by the parched, thirsty grass. The train stopped, violently reversed to reconnoiter the situation, and stopped again. We could feel the train worry. Now it nursed itself forward, we supposed, in a dare to make passage when the winds shifted or calmed, or the fire waned. Our proximity put us in the heart of the fire, where it circled around near the rear wagons and sparked color into the night in every direction. We gazed out the corridor's windows. Our remoteness left us in a wilderness without promise of rescue or guidance; the fire would be unchallenged by men or equipment. A plume of diesel exhaust eclipsed the beauty of the fire in the pit of night.

"We have a diesel engine?"

"They must've put it on at the border" Dad answered, not understanding my panic.

"Do the math! Add one fire and two fuel tanks and see if you get 72 travel-ready virgins. Judging by the scenery, this says eternal damnation to me."

"Isn't *this* remarkable," Sean exclaimed. "Brent! Is this in the guidebook?"

'It's under the DOs and DON'Ts…. I'm fairly sure it's a DON'T!'

Other cabin doors opened. We could do nothing but watch the advancing dance. And wait. Which, by now, all 400 of us on board excelled at. Seconds passed slowly, as if choked in smoke. The engine compartment, I thought, must be a sight. A fifty-five-ton diesel locomotive. Was there enough sweat pouring off the crew to fill a bucket? Would they appreciate God's swift intervention? Were they bouncing heads off the dialed panels? Playing Rock-Paper-Scissors? Projected onto the theatre of my mind was an image of me dying in these flames. This was one of those mistakes in life that shouldn't be fatal, I thought, countering that there was a certain romance in having one's spirit set free in a train wreck in Mongolia: it is better than being killed at home hit by a bus.

The train's brusque movement threw us all a step back. Acceleration climbed to top speed. Flames beside the train stretched to almighty heights. The locomotive pulled us through and beyond.

Not tonight, dear little ones, I heard a passenger's voice say, *not tonight.*

Sleep after that was impossible. Rest came and went. A heavy pounding fell upon our roomette's door in the Mongolia morning. A lazy voice yawned in the distance. It was our wake-up call. I rolled over the short lip of the top bunk and free fell onto the food bag, causing my head to ricochet off the doorframe. The sudden collision threw stars across my vision. Sean spun himself awake, grazing his forehead on the steely underside of the top bunk as his foot shot into the bifurcation of my legs. He clutched at his skull; a small scream escaped from his lips. Dad stirred and we both told him not to move a muscle. Not just yet.

Our morning was held hostage by a Mongolian sunrise.

The 232 mile (374 kilometer) trip marker raced by the window. Ulaanbaatar, inshallah (God willing), waited at 251. Dad left to run a bath for our coffee crystals and was instantly checkmated between the samovar and a Mongolian's stashed belongings. The aisle was piled with luggage–all packed, stacked, and precariously balanced. Early-morning command of any language relies on nods and shrugs, and with it he negotiated his way back to us.

"Mongolia, kid," Dad smiled to me. The country's magical name enchanted him, as would Zanzibar or Marrakesh. I grabbed my steaming mug. With the shells of exhaustion falling around me, I nursed the third-degree froth off the beverage and leaned into the window. Our immediate plans for Ulaanbaatar included a room booked for three nights in the Bayangol Hotel.

Ulaanbaatar (also known as Ulan Bator and Ulaan Baatar) snuck up in small fringe-housing developments lining the valley slopes in gentle, shaded relief. More than half a million people were scattered among the low buildings amidst the shrapnel of this urban district–which was devoid of cloverleaf junctions, thoroughfares, overpasses, and any of the infrastructure one might see in other major cities.

We stepped from the train's vestibule to the station's platform in what had become a common motion this far into our journey. Though the exhilaration of planting my feet on Mongolian soil for the first time left my soul giddy, I felt the need to maintain an air of sophistication during the attempt. A young Mongolian woman dressed in a suit wrapped in a red cape called out. She was attractive, smiling and calling me by name. I was in her shadow before she drew another breath.

Tezhlemsa Ravdandorj (or "T" for short) was a representative of Zhuulchin, the state tourism office that, she explained, had a share of our trip funds. Beside her stood an older man in a fitted wool coat and leather beret. She greeted me with a swift bow and introduced Chuuka Galsan (I shortened it to Chook), the tourism office's driver. Chook's face was etched with a lifetime of smiles and sorrow.

"Are you alone?" Tezhlemsa asked, flipping a piece of foolscap. I thought of answering, "Yes," and leaving with her right then, just me, alone. Before I could, we heard a holler using my first name. Sean clasped on the vestibule's handgrip, fighting it like a fish just pulled from the water.

"Dad, Sean, this is… is... "T." She reached for Sean's open hand.

Tezhlemsa led us through the parking lot to a shiny brand-new van, the brightest I'd seen since Moscow. It was clean, fresh, screaming yellow–the opposite of every vehicle around it. This was local prestige. Chook drove us through narrow streets to our hotel. Tezhlemsa explained our reservations had originally been made at the Bayangol, the usual travellers' destination, but renovations were being made to those elderly lodgings. Instead, we were booked at the recently completed Hotel Edelweiss. As we circled into the driveway of the Swiss chateau clone, our good fortune was apparent. The Bayangol, with its sad Soviet-era ambiance loomed behind us.

The Edelweiss (or *Otlas*, as the front-desk clerk pronounced it) opened six months prior. It stank of new. German financing lent the Western amenities of an extra star to its three floors. We were booked in two of its 16 rooms. I was sentenced to bunk with Dad.

Our window faced southward overlooking the etched groove of the Selba

River. Either side of the precision-straight aqueduct was a flat, gravel desert. The river slid west through barren hills. Near us, a village of plump and portable accommodations–nomadic *gers*–clumped together, surrounded by a wooden fence. Gers are generally a large circle of cloth or animal hide stretched around a wooden frame and domed by a similarly styled roof. They serve as living quarters for entire families. Skinny tin flues poked up from these gers and from a handful of wooden shacks, trailing ashy smoke. The perimeter fence enclosed this suburb of poverty. In contrast, across the Selba stood Soviet-style apartment buildings shoulder-to-shoulder in mock prosperity.

The occasional passerby was dressed in traditional Mongolian garb, usually a blue silky robe called a *deel*, with cuffs that hide the fingertips, baggy blue pants, and black footwear that curled the wearers' toes back.

The magical wand of travel waved.

We entered the lobby restaurant, each presented with a breakfast egg and two wieners. Before leaving us, Tezhlemsa said, "You have the day to wander," and "Show up at the Zhuulchin office to explore possibilities," which was code for us feeding her company our funds in exchange for an excursion.

Following our intuition–"city to the east and sparse vegetation to the west"–we followed the lazy Selba to an abrupt transition: the cosmopolitan core. Ulaanbaatar was a tranquillizing dose of a small town built big by the Russians, who then left. Grumpy trolley buses spilled people onto the streets. Schoolchildren darted through the suits and skirts of a corporate crowd. Muffler shots rang out from beneath the thin traffic of vintage Chaikas, Ladas, and Jeeps. Two men in wooden carts snapped whips at their horses as the traffic light turned green. Peace Avenue–Main Street Mongolia–was a wide, tree-lined boulevard with as much road as side-walk. Paint colors that had faded from the Western palate in the 1970s covered everything that wasn't moving.

Fresh coats of traditional Mongolian script overlapped–or were next to–washed out Cyrillic billboards, all aimed at enticing shoppers. Mongolia's loose alphabet script fit the country's exotic personality, as Cyrillic reflected Russia's.

A monstrous statue of the revolutionary Damdiny Suhbaatar, gallantly poised on his horse, dominated Suhbaatar Square. At the time of his death in 1923, when he was only 29, he had been the nation's most distinguished revolutionary hero, minister of war and commander of the army. Suhbaatar raised a welcoming hand in triumph. His horse, however, seemed concerned with the bit lodged at the back of its smile. Statues depicting warriors on horseback indicate their fates. If the horse is rearing, the dauntless rider died in battle. Four hooves on the ground convey that the hero died of natural causes outside of fighting. If one front hoof is planted, the other raised, as was the case of Suhbaatar's, he was wounded in battle. Suhbaatar died "officially" of natural causes but, "unofficially," he was poisoned to permit the succession of Choibalson. Whatever the truth of his battle-stance horse, a crowd sat in its shade.

Our day continued to be one of vignettes. Two men, so old we wagered at least one was dead, were playing chess on a small pine bench. We stood over the game, watching, speculating, and waiting for an epic move. The pieces were dull and worn from years of perspiration. One of the players tipped forward, poised to fall on the board. He held himself there, violating gravity for many minutes, but did not move a piece.

Dad's treasure of Mongolia became a pencil-stippled sketch of a crazed horse and rider backdropped by local hills. He was overjoyed with the framed print bartered from a merchant inside a marketplace, and held in his hands for minutes until we were outside and he passed it to Sean, who dropped it. The moment it shattered along Peace Avenue, shooting splinters and right angles of glass in all directions, we were family in name only. And that was considered worthy of changing. Listening to the war of words between them, I felt a tug at my shirttail. Turning, I saw the dirty face of an impoverished boy with cupped hands. He pointed to a rudimentary shoeshine board and pleaded with long eyes that I use his service. He could have been no more than six. I placed my well-travelled heel onto his sheet of paper. The boy squatted, leaning his arm for support on a shin-high iron fence (an ugly little oddity that ran throughout the city.)

Following a map on which Tezhlemsa had drawn a route, Sean poked into every storefront we passed in his determination to find a national flag but turned up nothing. In the shadows of apartment blocks off Stalin Avenue, he found a shady cottage selling artwork and Mongolian kitsch and stopped to inquire about a flag, particularly one that had been used. He mentioned one he'd noticed fluttering atop a specific government building. He was told to return the following day.

A wind picked up from the south, blowing enough dust from the streets to haze the mountains and turn them blue. We made our way to meet with Tezhlemsa and hear her offered diversions. We decided to ask Chook to escort us the next day to Terelj, a soul-answering retreat a few hours' drive southeast of Ulaanbaatar. There, we would be able to ride horses, climb around a cave, and spend the night in a ger–all for $50 each. With that plan in place for tomorrow, I sought time alone for the evening.

I wandered alone behind the Edelweiss Hotel and the long look down from the Gandon Hiid monastery. A young man came from behind a hut and spun the cylinder prayer wheels mounted on a small fence. I followed his motion, and spun them as well. As I inhaled the sight, something ran up my pant leg. I leapt around prepared to meet the Master Monks of the Mongolian Monastery Security force, but instead met the soft eyes of a calf with a warm, spongy tongue, licking my ankle. In that span of a few minutes I'd found serenity just off the avenue bearing its name. True travelling is the experience of discovering a place where you feel out of place.

Calmed, yet not wanting to be, I found a bar and spent hours throwing back cans of Tiger Beer. The bartender matched me drink for drink. He pulled a compact disc from his knapsack. Through a series of air guitar gestures, I gathered it was a recording by his band, Camerton, and made the mistake of nodding approval. "Yes," he'd cry at the end of track 14. I would smile, then track one would begin. Again. Over and over, at a volume that made the cigarette smoke dance.

We were to depart Ulaanbaatar after breakfast for our arranged side trip to a remote village. Chook entered the dining area with his leather aura as we sipped our 3-in-1 coffee product: a small package held a cup's worth of freeze-dried coffee, sugar, and powdered creamer. The novelty, and eventually the lingering taste of whitener, caught me off guard–and, lo, I was addicted, and would be for decades.

We tackled our van with keen anticipation over the trip to Terelj. Tezhlemsa had promised we'd find proof of dinosaurs off in the hills. Mongolia, primarily on the northern plains, comprises some of the world's richest fossil deposits. The road was anorexic in its thin single lane. Flipping on the radio, Chook slipped in the

Power of One soundtrack, a gesture that forged a Mongolian soundtrack for our travels.

Chook pulled into a small incline, shut off the engine and led us to a large pile of rubble–stones, ribbons, broken glass and one bovine skull. At the pile's seven-foot peak, a stick jutted out in the searing heat, holding a tattered blue cloth to capture the breeze.

"*Ara*," he said. Chook rarely spoke and had not yet attempted English. "Prayer flag."

"Walk." Chook held up three fingers and we circled the shrine three times. Then he bowed in humble devotion. "To Buddha," he whispered. His strong hands were pressed together and he bent forward a second time. "To Dalai Lama." Something just beyond the senses shifted to me, to us, to time, to the space between us. There was a stirring of magic in the *Ara*. Nothing mattered more than just being itself.

Chook worked the van down a grassy meadow of billiard-table felt into a valley. A few gers nestled on the edge of a vast plain beneath a sheer cliff 400 feet tall. I thought the steepness resembled a turtle. "Turtle," said Chook as confirmation. We descended into the rippling plain to the Lohan Khentee protected area and the Gorkhi/Terelj National Park. Winding down from the hillside roads, we crossed a long and frail bridge. At a straw-covered crest, I spotted what looked to be the shell of a bombed-out building and a handful of shiny white gers. Chook turned, palming the wheel to the right, and sloshed through the muddy gate of a decrepit compound of Terelj, Zhuulchin's camp. A young woman staffed the bar/restaurant/front desk. She handed Chook a key. Chook led us the short distance to one of the gers and twisted the key in the padlock on the purple door of our night's accommodation.

Four beds tucked into the ger's wall. Chook bent down and fed a few sticks into the woodstove, sparking it to life. A timid knock rattled the hinges of the door, which Sean opened to reveal a man dressed in traditional Mongolian attire. "*Sain bainuu*," he said as he entered, ducking to avoid the low frame.

"*Sain ta sain bainuu*!" Chook took his hand.

"*Sain bainuu*," said the man again. Chook turned to us and fumbled for an explanation.

"Eh… Bat." He cocked his thumb at the man. "Horseman...."

"Yah!' Bat laughed.

We followed Bat out of the fenced area and into a ravine where five horses, tied to a tree, stood in mud. Bat's son, Bold, was feeding them a sloppy bucket of oats. The horseman's son could not have been more than 10 years old, though his youthful face showed all the determination and wisdom of his father. I was motioned toward Borra, a brown mare freckled with orange and white spots. We mounted up, and with clumsy rump-banging steps, rose from the ravine camp to a plain. Mongrel dogs scouted ahead as we left.

"*Toosh-toosh*," Bold said, encouraging his horse to gallop.

"*Toosh-toosh*," I whispered to Borra.

But Borra maintained her stumbling gait and turned her head, batted a big black eye to say, *"as if,"* and continued at the same sleepy speed. The dogs ran far ahead, frolicking over one another, barking at a grazing yak.

Grassland spread before us. A silence swallowed everything but the wind in my ears. Bat sang a mumbled calling of foreign sounds that caressed the moment. His son clicked his cheek, drove his heels into the belly of his horse and joined his father in song. The tune was proud, as natural to the herdsmen as was the herd itself. The low-sweeping grass burned with the golden touch of high noon.

An hour or more later the small black line on the horizon gave way to a village of gers, each anchored into a small plot of land by an adjacent wooden shack. A fence of sticks, twigs and logs enclosed each area. In the center of this village was a stash of dung four feet high used as fuel for the gers' stoves. Despite a community with dozens of gers, there was no one to offer us welcome.

Bat grabbed our reins, hitching them to a post. He had brought us to his home. It must've been 110 degrees inside, a testament to the power of the smoldering excrement. Bat's father-in-law, wife, two daughters and young son, Y, bowed excitedly at us. Bat quickly positioned three stools, encouraging us to sit. Bat went to the kitchen–actually, he went to the corner of the round tent–and rattled cutlery and plates. He passed around a frothy bowl of *airag,* or mare's milk. Sean pretended to swig a gulp, feigning pleasure with the taste, smiled happily and passed it along. When it reached me I smelled it and at once was fully aware that one sip and I would coat the ger. I didn't chance it.

The grandfather pulled out a small snuffbox from beneath his pillow. He drew a thumbnail full, which he snorted before passing the container around. From my hip pack, I produced a can of Copenhagen chewing tobacco I'd brought along to stave off the ghosts of my own addiction on the airplane. I demonstrated for grandfather how to secure it against the teeth he had left and reinforce it with his lip, and offered him a pinch. He swallowed it. This isn't supposed to happen. I could tell because he grabbed at his neck as if strangling himself. He hobbled outside where sounds made it clear he was not a fan of chewing tobacco. I smiled apologetically to the family. And kept smiling despite the groans from outside.

I asked Bat, through a series of gestures, where I might find the restroom. He pointed out the ger's only door. I exited to find grandfather spitting at the fence and fingering his tongue. I found a small boarded outhouse, the floor of which had been axed out. When I emerged, both families were a yard away with looks of anticipation on their faces.

Bold and Y kicked a withered ball at me and I pinned it to the ground and kicked it back and it went wide down the pathway. For half an hour, the eight of us chased the ball through the village and into the fields, and back again. One of the kids kicked it to Sean, the family's soccer fan, who heeled it in the air to dad. Dad bounced it on his knees a few times, to the delight of the children, and then launched a fierce kick that quite simply killed the ball. It bounced off a camel's head before landing at Bold's feet, deflated and dead. Game over. And probably months to sew a new ball together.

Bat swept his hand in the air toward the horses, as if we'd robbed a bank and it was time to escape. Sean mounted promptly and efficiently. I swung my foot high and over, landing in the saddle and cringing at the contact. I locked eyes with grandfather who was whipping tobacco spit from his chin. Dad gave up trying to revive the soccer ball, handed it to one of the kids, and hauled himself onto his horse as though nothing had happened.

We trotted off at a leisurely pace with the mongrels leading the way, and the village receding over our shoulders. Suddenly, Bat hollered to Bold, who'd been minding the rear. Soon the two of them snapped their whips on the flanks of our horses. The beasts leapt with lightning bursts of speed. The five of us rode in the fury of Mongolian tradition, screaming the cries of Genghis Khan. Galloping hoofs ate the landscape. The rough wind combed Borra's mane and rifled my beard. The saddle rocked violently, throwing me around. "*Yah! Hee-ya!*"

Dad's horse buckled its front legs, flipping dad into a catapulting vault, landing on his back. All seven dogs, unlikely to have ever seen such a display, circled back and licked his face.

It was early evening when we reached the compound, its entrance guarded by a herd of cattle. In a series of quick chevrons while on horseback, Sean guided an errant cow into retreat, opening a way through for all of us. We dismounted alongside the creek. I stroked Borra's mane and thanked her, and we climbed the gulley wall back to camp.

Chook was relaxing in the ger. With hand signs he said it was time for dinner. We were the only people on the grounds. After dinner of mutton balls–possibly sheep gonads and not balls of mutton meat at all–we sought the fresh air of outside. We shuffled toward where the sunlight sank on the hillside we'd ridden earlier. I took leave and climbed a hill, approaching the forest that blanketed its upper quarter, and finally reached the top. There stood a small wooden gazebo. It was so quiet I could hear my hair grow. With my penknife, I added my own to the dozen or so names and dates carved into the railings by lovers and lonely souls. Below, I could see forever across Mongolia. My pulse quickened at the landscape's immensity. Dad, a mere blemish on the fold of a ridge, hollered against the wind.

"Do you know where you are?"

I yelled back: "Mongolia!" Sean echoed.

Damn fine.

We were lying in our beds, reading by the light of the fire. Oily shadows leapt at the top of the ger. I left the tent to go write inside a small hotel (the building that looked bombed out) where it turned out Chook was spending the night. Soon afterward, the hotel lights–indeed the whole camp–went dark after a scattering of sparks from a fuse panel. The staff lit candles and gave Chook, the hotel's lone occupant, instruction to escort me out of doors. He did, and left me there.

I wandered to the edge of the camp's fence in the darkness. The Hale-Bopp comet was sailing high above, teasing Orion. The dogs from our day's ride followed me and when I stopped to gaze, they parked around me. In a few short hours it would be my birthday. Number twenty-seven. I'd spent my most recent birthdays in Washington, D.C. and Estonia. Now Mongolia. I hummed a little tune, scoured the sky for a star to wish upon and went inside the ger.

The next hours will forever remain disputed, argued as family fiction; depending on whose side you take. To be honest, they're a little fuzzy which may make me guilty. Dad and Sean appreciated the heat thrown off the embers but I couldn't bear it. When a firewood lady entered and stoked our stove to a flaming life, I noticed power had been restored. I followed her outside, heading back to the hotel to write my journal. As I left— the ger door caught a trifle of a breeze and refused to stay shut. There was an open padlock hanging uselessly from the latch; I slid it through. Allegedly.

At this late hour, the hotel attracted local Mongolian men and their wives who arrived on horseback. A few of them approached my table with a tumbler of vodka, offered it to me as a gesture of friendship and eventually lured me into a back room where men were shooting billiards. I was pulled in to play the game's winner. The roused crowd made it clear they favored me to win. My moral support came from their shot glasses brimming with Genghis Khan Vodka. Billiard balls rolled their trajectories, tapping and sinking. With eager voices, the group directed Mongolian sarcasms at my opponent, Chun. When I called a double bank of the eight ball to slide past his remaining ball and into the corner pocket, the room went quiet. I managed an irreproducible shot. The room stayed silent as the ball fell in. I broke into a touchdown dance and pointed to myself, repeating "Khan! Khan!" When I looked closely, my opponent was the soul of restraint. "You always let the boss win," said an echo in my head. But I didn't know he was their boss.

Post-victory, I passed long hours inside the hotel with Chun and his girlfriend, Myla. They were from a village an hour's horse ride away. He made it clear he owned 140 horses. I made it clear that I owned two cars but kept to myself that the second was used to replace parts on the first. The combined horsepower of my cars was about 180, so I was ahead of him by 40, or so I explained the math to him. Chun and Myla wanted to learn English words they could drop into their conversations. We chanted "floor, wall, ceiling." As the clock hammered 2 a.m., Dad and Sean burst through the building doors.

"What the…?" I asked from my cozy sofa, preparing to introduce them to Chun and Myla.

"You stupid dick," Sean yelled (unchallenged).

Dad scowled. "You locked us in the ger."

"Huh?"

"Four hours," Sean managed. 'Four hours in that oven. The stove lady let us out." Sean swatted the back of my head. Dad swatted the back of my head.

I stumbled for an exculpatory response. "It's, it's…. It's my birthday." Shifting the topic, I blurted, "This is Chun. He has one hundred and forty horses."

Into my early morning hangover halo, I heard Chook rap on the ger. He walked us one by one to his second-floor room to use the shower, me first as it was my birthday—plus Dad and Sean weren't talking to me. Chook's quarters were of Third World prison standards. The plumbing shook as I ran the water. A warm liquid spat from the nozzle, slid through three shades of brown, then turned cold.

In the dining room, I joined my ger companions–with their campfire hairstyles and burnt corpse breath–to celebrate. Dad had dragged a collection of birthday plates, napkins and cups halfway around the world in secret. My eyes welled up with their rendition of "Happy Birthday," to which Chook moved his lips, having memorized the international anthem. Dad stabbed candles into my onion omelet (looking as yucky as it sounds). They teetered in the half-cooked gel.

Bat came to see us off. Dad lit his pipe. Chook and Bat took it from my father and sucked in a lungful each. Smoking has, is and will forever be a great unifier of people, if only temporarily.

Later that morning we arrived back at Ulaan Bataar. I announced my quest for a birthday lunch, and Tezhlemsa arranged for a young Zhuulchin commando named Smuk to drive us to a few places as part of this search. The five of us loaded into a clean blue Mercedes and set off to find my chosen pizza, which I thought straightforward. Tezhlemsa said the prospects of finding a "How do you call it? Pitza?" were quite low. After several aborted stops where chefs replicated her term "Pitza?" we found a place willing to make the attempt. Tezhlemsa had never experienced pizza and ran her finger down the list of available ingredients, like corn and fragrant herbs. Sean, Dad, and I chose the plainest—Margherita— since suspicion of the simplest Mongolian foods reigned among us. The restaurant staff, and a few street people, sang "Happy Birthday" in the manner of those who learned the tune minutes before. I am not exaggerating with flair when I say it was the best pizza I ever tasted. Nor when I say the worst pizza was in Venice.

We told Tezhlemsa we would like to visit a market or bazaar where we could poke around and pick up souvenirs. "The market?" She made eye contact with the driver. "Yes, there is an open-air market north of town. It's crowded, quite unsafe. There is nothing to see there."

"Well now," I said. "You've gone and made it a must-see event."

The market spread over acres of dusty sand. People–Dad's estimation put it at 20,000 Mongolians–drifted around tables, carts, trailers and stands. We were the only Caucasians in the swarming mass. I recognized what a new immigrant might feel–helplessness in a sea of strangers who know each other better than me.

The market's tempo was a notch below that of a riot. Pushing, shoving, fighting, haggling and (no doubt) thieving were rampant. I experienced a sharp pain in my lower back. An elderly woman, for whom the chore of motion was hindered by her hunched height, drove a thumbnail into the lower backs of anyone who stood between them and a bargain. I was but one.

Tezhlemsa watched as I flipped through a stack of bootleg tapes on a table and pulled one out. The cover had been photocopied; the members of Guns N' Roses were smudged black. Tezhlemsa bent in and stopped me.

"Give me the tape," she said. I handed it to her. She ejected Abba from a nearby sound system and inserted my choice. She pressed play. The speakers crackled, but no music. The tape was blank. The seller pulled a half smile and a half "unimpressed" smirk.

"You have to check first. Everything you buy here," she admonished, transferring the responsibility for honesty to me.

Another short woman finger-nailed me out of her way. A table displayed carton upon carton of Marlboros. Hundreds of them sat in the hold of a trailer behind the table. *Well*, I thought, *this has got to be safe*. One side of the table quoted 7700 tugriks, the other said 5500. Tezhlemsa grabbed one of each, tilted them, and explained: "The codes on the bottom of these two seemingly identical cartons are different."

"2A3 is a fake code, made in China, garbage tobacco, *if it is tobacco*. 2A4, made here." She pointed. "These are real. The ones for 7700 tugriks are authentic."

"Well, I'll be damned." Without her Mongolian street smarts, I'd have purchased a couple of blank tapes and 10 packs of bush leaves.

Our next goal was to purchase a bumper sticker showing "MGL" for Mongolia. Sean and I covered our cars at home with such bumper stickers of different countries we'd visited, and I'd found the only one from here. After a long drive, we pulled into a dealership with as much rust on its cars as on its promotional sign.

There among the dust was a sticker with flag symbol and our desired abbreviated capitals for Mongolia; we bought it

In front of me were a much-dented Mercedes Benz and a mud-caked Audi. I asked T how they got to Ulaan Baatar. She said, "People from here went to Europe and drove them to Mongolia to sell them."

"But," I pointed out, "there's no road from Germany to here."

"There are paths beside the train," she said "You must have seen them "

"We did see them, but they ran beside us, then slipped into a marsh for a mile or so. Then they surfaced beside us again, and then once more disappeared. They weren't really much of a road for someone to drive that distance."

"This is their job," said T. "Usually four men will take the train to Europe, buy the car and take turns driving all day and night to bring it back here. It takes them two weeks." That meant driving the grueling road, and climbing onto the same live train tracks our train used when the road disappeared into the marshes. I immediately wanted to do it. For now, I had to be happy with that we found the sticker.

Back at the hotel, Sean left for the art store get his hoped-for Mongolia flag, only to be told to return at 6 p.m. as the young man said they may have one by then.

I decided to alter my appearance at a hair salon. It took three minutes to elevate me to Mongolian-styled clean cut. The stylist must have been raised with scissors in her hands–they blurred as the blades spun around me. The cost was one dollar. No coupon needed.

Sean and I returned to the art store at the appointed time. There was no flag to be had. However, when Sean pointed out that there was only one flag flying in the neighborhood, and it was atop a government looking building, the young man accepted the lead. He offered an arrangement for what sounded like a contraband, perhaps stolen, flag. Sean shook hands on the deal.

Hours later I walked to an address with Sean on what now seemed a covert operation. A tiny bell rang our entrance into a dim shack. Of the three men at the counter, one quietly slid behind us and locked the front door. Another closed the drapes. The third put a thick package on the glass case and unfolded a Mongolian flag. It was a real flag soiled by dust and faded by sunshine, one that had, only minutes before, been waving atop a government building.

"Forty dollars," said the man as he unfurled the stolen flag.

Sean swallowed. In the room's pasty orange light, it seemed heroin would have been a safer purchase.

"All I have is ten American dollars" Sean threw two crumpled fives next to the flag, just as we'd rehearsed.

"No deal!" The man started to fold the flag.

"Wait," I interrupted. "I'll lend you five and, boy-oh-boy, you're gonna owe me *big* time." I clucked my cheek.

"That's 15," Sean said, meeting the thief's stern stare.

The salesmen's eyes ricocheted between his fellow entrepreneurs' cool gaze. I read it as *"Damn. Only fifteen dollars for committing a federal crime."*

Our shifty eyes worked between us. Sean searched through his hip pack and tossed 77 tugriks amongst the bills. I dug into mine and found 7,000 Russian rubles, which I tossed on the table as though icing on a cake.

"Chit," said the boss man. He collected the 15 dollars, even took the 20 cents in tugriks but pushed back the rubles.

That night, in the dimness of the bar where I'd gotten drunk with the bar tender the previous night, the three of us sipped Tiger Beers while carving best wishes onto postcards that would never reach home.

"More than anything else right now," Dad said, "I'd like a plate of nachos. Mongolian nachos."

"You dream big, Mr. Dad. Big," I said.

He summoned the waiter and, detailing the ingredients with his hands, described nachos. The waiter nodded proudly and there was no doubt anything of Dad's elaborate request had been misinterpreted. The waiter certainly looked as though he had a complete picture of the plate of nachos in his head. After 10 minutes of Pavlovian anticipation, he returned. Dad rubbed his hands as the plate hit the table.

"What the…"

The contents were repulsively un-tortilla and un-cheese. Slabs of jellied meat, suspect grey vegetables, cubes of squishy fat and a few items that looked like the pink noodles of a small animal's digestive track proved to be the man's interpretation of "nachos". Dad and Sean pushed fingers through the plate and found a cracker, which they shared. I did not eat.

In the twinkling last light of that mid-April day, we exited the bar's doorway. We watched darkness descend on the four sharp hills that surround Ulaanbaatar at roughly the four points of the compass. These hills are considered holy. In the crisp evening air, Songino Hairhan, the western peak, was prism-like with its own crown of light.

Dad broke the silence. "Mongolia, guys."

Men stumbled past in their traditional attire of *deels* and *janjin malgais* and disappeared into the village near our hotel. One long cloud burned pink, then spread into the sky. Sean rewound his tape recorder and played the herdsman's song from the previous day. We heard the dry, raspy voice of Bat fighting the wind as his voice embodied Mongolia to the rocking of our horses across the endless plain. Where Man, Earth and God met. Mongolia had opened her heart to us.

Loose strands of daybreak dragged across the Mongolian plain. It was 5 a.m., a time of day reserved for attacking another country, when street cleaners book off, really good parties start to taper, people dial wrong numbers, and those wishing to make the east-bound *Trans-Siberian/Trans-Mongolian* in the heart of nowhere are nursing themselves awake with mildly warm water and freeze-dried coffee crystals.

"Hey, kid," said Dad. "Sleep well?"

I eyed him standing there, fluffing his pillows. My eyes were slits. "Has anyone ever confronted your snoring problem?"

"I snore?" There was a degree of shock in his voice.

"It's like sleeping in a room where the dryer is on and filled with tools."

"That doesn't make any sense at all," he rebutted.

"I prayed to the God of Apnea to rescue me."

"You're in a mood," he concluded. "Maybe you should drink less."

"Sharing a room with you requires passing out."

His eyes jumped past me to out the hotel window where Chook paced in the roundabout.

"This isn't over," I said, quickly leaving the room. "We're going to get you help. Maybe there's a Chinese herb. Or a Chinese laser."

Streetlights harmonized with the rising of day, catching the mist burning off gers as we drove through a quiet town. We coasted to the train station's gate where Tezhlemsa stood impatiently tapping her foot. Words passed between her and Chook, most definitely to do with our tardiness. Our train rolled its romantic clacks and slowed to a stop at the platform as the five of us and our luggage made ready. As the last pack was thrown onto the vestibule floor, we turned to the two people who had given us Mongolia. Chook patted his pocket and withdrew two coins with a brash Genghis Khan pressed into the nickel. Sean and I accepted them and promised, as the situation demanded, to return again soon. I offered Chook a pack of cigarettes from which he drew only one, placed it behind his ear and handed the rest back.

A *provodnitsa* hollered from the top step, and the train shunted. We waved from behind the filmy windows as the metal stairs were pulled up, the door secured, and movement began in earnest. Sean pointed to the government building where he'd earlier pointed to a flag flying. No flag flew. It was in his pack. I retreated to the bathroom and looked out the window in time to see Ulaanbaatar and its Soviet skyline blur into the distance. I was sure that Dad and Sean had worked out any differences in settling our share of roomettes, taken their own beds, and stuffed their luggage on mine.

Dad borrowed my cassette player and kept a beat with his thumbs on the seat. I debated telling him that it had no batteries but decided to keep his spirits up. Lying across the bags, I gazed longingly at the remote landscape that was catching daybreak from the sheltering mountains. Sparse fields rolled away and unfolded at the foot of the low hills where the earth bowed under its form.

This was the edge of the Gobi Desert. It was sheer desolation; loneliness would be an improvement. *God should've spent his seventh day here*, I thought. Yet I loved it. The world was shrinking, and the farthest distances still remain in the heart.

I went to the restaurant car. People sat down and ordered each other around with civil tongues. Russian country folk, booths away, revitalized themselves with a bottle of vodka. Within minutes their conversation grew into an uproarious battle.

Sean dumped himself and his journal across from me.

"Do you think they would turn up the heat if I asked?"

"That's the Gobi Desert out there," I replied.

"No dunes, no nomads, no camels, no sand."

It was true. The Gobi is primarily grassland. Sand, which I felt was the quintessential desert requisite, was scarce. A tenor-voiced Russian woman with uneven breasts approached us with menus.

"You ever had a vodka breakfast?" asked Sean.

"I should think not–but not remembering may be a side effect."

"You wanna try it?

"Oblivion is a dish best served drunk!"

"One hangover-in-a-bottle coming up." Sean grinned like he was about to get away with reusing postage stamps. "Temptation is my only vice; giving in is my only sin."

The waitress passed us one bottle of Genghis Khan Vodka and two shot glasses in exchanged for seven American dollars, the price in tugriks being nearly twice that. Withered labels from multiple washings were evidence the bottle had been recycled frequently. The cap's seal had been broken prior to our purchase, sending off alarm bells that went unheeded by us. The mouth tipped around the glasses, splashing generous portions. Raising glasses to make a clink, we mouthed, "*Erool mendeen tuloh*," the Mongolian toast we'd come to know

The scenery didn't resemble desert so much as deserted. I waved to the waitress, who was cleaning the aftermath of the loud Russians' table. On the last page of my notebook, I drew a reasonable dromedary facsimile (RDF) and an arrow meant to convey, "Where are the camels?" Inappropriately, I pointed the arrow just below the tail. The waitress rested her wrist on the table and looked outside. Two hours, she indicated by tapping her watch. They would come, I gathered. They would come.

Heat rippled the desert and the wagon, where the windows were stuck closed in the locked position. Clothes were shed. We poured another vodka. The train headed southward, breaking off from the symmetry of Mongolia. We saw our first nomadic ger in the distance. On a curve, we noticed only a single pair of tracks belting the way for us; we were as remote as train travellers get.

The bottle of vodka met its demise in early afternoon as a lunch crowd formed around us. With caution, Sean ordered another. The sun had spent the day riding slowly towards its pinnacle but was soon bowing into the desert, efficiently slanting across the tabletops. A few gers, raw with age, sat just beyond our window. I wondered if their occupants were lost. Being a nomad was not yet trendy and I could easily believe the gers had been set up beside the tracks to provide the visual stimulus in the stark surroundings. The waitress pointed further out the window.

"Camels!" I cried.

It was hard to determine whether they were camels or lumpy horses. Seconds later, they were gone.

The train stopped at a village besieged by grass and sand. Makeshift homes appeared empty and lifeless. Blended ever so closely with a wall stood a bored, mat-coated and thirsty-looking camel. The two of us exchanged a long sympathetic stare.

As dusk purpled the sky and the temperature dropped to a chill, the waitress stoked the heating stove with coal. Dad entered with the early dinner crowd and began his active interaction with humanity. He had read and rested in the cabin all day and remained one big step below consciousness.

"So, guys,' he said, 'last night on the train?"

"Brent and I covered that earlier today," slurred Sean.

"We've been conducting subjective tests of vodka digestion in desert environments," I said.

My eyelids were darkening my forehead but I wanted to add, "I never imagined we'd be completing this trip. This has been the absolute finest father/sons thing. We are slicing through the Gobi Desert on a goddamn iconic train. What can we do next? How about the Sahara? We could cross it on camels. Or Antarctica? How about Antarctica on camels?"

Dad smiled, off in a little corner of himself. Our ability to work, travel and stay together had been a success. Lines that should not be crossed had proven fluorescent and impenetrable. There was little, I sensed, that we could not deal with. Dad looked out at the arcing Gobi Desert and suggested we plan another train adventure. We creased my atlas open and sank into an hour of hypothetical routes. We were the loudest table in the car, pouring shots of vodka and interrupting one another. The waitress smiled. I smiled back. She winked.

Somewhere during the evening's Gobi Desert crossing, Dad and Sean left me alone in the dining car.

The carpet of ink-colored desert was devoid of the odd glow of settlement found even in the far reaches of Siberia. Across from me, a Mongolian party of two men and their wives were pouring through their second bottle of vodka. When I made passing eye contact with the larger of the men, he felt obliged to pull himself up to our table.

He introduced himself as Suhk and garbled my name into something like Blech. Suhk hollered the few feet over to his companion, repeatedly calling, "Turg!" Turg leveled out next to Suhk, who then pointed to the two ladies and encouraged me to repeat "Udval" and "Olyuun." What should have prompted a small wave instead heightened the women's resentment: *"Aw shit. Suhk's taken to another bastard who made eye contact with him."*

Suhk took my pen, flipped opened my journal to an arbitrary page and drew out the original Mongolian alphabet. He realized he'd forgotten a letter and squeezed it in before taking another page to illustrate parts of the Russian alphabet, butchering through the Cyrillic and dragging his hand through the ink.

Meanwhile, Turg fell lengthwise to the train's floor. Pulling himself up with a slight chuckle, he used the table to guide him towards the women. He was navigating the Twilight Zone of Excess, part of which I've mapped out myself. All the while, Suhk continued to work over the letters–counting fingers to keep track.

Turg sunk into his seat and spoke to Udval and Olyuun in a one-sided conversation that ended with "Heh, heh, heh..." I wish I'd understood precisely what he'd said to warrant what followed. Olyuun picked up her tumbler and smashed it openended onto his forehead, leaving daggers of glass impaled in Turg's quizzical brow. Blood seeped but pain had yet to penetrate.

"Heh, heh, heh...," Turg grumbled.

Together, the women rose in a huff and left by the rear door. Turg looked over at Suhk and me with a vacant grin, blood curving around his cheeks and puddling into his lap. Suhk broke into a cackle and continued to letter in my journal. The waitress snapped her cloth at Turg, scolding Suhk to trail Turg out the door.

"*Slovnitchki*," she said to the empty air. *Piss-ant little nothing.*

The train continued to eat through the final hours separating us from the Chinese border. Or, depending on one's geopolitical ethic, the point where the frontier of "Inner Mongolia" began. In many respects, this situation is not unlike the Tibetan syndrome. Though Mongolians claim the Chinese unjustly occupy their land, recent combat is limited to wrestling and equestrian endeavors. These might prove unpersuasive against a nuclear power. Mongolia proper felt nearly over. My sorrow inspired me to pour out my melancholy in a poem I titled "When Apples Bruise," and to order a beer.

During the train's slow linking of destinations, I yearned to be back a week in our travels, crossing Siberia, locked in birch forests; in Terelj's hotel, shooting billiards; or in Irkutsk overlooking Baikal's frozen shelf of ice. I wanted to be in Beijing knowing the trip had been successfully completed as much as I wanted to be reliving the first few inches of track leaving Moscow. But I *wanted* most to be right here—to be in the Gobi Desert reflecting, and writing poetry about bruised fruit.

We saw a sweep of sulphur colored lights in the distance. When we reached the rail yards of Erenhot, I yelled aloud, "Ladies and Gentlemen, the Mongolian/Chinese border."

⫛⫛⫛⫛⫛⫛⫛⫛⫛⫛⫛⫛

Sean entered at dusk, a longer process in Mongolian than most countries since the horizon never ends. I rose to slap an imbibed hug on him. He quickly shook it off.

A low, broadcasting glow sat on a clay wall outside the train's window. The teetering and rocking, evidence of many tracks splitting off with the wallflower grunts of the freight yard, signaled the end of Mongolia. We raced the hallways to our cabin, hurdling over luggage, traders' crates and boxes in the corridors.

We readied our stowed bags for customs officials. Passports, visas and funds were prepared for scrutiny. The train's entire population was hopeful we'd all have our passports stamped for entry into China.

A young Mongolian agent finally appeared, dressed in a uniform older than he was. He straightened his face and, with a confident hand, ran his fingers through our documents before leaving with them. Two hours passed. Voices drifted down the hall, accompanied by shuffling, banging and the occasional thud of descending luggage. Four guards stood before us, one of whom handed over our stamped passports. Two others, a young man and woman, entered our cabin and swept their eyes in the places our luggage was not. The two "souvenir" train signs lay shrouded in a curled sleeping bag, neatly bandaged with tape. In the Alps, they would have undoubtedly been skis. Here, I suspected they'd be highly suspect as extreme chopsticks.

Without warning, the customs man leapt onto the bottom bunk and peered into the empty bulkhead that arched from the cabin over the hallway. He waved his arm inside of it. It was intimidating being at the mercy of ambitious guards in their early twenties. Their search was not precise, and they passed beyond our door to infiltrate the neighboring traders who greeted them with guilt, contempt and disdain. Banging ended with these passengers being escorted off the train. "It could have been us," said Sean.

The train jerked forward with each wagon in succession echoing off the sitting freight cars. We crossed into China through to a sulphur-lit shed. Here began the ceremonial changing of the wheel assemblies or, in railway lexicon, the *bogies*. The Russian government, fearful of invasion, decades ago committed the Eastern Bloc–along with its buffer zone and protectorate countries–to rail security by using a wider rail gauge than that of its bordering countries. The five-foot wheel width also afforded greater wagon engineering than China's four-foot-eight-and-a-half width. In the confines of the machinery shed, each train crossing the border underwent an exhaustive conversion from one size to the other.

We were neither cautioned nor warned. The wagon we were in was elevated above the ground in such an un-disturbing fashion that we did not notice the initial movement. Rows upon rows of bogie gauges of both sizes stretched beyond our view. Huge electrical lifts, four to a car, raised us just high enough to expose the assemblies.

Against the Trans-Siberian handbook's better judgment, and in my vodka-shot wisdom, I descended the available stairs, wandered about, and took pictures.

A team of frock-clothed workers pushed the wheels from beneath our car by hand. A woman in an aerial crane raised the bogies and placed them aside. She maneuvered the smaller-gauge wheels and cradled them into the guiding arms of the ground crew. Taps, hollers and a surgeon's dexterity slid them underneath the coaches. The wagon was recessed into place.

Two hours had passed in the middle of the night, with me alone outside the coach. Eventually, the track spun. I re-boarded. Soon a new engine stammered to the lead. We were in China and, to use the appropriate coinage, ready to roll.

Dawn soon broke over rocky hills of China. Hundreds of farmers' fields spread from the railbeds. Some were flooded, others dry. People, crowded shoulder-to-shoulder, bent over, pulling at rice. Minutes later, empty ditch-like expanses rolled by with no one seemingly occupying China at all.

The commotion of disoriented travellers embarking in the city of Datong six hours after entering China disrupted our slumber. Through the fog of chintz curtains, I spotted the sweeping eyes of the platform dwellers. One hundred and eighty-six miles (300 kilometers) separated us from Beijing.

After Datong, our train paralleled a distant spine of mountains. Creeping along its top was a snaking line of dim orange: The Great Wall of China. Since as a young boy I first encountered a set of classic encyclopedias, I've always wondered: Would I see it one day? And here I was, at the foot of a childhood dream.

The rail line rose into the foothills. Craggy postcard mountains thrust at the sky. Runoff from the winter's snowpack ran in crystal-blue falls close enough to spray our windows. Mist hovered over canyons, shrouding the ridges. Spring pulled sunflowers and berry-clad bushes from the ground to wave in our wake.

Sixty-five miles (84 kilometers) outside Beijing, we stopped in Kanzhuang. An extra engine was mounted to help our climb up to the Nankou Pass. We rode on for 8 more miles and chugged up to Qinlongqiao, where we held our breath at the mountain view locked in by old-script artwork and feathery hills–the kind that ascend in a fanning display of plant life transcribed onto burned earth and the loose arms of old plant life. The train vestibule was a cool shell, and passengers threw back the solid metal door without warning. We stepped out.

Set into the rock face, a length of the Great Wall dropped down to the far side of the tracks. Time had silently withered the stony edifice. It was rubble, mostly. Thousands of stairs were worn into the surrounding foliage leading to it and away from it. To have such a moment alone with the Wall was my trophy wife of travel.

The *provodnitsa* shouted it was time to climb aboard just as the train started to move. After a switchback descent of metal-twisting groans, we reached the plains.

Beijing came into view. Droves of bicyclists pedaled on the roadway alongside the train, flowing in the shade of the trees lining the streets. Laundry lines snaked across low apartment complexes. Automobiles and pedestrians were seamlessly woven into the scenery until the monoliths of urbanity overtook. Soon, a homogeneous fleet of cars, trucks, tiny yellow taxi-vans, pedestrians, and bicyclists covered every asphalt surface in our view.

A delta of tracks spilt into the rail yard. The train coasted up to our final platform in a sea of iron. The undercarriage wheezed to completion of our trip's mileage and time zones. Beijing Rail Station. The kilometer sign read 9001.

Moscow + 7.

There was a choking conclusion to the appetite of journey. I wanted to be in the midst of a transition between destinations, in a fog of timelessness, content to watch it all go by. I bent and kissed the train; she was now a love, something that had touched me deeply, and we were parting. There is nothing like the disappointment at the end of a journey, when the best of what was ahead is behind.

China's capital was enveloped by the energy of an unfathomable city. Beijing blended poverty and excess with its neo-architectural skyline and tree-lined streets, storms of dust and residential alleyways, brown brick buildings, racing traffic, and rickshaws stacked to great heights with boxes. People, eleven million of them, lived in the endless urban districts surrounding the heart of the Forbidden City. Traffic on the lane-less streets honked with impunity, guided by the white-gloved pantomimes of police. Bicyclists–old and young, fat and skinny, professional and peasant rode on the spoked tires of dimly colored single-speed bikes.

Taxi drivers were outlaws, and the horn their weapon. Taxis charged differently to reflect the quality of the vehicle and the driver's honesty. Each taxi had a red passport-sized sticker with the price per kilometer posted on the rear window. The range spanned from one to four yuan in 20-fen increments. The one-yuan minitaxis were yellow Japanese-designed Miandis vans, known in Chinese as *Mian Bao Che*, meaning "bread loaf vehicle" due to their odd, skinny shape; the government was trying to phase them out. Twenty-two thousand of them alone roamed Beijing, causing a fifth of the pollution. We were cautioned against using them. At 1.20 yuan were the Mercedes and Audis. For four yuan the driver opened the door, buffed up the vinyl and did not sing along with the radio. Their driving habits were similar, regardless of the price, and represented a choreographed performance of meander, mesh, and merge.

Outside of the main thoroughfares, Beijing conducted its affairs as if it was an overpopulated small town.

Sean and I set up at the Exhibition Center Hotel, the day our own. We were north of where Dad had gone to meet Janice (future mother-in-law) at a hotel for the conference they were attending. Our hotel was a star below the places that fold back the corners of your sheets and leave extra towels on request. It was recessed a block in from Xizhimen Wai Street, a popular commercial strip alive with thousands of people working the storefronts and restaurants. Chinese characters sparkled on rotating advertising columns, buzzed in neon, or were skillfully painted on sandwich boards. The written Chinese language of pictographs cross roaded with the Roman alphabet in a soupy mash-up called *pinyin*. It was through this medium that we read our sloppy Chinese and conducted ourselves with a stubborn grace as the merchants tried to appeal to Romanized visitors: Happy Panda Restaurant, Old China E-mail and Fax, Happy Lawyer Divorce Services, Duloug-dongalachinaqinouwang Shoes for Happy Feet.

Stiff smells of body odor, steamed vegetables and burning skewers of pork choked the air. Music pounded from the Beijing Music and Plumbing Store on the opposite sidewalk and we soon understood what navigating the street signified: pedestrians rank below dirt. Tsunamis of vehicles sped along as though all eleven million of us were ghosts. It is best to let an experienced local pedestrian launch across a street first, then follow en masse. Only when confronted with a mob of bodies that could damage their undercarriages would the vehicles slow down and honk. At night, the street came alive with electric color. Silent trolley buses sped by without headlights, dragging sparks from overhead power lines.

The following morning, we taxied 6 cross-town miles to the Kempinski Hotel, where Dad was staying. His fiancé Janice had arrived the evening before on a late flight from Vancouver. Dad looked like a fresh stack of traffic tickets with his newly groomed beard. Janice had brought him fresh clothes and a nudge to clean himself. The four of us walked lazily for an hour. A dust storm billowed above the buildings, coating the streets and dimming the lights; locals will tell you this phenomenon is from the Gobi winds that tear across the desert, and point with blame and disgust toward Mongolia. It is also the consequence of the Chinese denuding their forests, the erosion of their own soil at work. People wrapped scarves across their faces and leaned into the grimy wind. I spotted a barbershop and, jealous of Dad's return to decency, felt it was time to tend to my beard. I proposed that Sean and I get goatees.

Dad said, "We'll meet you at Tiananmen Square in an hour." We agreed. Unlike Dad, Sean, and me, Janice responsibly wears a watch and is known to be the kind of 'prompt' that has her actually meet people where and when she says she will— unlike Dad's Hour, which runs on the axis of his selfish convenience.

I plunked myself into a vinyl-covered barber's chair and drew out with my fingers, the perimeters of a healthy shave. Armed with a straight blade, the barber restored dignity to my visage.

Sean looked on, wishing he could grow a beard, ribbing me: "You've gone from looking like a bum to looking like a pimp".

At the appointed time, Sean and I went to meet Dad and Janice as decided. The back-alley streets doubled their width at Qianmen. The featureless panorama of government buildings ruled the sidewalks, then parted, revealing the hazy expanse of Tiananmen Square all the way to the high red walls of the Forbidden Palace. It had seen the bloodshed of student uprising and democratic rallies and the ensuing clashes. The resulting crackdown left a timeless silence stolen by the past. Large red numbers on a 100-foot high electric sign counted down the seconds to July 1, 1997. A Chinese agriculture student from the University of Beijing, named Virginia, spotted us trying to decipher the lines of script and offered to translate. "The clock counts down the time in which the Chinese government will take back Hong Kong," she said, tapping an extended finger in the air and reading the numbers off: 73 days, and 245 minutes.

Virginia wandered along with us, armed with her knapsack, fleece sweater and narrow spectacles. She was too young to have been involved in the latest protest at the square but told us her brother received two broken arms for his beliefs. We approached the Forbidden Palace. Throngs of people were sewn together in front of the imposing face of Mao Tse-tung, high above the entrance. Virginia pointed out the two banners of characters flanking Mao's portrait. "Salute to the People's Republic of China," she translated, "and Salute to Global Unionization."

"Virginia!" A young man called out to her across a sea of people, his arm flapping.

"My boyfriend. I must go now." She disappeared.

Beneath Mao's profile over a stone bridge, we crossed a moat to the conical entrance hall. Roofs angled out from the commanding walls with a harmonizing face of imperialism–The Gates of Prosperous Harmony, the Imperial Library, the Palace of Heavenly Purity.

I thought I heard Mao moaning beneath the clutter of conversation and commerce. Lashing stone dragons, cold marble lions and castings of tigers were for sale. Staff dressed as Imperial guards. Branches and flowers waved in the breeze. A dust eddy wound around the main corridor of trees, carrying a Snickers bar wrapper. A Fuji film tube rolled between the legs of visitors. The Palace was cleansed of importance; it was an amusement park where once it represented the fierce mind of the largest country on earth.

After two hours, Sean and I realized that Tiananmen Square was so vast, smoggy and crowded that it was like saying you'd meet somebody in Paris. Hailing a 1.40 yuan taxi, we returned to our quadrant of the city.

That evening we lounged over beers with Dad on a park deck near his hotel as dusk turned to dark. Home was a foreign concept that we would adjust to in 24 hours.

"Thanks for a good trip," Sean said.

"Thank you, guys," said Dad.

"And," Sean added, "thanks for being our dad."

"Yeah," I smiled. "Thanks for the chromosome."

I looked at the sky, the stars hidden by Beijing's brilliance. A few hours later, I would rise early and discover a manmade acre of lake, crisscrossed with tiny bridges, just beyond the shadow of our hotel. I would borrow a fishing pole from an elderly Chinese man wearing an old circle-brow hat. He would show me how to mold the bait onto the hook before I cast my line out. I would inhale the setting of the backstreet, the grimy windows of the brick factories, and know I was accepted. He would smile his rural grin of missing teeth, position his hat to block the sun and re-bait my line. I would again cast away, farther this time, far enough to catch someone else's bucket on the next bridge over and spill its bait into the lake. And still be accepted, as hosts around the world accept travellers.

Sean and I would then take a taxi to the airport, staying silent from the displeasure of going home. The trip would become memory as our wheels scraped the runway at home in Vancouver.

But for now, I was content to sit in the dark and enjoy the company of my dad and brother, trying to slow memory's spinning wheels. In the quiet of the park we each fidgeted with the looming departure. I noticed Mongolian horsehairs on my tie. Dad found a thousand rubles in his pocket. Sean found the missing batteries to his Walkman.

Train travel had made me a muser. Because of how well we travelled as friends, we restored pride to our interpretation of "family." People need an interlocking set of principles in their travel companions to face challenging scenarios. Like a Swiss Army knife of qualities, Dad, Sean, and I had found that gadget of camaraderie.

Dad could have tried on various masks throughout our three-way cohabitation on the train but he chose only to be himself, flaws included. I realized Dad never left the family structure because it didn't work on its own grand and lengthy level of love. One could say our family broke up because there was too much love. And that love is stronger than a divorce. As a redefined family, we were discovering that train travel provided the ties that bind, just as our friend George the restaurateur foreshadowed.

At this end of our last night together, we crushed hugs then stood arm's length apart.

"That's it," I said, anxious at the parting. "Walk away."

Dad squinted. "Safe passage home sons."

"Call when you get back," Sean said.

"Walk away…" I repeated.

We stepped back further, eyeing one another. Then Dad turned left at the streetlamp and was quickly enveloped by the park's darkness. Sean and I waited for a taxi to roll by. We said nothing. A voice rang out from the night with the phrase that had taken us around the world. It was the voice of a man who pursued the dream of taking his two sons on the *Trans-Siberian Railway* start to finish. Together they'd gone to places that once lived only in their imaginations.

"Guys…. *Do you know where you are?*"

SECOND JOURNEY ~ HALIFAX-TORONTO-VANCOUVER
"THE CANADIAN"

Three years later we decided to take the second-longest train trip in the world: *The Canadian*, from Halifax, Nova Scotia to Vancouver, British Columbia. Since our first journey, we'd each passed many personal mileposts. I had earned a teaching certificate and was ready to teach English in foreign countries. My country of choice was Russia and that was about to happen. I self-published a slim volume about our first train trip that I gifted to friends and family, titled *Moscow +7*, which was being excerpted in a Russian language magazine, and a newspaper in Russia. Sean began dating Hilary and both were working in hotels; indeed, she'd been his boss when he began working the front desk, and they were en route to being married. Dad's career in tourism had him involved in launching the bid to bring the Winter Olympics to Vancouver and Whistler for 2010, a process still underway; he and Janice had married the year before.

George at Neighbours Restaurant was well aware of our unfolding lives as we frequented his establishment. Whichever of us arrived first soon found a complimentary serving of calamari on the table, which, among the three of us, only Dad (and George) liked. Happily for us, George always sat at our table for part of our evenings, despite attending to dozens of other patrons. When he heard our idea to fly to Halifax to start out next train journey, we learned that as a ship captain in the Greek mercantile business, George frequented Halifax harbor and its shore life. He told us, "It is beautiful, heaped with history of the near term—when compared with Greece—and backdropped by a party city, ...or so I recall." His eyes hinted at mischief with those last words. The night our plans for training across Canada firmly came into focus in his restaurant, George offered a gruff blessing in Greek shorthand: "May the love of family trump the travails of travel."

Halifax to Vancouver is 3,946 rail miles (6,351 kilometers). Boarding VIA Rail's train at one side of the country and travelling westward is a dream held by many but realized by too few.

The aircraft's wheels kneeled into Nova Scotia's capital runway. Downtown Halifax knocked us around its streets. The city has a geographic battle with the ocean, a shoreline with dozens of coves, harbors, ports and marinas. At our hotel, Sean and I took the smaller twin room, while Dad eased into his single. The arrangements felt family familiar.

Dad called Sean and me on the hotel phone–a mere foot away from our room through the adjoining wall–and spent five minutes outlining the itinerary of our first night in Halifax: Walk around town, have dinner at Privateer's Warehouse, and then drain away the jetlag in bed. The family was comfortably back in travel territory, crawling toward food and drink and learning.

A sharp and persistent crosswind kept the city free of wrappers, napkins, and Tim Horton's' coffee cups. Our jackets billowed into sails as we crossed a few streets to the rails beside the harbor. It was here in the undulating grey waters of Halifax Harbour on the morning of December 6, 1917 that the SS *Mont-Blanc*, a French munitions ship, exploded after colliding with another ship. The most powerful unintended explosion of the First World War killed more than 1,600 men, women and children. Nine thousand others were wounded, 12,000 buildings were damaged–and barely a single pane of glass was left to keep out the winter weather. The destruction covered 300 acres. The war had come to haunt home soil.

But on the harbor now, in front of us, stood respectable wharf-friendly hotels, pubs, and restaurants; one would surely have a spot for three anxious and weary travellers. Space was a scarce commodity in the Good Times Pub; you couldn't fit another half body inside the place. Pints of Maritime brews crested safely over heads of the young clientele to intended imbibers. A band from Newfoundland invested heavily in a fiddle solo and was rewarded by deafening applause and whistles. The music stymied casual discourse and we were left leaning against a wall to watch the frenzied weekend crank up. Lobster, bread and beer; doesn't get much better than this. Brits, Americans, Germans, and Japanese; everyone feels like a Canadian when in Halifax.

I awoke first the next morning. The others groggily offered hugs when reminded it was my 31st birthday. Shuffling to the bathroom, I looked in the mirror of vanity and gave myself unbiased permission to like everything in front of me on this special day. My birthday treat was a trip to Peggy's Cove. I got to drive while Dad and Sean fought over control of the music.

Peggy's Cove is a winding, tree-lined, half-hour drive from Halifax in which the forest peels away to expose a low rocky coast and the Atlantic's horizon. Ships stood at the dock in the sheltered cove, tilting weakly to the scattering waves. Beaten-up buoys, lobster traps and webs of netting were piled for loading. Idyllic, postcard-worthy homes were strewn on a brow of hill as the road fanned into a parking lot. The homes' exterior colors, faded by years of salt and spray, softened the landscape in shades that couldn't be duplicated without time and specific geography. The most-photographed lighthouse in the world towered in bleached white over the shore's stonework. A spiral of tiny windows reached up to the red crown of the lantern, falling against a deep unpolluted blue.

As the wind drove into our faces, Sean ran ahead to read signs warning of likely harm or possible death. On a rise that slipped some short slippery distance into insanity, we took pictures and tempted fate.

In the moment, I imagined myself onboard a 14-crew ship that hadn't seen land for near to three weeks.

It was rumored that one of the crew had lost the ship's compass in a game of cards at their departing port. Our guiding stars had stealthily left at midnight while the moonlight hid after running the outlines of an inky cumulous front. The flat sheet of ocean began to rise and then came the fierce whitecap slaps on the hull.

Land was surely close, but how close? The men came up from their card game to ask redundant questions or talk of mutiny. I sat behind the cabin, leaning on barrels of Fifth King whisky and smoking something Chili the cook had sold the deckhands at lunch. I could hear the laughing and smashing of night in the canteen. When the men were drunk enough, they would sing fishing songs they all knew bilingually.

Blackness. Even the railings were lost in it. The ocean spray developed into drenching sheets and hammering thuds. Then eerie silence. The bow dipped and crunched into an avenging mountain of water. I slid across the deck and crashed into the oversized whisky barrels. The rivets told me I was against the iron rails as I grasped at air. Water slipped a foot across the steel and disappeared into the night, carrying my tobacco and pipe with it. A lone bulb on the weather mast flickered twice and died. Nothing reached that edge of living darkness. Terror teemed out there, hovering, groping. I heard two mates open the door and holler for help before being silenced by a lethal collision. Then, like falling on steel, a deathly cold knocked me loose.

Loose into that fatal night. No life left to rage against the light....

— MY DREAM SEQUENCE 09/01/01

The time-eaten rocks near the shoreline beside us that day at Peggy's Cove were juicy with marine life. Tidal pools refilled with every hypnotizing rotation of the waves. My Zippo sputtered in the wind and went out; it took half a pack of matches to light one cigarette. Seagulls, suspended by the winds, rolled around in the sky. Dad had gone for a solo stroll and so it was just Sean and me against the sea.

"Imagine coming here in a storm," I said, leaning into Sean.

"Imagine you're on a ship offshore," he replied, fighting the wind, "and you spot the lighthouse's beacon between the waves."

I looked up. Way up. Up to the iron lantern and its hyper-radiant lens and the windows that brightened with every cycle of the guiding light. As if in a trance, I saw myself in the gusts, fumbling with the keys while mounting the steep steps to light the pilot again. I looked out at the rumbling ocean turning waves into Poseidon's fists. A foamy wave thwarted a skull of rock, spitting furiously and taming it to shore.

We walked to the gift shop, where trinket-y gadgets–from ashtrays to snow globes–sat expectantly on the impulse-buy racks. Beyond these were the local crafts and shipbuilding manuals and other treasures ending at a rack of colorful postcards. There were cement, ceramic and solid oak lighthouses; punch-out, die-cast, puzzle lighthouses; lighthouses in papier-mâché, wire, and glass. There was intricately carved art from First Nations groups.

"The Ship-in-a-Bottle sale ends Thursday," the saleswoman announced. She pointed to some precious, impractical pens with a lighthouse thermometer that headed south when turned. A nearby family played with a battery-powered light-house that emitted endearing sounds from mechanical birds.

At the restaurant attached to the gift shop, Sean and I each ordered a Broken Oar omelet, a bowl of honest-to-God stick-to-your-ribs, hot cereal, and a side of home-style breakfast fries. Our schedule was tight, according to the clock in the kitchen. Our train left Halifax in less than two hours.

Dad rejoined us from his walk on the shore. After scanning the postcard racks, quickly pecking at the food and acquiring some "been-there" souvenirs, we left the lonely town on the bluff. I drove, following the rocky coastline two miles west to a memorial for the 229 souls lost in these unforgiving waters just two years earlier.

Transcript between Swissair Flight 111 cockpit and Halifax air traffic control, September 2, 1998, night. (Edited by author for clarity.)

Swissair 111: Swissair one-eleven heavy is declaring emergency; Roger, we are between, uh, twelve and five-thousand feet. We are declaring emergency now at, ah time, ah, zero-one-two-four.

Halifax, Nova Scotia control: Roger.

Swissair 111: Eleven heavy, we are starting fuel dump now. We have to land immediately.

Halifax: Swissair one-eleven, just a couple of miles, I'll be right with you.

Swissair 111: Roger. (Sound–probable autopilot disconnection.)

Swissair 111: And we are declaring emergency now, Swissair one-eleven.

Halifax: Copy that.

Halifax: Swissair one-eleven, you are cleared to commence your fuel dump on that track. Advise me when the dump is complete.

Halifax controller: Swissair one-eleven, check. You're cleared to start the fuel dump.

Swissair 111:———.

With that haunting final silence, Halifax control lost radio contact with the airliner seven nautical miles from where the memorial now stood. Swissair Flight 111 broke into the face of the dark Atlantic. The MD-11 fragmented and all 229 souls onboard perished.

Peggy's Cove (population: 60) was soon overrun with law enforcement personnel, search and rescue teams, recovery divers, the Coast Guard, Federal Aviation Administration (FAA) personnel and other aviation industry representatives. The area was taped and sealed off from the public overnight. With their boats out searching for survivors, the townspeople paced their days offering food and warmth to those who needed it. Local fishermen talked in low tones of the grisly catches they'd be pulling in. The cove's famous lighthouse, an icon of safety, became associated with a tragedy it could not have prevented.

Now, two oval stones stand upright in a concrete compass embracing the bay. Someone had, almost forbiddingly, carved the number 111 deep into one of the stones, perhaps as a way to expose the untamed Atlantic. As a member of a family in which someone is inevitably flying somewhere, we read the inscriptions, and paused hard at risks and odds. The fierce wind provoked an almost sorrowful groan as it came ashore.

Ticking out time with large iron hands, the Halifax train station clock pulsed to departure. It revealed we had 20 minutes before our train left the platform. Ours was the end car. Having learned the value of personal space and comfort while railing, Dad, Sean, and I had booked a three-bed sleeper. We readied to board the *Ocean-Limited.*

A smartly uniformed man greeted us as we hurriedly approached our car. Franc was the attendant for the dome car and planned to be along for the ride as far as Québec City. We introduced ourselves and stepped back. With a deft slide, Franc managed our bags onto the vestibule and guided us down the hall to the last sleeping quarters on the train. We forced the packs into the room and slammed the door.

It was time for me to get settled in the bar car, feet away.

Michy delivered hors d'oeuvres from the kitchen and Franc opened the bar. While Dad slipped back into our room to stack the luggage in his favor, I made my way to the end of the coach and embraced that "identified-as-a-smoker" feeling. I found a seat in the exclusive corner, built to accommodate eight smoking passengers.

I pushed the Trans-Canada guide across the table and noted the uncomfortably high windows in the narrow bar.

"Franc, why are the windows so ridiculously high?"

Seven others turned to Franc. He threw an empty beer can in the trash and padlocked the fridge door before landing at the counter, grasping it like a podium.

"The cars, all of those in this train, were built in the early Fifties." He moved a rag along a vinyl rail. "At the time, you could not be allowed to show alcohol on sale."

We all looked around, then at each other, with renewed appreciation of the out-of-date décor built for out-of-date values.

"First call for dinner in dining car,' Michy interrupted. "*M. et Mme. Première appel pour le diner... pardon? Celui-la, oui, c'est ca.*" He carried on up to the domed portion of the coach and out of our view.

Three men sitting near me sucked their cigarettes to the filters and left. I lit another. Time was on my side. Sean had reserved the third dinner seating, hours away.

The town of Truro came and went as the train trundled through. A rail line cut through forests guided us into the province of New Brunswick; our "stay" in its capital, Moncton long enough only for a stroll along the platform. It was quite a change from Russian stations of our last cross-country train ride; a hedge ran across the horizon with a suburban residential area on the other side. Once we re-boarded, the afternoon grew dark, and I decided to nap.

Sean shook me violently.

"What?"

"It's dinner! We've called you twice. Either get a Medic-Alert button or be ready when they start calling names."

VIA Rail trains have skinny halls and heavy metal, which is to say you can't walk a straight line on a moving train without looking like you need assistance or would fail a breathalyzer. It's is a matter of countering bends, the train's surges and its braking. Every second is fraught with these conditions; shaving is not advised.

For me, walking four coaches to the dining car was an experience close to derailing, all while maintaining politeness towards anyone–or even anything–you bump into.

"Sorry." My apology, though hazy, was entirely genuine.

"Sorry."

"My fault. Sorry."

"No, I own that. My bad. Sorry."

I took a seat facing backward in the dining car.

Sean argued that he could only sit facing the direction we were headed. "I get sick if I sit backwards."

"You serious?"

"I do, too," said Dad. "That's why I'm sitting here."

"So neither of you two can sit with the scenery passing you from behind? Do you have a doctor's note?"

I sighed and focused on the menu: fresh salmon, lobster and one–lucky for me–item of turkey. Seafood and I have issues.

The waiter walked over and pointed his pen in my direction. "*Êtes-vous prêt à commander?*"

Just then a young woman with a nose ring touched the back of the empty chair beside mine.

"Would you mind if I sit here for dinner?" she asked. "I reserved a seat and they put it here."

"This is a drop-in family," Dad said, pulling back the chair by its leg. "Please sit with us."

"I'm Carolyn." She traded handshakes around the table and settled in.

Carolyn smelled like Raid, which had undoubtedly played a role in the breakup with her boyfriend, Charlie. Through discussions and desserts, we opened Carolyn's mind and tinkered with her romance receptor. She hoped the memory of Charlie would float away with the passage of time–but not before she wrote a goodbye letter using spray paint on his house. Our dinner guest had a clinical diagnosis that was visible from across the street; she was all over the spectrum. We shuffled uncomfortably in our seats; we had played along but now the stop signs had started appearing. The trick when travelling on a train is to not go about interfering with someone else's life-altering narratives.

Soon after dinner, Carolyn left for the front wagons–the economy zone. The restaurant car is the point where the coach classes collide and where those closer to the engine are expected not to cross the threshold into the rear. There was no unspoken rule preventing the reverse. I used my napkin to clean crumbs from my Velcro-like beard and then headed to the front of the train. The first people I saw were watching a movie about dinosaurs on their laptops. Another few doors brought me to cars lined with seats. I cannot fathom crossing 3,000 miles (5,000 kilometers) sitting up; it violates the Geneva Convention and would be akin to driving to Québec in a Boeing 737. Plus, sleep in that position looked unlikely without drugs.

On my return, I found Sean in the smoking section, squeezed among eight people engaged in a riveting debate over where we likely were. One woman, a frequent rider between Halifax and Rimouski, said we'd crossed into Québec in the past hour.

"*Belle Québec*," I ceremoniously announced. After all, we were in the province once voted "most likely to separate." The woman said we were seeing Québec in a sad way.

"My father lives in Sept-Iles. From Rimouski, I take the ferry across the St. Lawrence. The Québec you will see on the train is not the Québec that is Québec. This provincial territory, despite unresolved border conflicts with Labrador, is nearly 580,000 square miles (one and a half million square kilometers) of the finest earth you could want. That is what you had better see to give an accurate picture of us who are Quebecois. You're only going to see politics in the cities. Visit Gaspé before you die."

Sean and I had heard a similar plea while railing in Croatia some years before, during the area's conflict. Zolan, an informed citizen with a taste for bad vodka had admonished us to see the true Croatia. The town Split, if possible. We arrived in Zagreb only to discover the tracks into Split and Bosnia had been blown up the night before. Sadly, that too was part of seeing the true Croatia in that time of war.

In our VIA Rail smokers' group, a man, late sixties with a dollop of grey hair and a short cigarette burning his orange fingers, sat across from Sean. He'd picked up on the border discussion. I didn't need to hear a second sentence to know he was German. Without a trace of alcohol apparent, he dropped into a monologue about how lucky we were that the Nazis didn't win the Second World War. He said, as if reliving it before our eyes, "You are so fucking lucky," and repeated that refrain four times in 10 minutes. A woman obviously uncomfortable with the man left. I sensed the speaker was lonely and living 50 years ago.

"What's your current mission?" Sean asked him, gritting a cigar.

The old man smiled and said, with a twinkle, "I'm going to Montreal to see my new grandson."

The woman from Sept-Iles announced the time. Sean said he was off to bed. Charny, the railway's southern link to Québec City, was expecting us at 4 a.m. I left with Sean. Three cars down, we found our room. Dad was snoring. I bent my forehead into something suspended from the ceiling. *The lights, the bloody lights are around here,* I thought, sweeping my hand through Dad's toiletries instead. Sean grabbed my belt as tripping on the food bag downed him. The fan whirred to life as I worked my way up the succession of buttons and switches. The light above the sink flickered on, revealing the small arrangement with which we had to work.

"G'night, dude," Sean said as the sink light went out.

"Yeah." I stretched out as far as a mummy could. "G'night."

Every early rising in a train compartment is a mixture of "get the hell out of my way" and getting the hell out of someone's way. It was a subjective social issue with apologetic pockets in Canada. I shoved anything I could identify as mine into my backpack and got out of the way of bunkmates who prioritize themselves as the only person who counts, Dad or Sean.

When the train stopped, I landed on Charny's platform in the still chill of darkness. Passengers carefully managed the staircase. A woman of profound beauty stood at the edge of the doorway. She looked like Marilyn Monroe with bedhead. When she stepped down, just five paces stood between us. She made eye contact, a simple feat because I was already watching her, and gave a coy smile of acknowledgement as she dragged her bag past me.

"Hi... I'm Brent... the First."

"Aphasia," she smiled with one side of her mouth. "*Bon matin.*"

And then she was gone. No one else had seen the unicorn.

Dad, Sean, and I walked out into the Québec City morning. The blues in the sky's hue indicated the sun was still in its housecoat and nursing a second cup of hydrogen. Outside the station's vacant lobby sat a single taxi and a driver who didn't want a fare for at least another two hours. He was, as he noted, in the fire lane, not the taxi zone. We convinced him we were only going up the hill to the Château Frontenac. After eyeing us–hoping he'd get a tip the size of his Christmas bonus for taking us to the finest hotel in the country–he pushed a button and let us pack our own luggage into his trunk.

Our driver stopped outside the most visually appealing building in the land and pushed the trunk-release button. Dad paid, borrowing money from Sean and me, leaving a nice but modest tip that made the driver so disappointed he vowed to be a separatist martyr *"peu de temps après le déjeuner*!" (Soon after lunch.)

Many who live in Québec have wanted to separate from Canada since France lost the battle against the British in 1759. The referendum to partition/secede 'Pakistanicize'/'Balkanize'/gain independence/achieve sovereignty/sleep-in-the-bed-they-hath-made ended in 51 percent of the Province de Québec voting in 1995 to remain Canadian, while 49 percent voted *"Oui–au revoir, fukerz!"*

A web of cobblestone streets spread over a hillside of cafés, churches, and thin alleyways that led to defensive locals sunbathing on their terrace, as well as an array of souvenir shops, bistros, pleasant squares, and stone houses dating back to the 17th Century. On this particular spring day, we encountered colorful awnings, hanging baskets in bloom, clinging vines, and cozy stonework of tenements stacked together like milk cartons. Soaring church spires, minimal vehicle traffic, French accents, customer service schools, endless breezes of fresh air, and the almighty Château Frontenac provided movie-set detail, yet also offered a reinforced sense that a visitor is truly touching the past.

Evening came. Québec City, as we wandered it, was experiencing the last of the day's light. Wrought-iron streetlights buzzed to life and threw sulfur shades onto the wet cobblestones. As shops rolled up their awnings and shuttered their doors, we ran into the lovely Aphasia—she of the earlier train steps moment—wandering along at a thoughtful pace.

"Aphasia," I exclaimed.

"Ah, the man from the train."

"Yes!" I bowed slightly.

Dad cleared his throat. I was being rude.

"Aphasia, my family. Family, Aphasia."

Dad intercepted her. "Aphasia. How is the city treating you?"

"Like it always does," she said. "I'm sure I lived a former life here."

"It can be transcendental," Sean said. Sean? He had a seriously serious girl-friend so possibly he was being sincere.

Before I said something profound, Dad invited Aphasia to join us for dinner. "There's a restaurant across that street. Looks like just the place to grab another piece of Québec."

Aphasia opened her mouth, possibly to decline. *Dad, say something*, I thought.

"My treat," Dad said with his trademark smile, the one that can soften stone.

"All right," she said. "I'll just go change into something more fitting. I'll be there in a half hour."

She shuffled away as if time was of no value. Dad, Sean, and I walked the dark streets to the restaurant in anticipation of relaxing conversation and a nice meal.

There were fresh flowers nestled on the sill and glamor radiated from the place settings, the diners and the exceptional standards set by Guy, the doorman, who doubled as headwaiter. We sat as three at a table set for four, stirring mochas and talking about the rich environs, their heritage value, and the city's distinctive value in the Wal-Mart and drive-thru country we'd become. While we spoke, Edith Piaf's voice poured from small speakers with the authentic vinyl hisses. As "*Non, je ne regrette rien*" ended in a sea of 40-year-old static, I stepped outside for a quick cigarette. I bundled myself tight into a stance of my own–all that was happening, where I was, and the timeless silhouettes of steeples, chimneys, and weathervanes. And, damn it, Québec *is* Canada.

I went back into the restaurant and sat down, avoided the argument about Spain that my table was host to, and looked out the window into the night. There, in a radiant pool of icy blue street hues, stood Aphasia, looking rather like a French angel dressed in a Molson jacket. The cue was the passing reflection of a door. When she sashayed toward us, I rose, unsettling the cutlery, and said "Glad you could make it. You look stunning."

Guy took orders off the wine list, one from the boring 'non-alcoholic' drink selection, and then two for steak, one for lobster and mussels for the lady.

God. Mussels? Can I even contemplate a future kiss if she consumes something as gory as an entire slug of a creature, from lips to asshole? I kept all of those words to myself and inwardly gagged as I watched her drain everything from inside the mound of shells set before her. And she chewed with her front teeth.

Eventually we were the only four customers remaining in the establishment. It was all civil, conversing like adults, while I was thinking like a primate in the spring when the females had thawed. Guy and the man who had been taking bills and munching on dinner mints began upending the chairs onto the tables. This classic end-of-a-romantic-evening hint was a prelude to Dad and Sean heaving their scarves around their necks and disappearing into the night.

Aphasia and I sat as nervous confidantes. She played with her watch and took it off and set it on the table. I tried it on snuggly over three fingers. It lay between us. I held it in my closed hand. Guy walked over to our table and blew out the candle. Aphasia and I talked. Then Guy put a bucket of dirty soapy water on the table. Aphasia announced she was a poet.

"How do you know when poetry is good?"

She turned her face to think. "When it harmonizes your philosophy and soul, when the words synchronize you with the rest of the universe. Mental honey. Maybe you wish you said it. That's because it is made of you."

"So why did it stop rhyming?"

She stifled a laugh. "Much deeper. Sorry, it is my fault. I spend my days around well-educated people, so it's a bit alarming to meet someone who isn't."

I rocked my spoon, wounded into retort.

"Why did you choose poetry? Why not astrology, saving extinct species, or non-profit fundraising? Poetry is for the poor or the independently wealthy. Don't you need money?"

"I don't think you understand me, Brent." Aphasia rolled that r off her uvula. "Poetry is unlimited, not constrained by the rigid rules of writing. I can have a point or be pointless, but the motive for great poetry is conjured eunoia put to paper."

"What is eunoia? It sounds like it belongs in italics," I said, feeling that if I'd known the word, we'd have made love on the wet cobblestone. But I had no intelligent reply, and sex on the rocks was slipping away.

"Eunoia means 'beautiful thinking.' It is the shortest word in the English language that uses all the vowels. And Brent, I am a good with words. I have a music degree. I play five instruments, and three parts of my body are insured. And as for poetry, my true love… I can taste the words, guided by eunoia as a rule, melt them over the charcoals of my tongue, add dashes of reckless prose if I'm in the mood, and then crack them into diamonds."

She mimicked these actions with precision. This woman was so far removed from my league, which was usually confined to drunk women left over when the bar lights were turned up. But I wasn't giving up on this marlin. All of this talking was sport; I just wasn't sure which one of us was holding the fishing rod and which was the marlin.

I leaned in and pinched her dimple. "You are charming… and you're as scattered as I am."

She drew her smile to one side. It said I didn't have the key to her lock. But she hadn't seen my key. I pulled a loving left hook off her cheek and brushed it affectionately. "You are a most courageous woman. Courageous from courage–"

"Courage from *coeur*," she said.

"*Coeur* to heart," I replied.

Tipping my fedora, I thought how never in my travels had I met such a woman as this. The texture of her voice, the way she ladled her tongue and spoke through the gates of her teeth with distinctive clarity and volume. I imparted this to her as we left the restaurant. Twenty dark steps from the hotel door Aphasia spun and drew a staggered breath.

"Your family has been kind to treat me well. Thank them for me, will you?"

"Of course, I could treat you more well if you gave me a longer first impression."

I bent in, whispered a soft couplet that would make a porn star blush and pecked her temple at the hairline.

She never whispered back. I found that poetic, non-verbal poetry. The loudest noise is silence. I really liked her.

Sean, Dad, and I, were aboard the aptly but boringly named train, the *Québec City - Windsor Corridor* the next morning. Over the day, we transferred trains and grabbed expensive station food to avoid the expensive train food. One train employee offered us homemade sandwiches. "My wife made them. Better than the onboard ones from the train company."

travelling from coast to coast in Canada isn't a straightforward endeavor. There had been a railway on the island of Newfoundland for 90 years but it stopped operating a few years before our journey. And so Halifax is the eastern-most start of tracks heading west to Vancouver. But the trains dead-ended and motor coach transfers to downtown had to be made in Montreal and then Toronto, detracting from the pleasurable sense of "journey" that one experiences in a sleeping car.

We had but one hour in Montreal, giving us enough time to witness a mugging and hear a church choir.

If any of this country's cities demonstrates solipsism and a diagnosis of "manic as an espresso with a Red Bull chaser on the Friday of a long weekend," it is Toronto, where, too, our stay was fleeting. The city's historic Union Station connects east-west trains, and also offers a southbound VIA Rail/Amtrak service known as the *Maple Leaf*, which links passenger trains between Canada and the USA.

++++++++++++

Upon one's departure southbound, the sky dances with the hue of Toronto for an hour. The *Maple Leaf* train skirts the northern shore of Lake Ontario until reaching the American border crossing at Niagara Falls. The Falls themselves are a breathing jewel that is also the Canada–U.S. border. There are two halves of Niagara Falls separated by a tuft of land called Goat Island. On either side of that island, billions of gallons of water cascade into a misty froth. Once it settles down, the Niagara River continues onward less violently into Lake Ontario. Although the border divides the two falls; the train stops a few miles away from them. There the engine crews are changed, customs inspection happens quickly, and suddenly the train inches into America, with the welcoming brownstone city of Buffalo, New York. That was a routing we contemplated. This was a potential journey, to end up in New York City.

But instead, our departure was westbound, where the sky also danced with the hue of Toronto for an hour. Travelling this way, as we chose to, the *Maple Leaf* train skirts the northern shore of Lake Ontario to cross Canada all the way. Our train continued northwest away from the center of Canada, away from the lights and Benetton and GAP ads, away from taxis and people rushing to and fro. We were in Western Ontario, and it was dark. We slept in our new configurations.

I woke first and noticed that not only had Toronto and its plethora of suburbs been whisked away but it was replaced with huge waterfalls, marble caves, covered bridges, tall trees, and an 1800s rugged feeling of being a part of the land.

This continued for hours and as we crossed into Manitoba, the beauty fell away, and the long stretch across three provinces with the same horizon began. I love the Canadian Prairies (American Heartland) except they're ubiquitously flat, a charm all their own. It is the land of cereals, grains, and wheat fields straight out to the horizon.

And so it was as we crossed our days aboard the train, looking out at wheat fields as far as one could care to see. Corn, sunflower, and wheat were all we saw for three Provinces.

We stopped in Jasper, Alberta for the night and quickly caught our train home the following morning. I must digress here, instead of explaining how beautiful my home province is, my Dad has already made his mark on the map with train stories about the West, as well as his celebrated, "Train Beyond The Mountains."

British Columbia is perhaps the most fortunate space on Earth. It has everything from hydroelectric dams to deserts, and tundra, to vast lakes, and soaring peaks. It has world-class skiing and snowboarding. But here I must refer you to my Dad's books because he's written extensively on railroading in the Western parts of Canada as well as his highly acclaimed book on the Rocky Mountaineer, a train that gives you British Columbia as no other experience could. So, I will refrain from saying how awesome Vancouver is, because my Dad has already done it. It is amazing though, and British Columbia is spectacular beyond what most countries dream of putting on their postcards.

THIRD JOURNEY ~
New York-Chicago-
San Francisco
ACROSS AMERICA

I love America. Until Russia came into my game, America had been my adoptive home and I was far more intimate with her roadmap, her state lines and her topography than those of my own country. I knew her. By the age of ten, I could recite the names of all fifty states alphabetically. I had seen more of America than anyone I'd met. But the glory was personal. Few people would choose to travel around the United States of America as I had done. Days of twenty hours at the wheel with static-afflicted radio stations and a worn-out cassette of Chris Ledoux were my solace, a dog was my companion, rest areas were my motels, and 24-packs of Pabst Blue Ribbon were my minibars. Watching people and listening to out-of-state country music were my entertainment. With those travels, I'd personally bonded with the USA. To cross the country by train would consummate our relationship.

It had again been at Neighbors Restaurant, where our 2003 train trip along the sash of the United States (2,567 miles/4130 kilometers) took form. Our Greek ship captain turned restaurateur, George, took in our stories of life changes noting, "You are proving the Greek prophecy right. You never return as you embarked, you are constantly new individuals and that interests me."

While our trips changed us, so had the intervening years. Sean and Hilary were back from two years of travel and work in Europe, spending the first year in all manner of dodgy and exciting places, from Sarajevo to Northern Ireland. I had spent a year and half teaching English at the Institute of Law & Economics in Russia, with side classes at the University of Voronezh, all situated midway between Moscow southward to Sochi. Dad was still travelling heaps for business, as well as meeting up with Sean and Hilary in Berlin, after which he'd flown to Moscow and spent time with me in Voronezh. Mom remained a constant in all our lives, as did Janice, and they got along well which eased all manner of family gatherings. None of us took good fortune for granted.

George summed up our need for a new journey, and encouraged us to keep leaving home and experience "elsewhere," as he called it. He quoted Aristotle's "Adventure is worthwhile."

The America we talked about training across was a changed America. On September 11, 2001, the 5,520-mile (8,891-kilometer) strip of international division that demarcated Canada and the United States matured from being the longest undefended border in the world to one of intense scrutiny. America suddenly became less accessible as she retreated into suspicion of the rest of the world. There was a speed limit to freedom. The border line-ups were dissuasive, as was the ugly insecurity that blanketed America.

For our journey, New York, with its wounded psyche still in recovery, was the place to start. Of course, everything in New York City was, and remained, New York-ish. It is the apex of city life with its blueprint of powerful avenues, residential streets, skid row tenements, tightly fit brownstones, and archetypal lofts. Kids play in water bursting from open fire hydrants, people are judged more for what they wear than what they say. And, beneath it all, Broadway wannabes, Wall Street stock market gurus, and all the mafias elbow their way to supremacy.

New York is a place of places. Even ice cream has its place. Across from our hotel, an ice cream shop boasted a large clientele trying to lick their cones before that first sticky drop hit the wrist. And, as many know, the day goes downhill from there. We noticed an empty table in the rear and fought against the crowd to claim it.

"New York City," Dad announced as he poached a sticky seat from another table.

"A Harlem bus tour leaves the hotel in a half hour," I said. "Who's in?"

Dad licked a pendulum of Rocky Road ice cream. "I think I'd prefer to walk around here. I've got a bookstore to visit and Central Park is a few streets up. This is America's 'walking' city."

"Well then," my brother followed, "I say that we wander!" A piece of his vanilla-cherry ice cream calved off the top scoop, slid through his fingers, and glopped onto the table. Both he and Dad reached for the napkins, making the table a predictably terrible mess–four square feet of dairy Velcro. 'Sticky' is the least virtuous of all tactile features.

Our hotel was near the south side of Central Park, east of Times Square and north of the bulk of Manhattan. The names of the city streets and areas were long familiar to me: Hell's Kitchen, Lower East Side, Harlem, and farther out, the boroughs of Queens, Brooklyn, the Bronx, Staten Island, and the East River. These all had a place in my mind long before their terrestrial quadrants were fixed in my memory. Superheroes had battled it out over the steel, glass and stone-clad metropolis (as if fighting in New York was fighting for the world), graffiti-covered subway cars slunk out of the Big Apple, steam vented from manhole covers, taxis came in yellow tsunamis, hookers negotiated at open-car windows as if orders were being placed at a drive-through restaurant, men used fire escapes when their girlfriends' husbands came home early, police officers strolled their beats while swinging their batons, security cameras caught little events and missed the big ones, light pollution hid any hint of the cosmos, and thieves with switchblades and eye masks hid in alleyways. So many ideas about what made a big city big were, to my mind, wrapped up in the image of New York City.

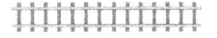

Central Park's green rectangle stretches from 59th to 110th Street and Fifth to Eighth Avenue–843 acres of landscaping in the middle of Manhattan. Though walled by soaring towers, the park is large enough to make you feel like you're removed from the chaotic traffic and pedestrians yelling, "Buy! Sell!" or "This conversation never happened" into their cell phones. Dad travelled to New York routinely on business and spent much of his free time in Central Park, which over-flows with paths and hillsides, Monet-esque bridges, birds, ponds, and soft knolls of dandelions. With more traffic than any other park in the country, and 25 million people strolling through it every year, Central Park has a huge force of laborers and planners–even its own police detachment–keeping every square foot of the park looking as it should and prepared for Central Park's full-frontal when Holly-wood settles in to film. Here, old trees play a quiet yet pivotal role, providing background atmosphere and ambient calm in every season. Small boys sailing their sailboats, zipping Pedi cabs, lovers leaning into each other, horse-drawn carriages clickity-clacking along, joggers sporting pulse/calorie monitors, old people feeding pigeons, and kids trying to keep their kites from tangling with the others–combined, they all make up the park's unique culture and tapestry. Though developers have wet dreams about converting Central Park into a parcel of build- ings, I'm damn sure New Yorkers would never so much as sell a leaf of this beloved green space–which they aptly call the "Lungs of the city".

The sun was setting low in the sky as Sean, Dad, and I left the park. But the night was bright as Times Square was fully lit up and firing off a galaxy's worth of photons. We were accosted with so many scrolling marquees, flashing banners, rippling signs, and colorful billboards that we didn't know whether to have a Pepsi or a pizza or see an over-priced musical. Companies arrest people electronically and captivate them with twisted neon, animated displays, synchronized monitors, dancing lasers and digital strobes. Storeys-high static signs for entertainment venues touched the sky and jumbotrons ached to impress you with thirty-foot revolving cans of Red Bull. It made me crave a Coke and a Buick.

Something was being filmed at Times Square Studios, home to ABC's popular *Good Morning America,* and the people who cared were ten deep. This was also the case at MTV's New York studio, where someone we didn't recognize was being interviewed and the sidewalk TVs garnered a cheering throng. Eventually, the hive of activity around the world's most famous intersection was behind us. We could now walk shoulder to shoulder, and talk without yelling.

"Amazing, eh," Dad said. "Times Square never fails to impress."

I said, "They should call this 'The city that *can't* sleep."

"Can you imagine New Year's Eve," Sean wondered aloud. "When the ball falls?"

"Can you imagine the lighting bills," I cautioned. "Some countries build dams or sell their oil to get this amount of power for their people."

Pairs of police officers loitered on every corner, joined by popcorn sellers and T-shirt salesmen–all hoarse after a day barking.

In our slow walk back to the hotel we came across the almighty of American architecture, the deity of skyscrapers–the Empire State Building. Following the destruction of the World Trade Center towers in 2001, the Empire State Building again became the tallest structure in New York City. It's a building that, despite its longevity, will–like Elvis's grave, survive on tourists. We looked at the there's-a-dupe-born-every-day priced menu fronting the restaurant and declined. I couldn't leave without a piece of the eatery, even though my days of taking small construction mementos–Roman Coliseum, Kremlin, Gobi Desert, Hollywood Cemetery, *Boston Herald*, Berlin Wall, Jack Daniels Distillery, Mount Rushmore, Atlantic City Boardwalk, Paramount Studios, Disney World employment office, Motley Crüe's dressing room, Vatican–were long gone. Once Dad learned that Sean and I had been collecting things from tourist sites, he gave us an eternal truth vis: "If everybody took a piece, there'd be nothing left."

'True. But we could organize a huge reunion and rebuild the Parthenon in the world.'

Dad often lays out laws, points and paradoxes that can't be argued with conventional wisdom or logic, and I conceded. I'd grown up. Now photo albums consummated my marriage with the world's finest places. It's a relationship built on trust, respect and sustainable tourism. I simply took a big hug from the Empire State Building.

††††††††††††††

Walking into a fine hotel room is a caviar moment of travelling. Dad had usurped the single room (hands up those who notice a pattern)–four floors and a football field away from us–while Sean and I shared the double. I dozed the night away. Waking, I knew that if I cracked my eyes open I had a good chance at stretching. In the middle of the stretch I noticed Sean wasn't there. He'd left the TV on. I wanted it off. I don't watch TV. Ever. Without breaking the comfort of the bed, I felt around for the remote but couldn't find it. I got up. There were no buttons anywhere on the TV to turn it down or off, and a desk blocked the plug. I sat on the bed knowing he'd done the TV thing on purpose, plotted revenge, then showered and pulled out a fresh stack of clothes. I called Dad's room and got no answer. I needed them; we had exciting plans.

This was a big day for us; we had tickets to see the Yankees play the Mets at Shea Stadium. One of Dad's numerous long-time baseball dreams was to see the two New York teams play each other. Sean and I were always in for a ball game and we'd talked about this day being one to remember. I was starting this perfect day feeling abandoned. Sean walked in and instantly became the target of my frustration. Nonplussed, he said he had left a note on his bed to let me know he'd gone for a walk.

"I don't look for notes on beds," I sniped (condescendingly, I hoped.)

My remark bounced off Sean without so much as ruffling a hair. "I went to get a paper and ran into Dad. So we walked around waiting for the sun to rise."

His calm response was chipping away at the list of grievances I'd been practicing in his absence. One last indignity sputtered out. "You left the TV on. You left a women's show on."

"Oh, the batteries in the remote were dead. I put that in the note."

Transit infrastructure in the world's larger cities can clutter up one's notion of simply going from point A to point B. The "7 local" was a long, single train to the stadium. It took us from lower Manhattan, across the East River to Queens. The spectacular graffiti started then; no building, no clean surface at any height was absent its share of art. Gangs had tagged their scripture on top of old gang rhetoric. Some buildings were entirely spray-painted with illegible names in strange fonts and abstract symbols, each one intended to obliterate any proof the former had existed. What an odd species we are.

Baseball fans crowded into our subway car at every stop and we were soon at capacity. This game is a part of America's brain. Professional baseball is so well woven into America's mosaic that even someone who dislikes baseball and never watches the sport will know the score. Today's was a big game and little kids brought along their little gloves, hoping to catch the ball that leaves the field for the stands. Their dads wore old team jerseys; some even carried their own ancient mitts in the hope that God would create a trajectory to their seat so they could die happy. Catching a game ball is the winning lottery ticket for baseball fans.

Shea stadium was open to the skies as we finally found our seats, high up from home plate. The sunny day had stormy intruders threatening from the north but, like a pack of wolves, the bad weather paced at a distance–a dare away from rushing into Queens. Eventually the teams were introduced, the national anthem played, and it was game time.

"Play ball," someone somewhere yelled.

With the first pitch came the walking concession stands. Vendors made their way up and down the stadium steps carrying large trays of snacks and drinks–yelling "HOT DOGS... POPCORN..." –, pausing only to toss bags of chips and other food into the crowd. They waited for the money to be handed over before starting up again: "HOT DOGS... POPCORN...."

"Go ahead," Dad grinned. I sensed he felt this was a rite of passage. "Order three hot dogs."

"Are you sure? Dad, it's the Yankees and Mets–top of the first and threatening skies approaching. Isn't this something *you* should maybe do for the memory? Hell, I'm 33 and I've done crazier shit than this...."

"One of the wonders of being a father is knowing when to give a moment you would love to your son. Besides, you've got the aisle seat."

Hot dogs, two ice cream dips and a bag of cold popcorn later, I was beyond the veil of innocence. I was now a worldly, well-rounded man. Life was just so much clearer now.

We first felt the heavy drops of rain at the bottom of the fourth. Ground workers rolled a large tarp over the infield. Thousands booed and wise fans deftly opened umbrellas. But the rain soon became a drizzle and the grounds crew got the nod to roll up the tarp as a beam of sunlight shone on the infield.

An inning and a half later, with the Yankees up one over the Mets, the sun left and the weather wolves pounced. The grounds crew again rolled out the tarp and thousands of fans without umbrellas sat glumly in the wind and the rain. It was torrential. Dad, Sean, and I had bought ball caps, which were now dripping colored rainwater. The loudspeaker crackled to life and a dejected voice told us that the game was postponed.

Disappointed fans funneled out of the stands in streams, down the staircases, and towards the Willets Point–Shea Stadium subway. The rain fell in sheets. It was a three-train wait, all of us fighting to get on board.

We headed towards Grand Central Station. A fellow transit passenger told us to cross over there and take the "6 train" to our announced destination: the Rizzoli Bookstore. Grand Central is far more than a place for merely changing trains. It's America's meeting spot. It's 76 acres and 44 platforms feeding 67 tracks, carrying more than 700,000 commuters daily. Because it is a terminus, trains from across North America begin and end their journeys here. Everyone was rushing to or from a staircase, knowing which subway went where and which train docked at which platform. We, however, got off at the wrong station and stood in the rain challenging each other's opinions about where we were. Dad declared time out by hailing a cab. Although the driver looked unhappy about getting his backseat saturated, he got us to Rizzoli without any English pejoratives. Rizzoli was Dad's favourite New York City bookstore; it was tall, calming, and loaded with sliding ladders and displays of prominent bestsellers and new arrivals. Sean was fixated on the final Harry Potter, which had been released that day. This rush consisted only of Sean. Dad was hunting for *To Kill a Mockingbird.* We left Rizzoli with a new book each, as one should do in preparation for a train trip.

We walked the longest of ways to take in the city. Hundreds of notes, cards, teddy bears, pictures, wreaths, ribbons, and extinguished candles were poignant reminders that we were standing where the twin towers of the World Trade Centers symbolized the might of America only a year and a half before. The events of 9/11 left a hole in the heart of the world. Construction trucks filled the yawning crater. As the rain lashed the faces of hundreds of silent mourners, I told Sean I'd be across the street beneath a canopy. Ground Zero wasn't my grail; I felt more like a curious voyeur than a grief-stricken American who had come to pay tribute or mourn. I didn't feel like I thought I should. That day stayed too fresh in my head and this excursion was like walking through a neighbor's house after a fire while it was still smoldering.

The rain worked its way through every cross-stitch in our layer of fabric, and our shoes squeaked as we walked away. In Vancouver, you don't wait for the rain to end to go outside. You surrender to it. And so we surrendered to our soggy state in order to fulfill our last objective: standing at the railing in Brooklyn Battery Park to gaze upon the woman in the harbor.

The Statue of Liberty was mired in a foggy skirt, obscured entirely by weather. As we turned to leave, Sean hollered, "Look." Lady Liberty's arm broke through the fog, her torch resuming its task as a beacon of hope and refuge. Just as I was about to say something about bringing your tired and poor, the mist enveloped her again.

We hailed a cab back to the hotel to call it a night so we'd wake up travelling. We were anxious to be on the railway. The next day would see us embark on the fourth longest train crossing in the world. After already tackling Russia and Canada, we felt ready for America.

As travellers often have, we woke, grumbled and headed for a train station. This was New York's Penn Station. Grand Central may be the largest North American train station but Pennsylvania Station is the busiest. A thousand passengers board a train here every 90 seconds. And all of them know where they're going. Not us, though. Amtrak signs pointed to various platforms and offered up names, while our tickets only had a train number.

I said unnecessarily, "This station saw 4.3 million successful Amtrak boardings last year. So three intelligent men should be able to solve this without having to ask for directions".

Sean approached an attendant and came back with a platform number, a boarding time, and a staircase that would drop us off in front of our coach. That first train on our cross-America journey was the *Septa*, which took us on a two hour slide to Philadelphia where we'd change to train number 49, the *Lake Shore Limited* which would take us to Chicago, where we would board the *California Zephyr* which would carry us across the country to San Francisco.

Expectation of our long days of rail travel ahead was stunted by our first train, Amtrak's *Septa*. It was a ride through New Jersey and Pennsylvania suburbs, reaching Philadelphia without our unpacking a damn thing. This was inter-urban commuter rail, the Trenton Line, with stops for long-haul workers, students, and people who seemingly get on the train for the thrill of a silent rush hour.

When we boarded the *Lake Shore Limited* Dad took the roomette beside Sean and me and within a few minutes our bags were stowed. Sean and I cracked Red Bulls and toasted our third train journey. When the train started moving through the hollow network of tunnels, Dad squeezed into our room. We dug out three more Red Bulls.

"New York City leaves us… What will tomorrow bring?" Dad said poetically, rubbing his chin's two-day-old stubble.

"Chicago," I said. "The lady clearly said this train goes–"

"The thought was lost on you, eldest son; 'tomorrow' means the idea of the journey's future."

"How many Red Bulls have you had, Dad? Is gobbledygook a side-effect?"

Dad replied, "See you tomorrow! However you want to interpret that."

Sean was reading Harry Potter. I was catching up on quantum physics and the search for the God Particle. As I delved into the subject, I knew that mixing Red Bulls with quantum theory footnotes was not going to work. I would either solve the God Particle or fry the part of my brain that dictates personality, humility, and use of long words.

One of the best things about train travel is that it can be uneventful. We lulled in the smooth passing of place and time, sleeping at will, wandering through coaches, poaching a meal together or on one's own. Trains in America lumber along, never sleekly skimming the countryside, but instead offering a gentler view of coming vistas and the slow fading of what has just been seen.

Except for one personal hardship: The *Lake Shore Limited* is 959 no-smoking-allowed miles (those miles took 18 hours). There was a brief stop in Ohio. I had been the squeaky wheel in cabin 42A and needed grease. I left. After inhaling two cigarettes outside the station in downtown Cleveland, I fled back to my train. There would be no more stops until we reached Chicago.

We awoke about an hour out from Chicago's Union Station. Trees and power lines masked the city's skyline, especially the signature Sears Tower and John Hancock Building. An entourage of smaller buildings rose out of the flat prairie as we passed through the southern suburbs. Our tracks joined others. A crowded commuter train nudged gently across from us, mirroring our speed. I sat on my bed looking at a smattering of employees and bosses, shopkeepers and students, on their way to their daily routines. Their faces showed no enjoyment. The few who were reading paperbacks probably didn't have the personal space to read; those on cell phones were likely disrupting other passengers. And, certainly, some among them were counting down the days or weeks until their holidays, to board a train like ours instead of one that commuted them to work. Only one thing was for sure: whatever they ritually did on weekday mornings was about to begin.

After stowing our luggage at the Union Station courtesy of a man who looked like he'd seen the inside of a prison cell for stealing stuff from luggage, Dad led us out into Chicago. The train that would take us across the rest of America left in eight hours, so time was precious. Chicago had to be visited.

The smell of fresh Lake Michigan air curled through thick traffic. The crowd of pedestrians seemed headed to the places I wanted to visit, so I followed, Dad and Sean in tow, south to visit North America's tallest office building. The imposing, black Sears Tower dominates the Midwest. Weighing in at 110 floors, you can see about 50 miles and four states (Illinois, Indiana, Michigan, and Wisconsin) from the top on a clear day. In terms of office space, the Sears Tower is the nation's second-largest structure after the Pentagon. We decided against visiting the top floor to verify these facts as stated in the building's brochure, so I walked over to a corner and gave it a big hug.

"Looks good on you, son," Dad said. "I'm sure you feel better now than if you'd taken a piece out of it."

"Sir," a security guard said from thirty feet, "no hugging the building please."

Sean smiled. "Brent, I don't know anyone else who knows the Miranda rights in three languages. I think karma has your address and waits outside for you every day."

Me: "I live my life in italics."

Sean: "Why was I born into a family of writers?"

Me: "It could be a family of mimes."

"It'd be quieter," said Sean.

Dad, who was trying to lead us away from the security guard while taking part in the conversation, said, "You don't think fate hasn't tazered you every few months?"

"I live in the present. Fate is therefore in the future. My life is just a few scrapes."

"Don't bullshit a bullshitter," Dad said.

"Why?"

"Because you just… don't."

"Tell me something me and my weather mast don't know," I replied.

"Pickles are cucumbers," Sean smirked.

He raised his hand to signal it was his turn to make a pronouncement. We stopped walking. "I think," Sean intoned, "I've determined an important cornerstone in our travels. Follow me on this but look at how we are talking. Brent hugs a building and that turns into Family War MCMLXIX, just like MCMLXIV. Look at the tiny components of our frequent train mornings. If we arrive in a city early and walk for two hours before having a coffee… someone gets ambushed. We attack the weak."

"Darwin in action," I stated, unaware I'd been ranked lowest of the three of us on evolution's survival odds.

Our meanderings took us through silent streets and busy thoroughfares where only Dad, Sean, and the L train running overhead made any disagreeable noises. The sun had yet to make much of its mark on the roads and sidewalks. In the busier business areas, Chicago's heart beats with suits and cell phones, a flotilla of taxis, and the occasional raising of the trunnion–or Bascule-style bridges–over the Chicago River.

Dad took us to Navy Pier on the open face of Lake Michigan. Built in 1916 for freighters and steamers to dock downtown, the pier juts into the wild winds that earned Chicago its nickname as the *Windy City*. After becoming a military property, it was decommissioned from such use to become public property. After a few ideas that didn't warrant being flaunted, Navy Pier became a civic area featuring theatres, convention space, rides, a huge Ferris wheel, and ice cream stands. On this day the skies were fair and only the incessant and driving wind troubled our stroll across the boardwalk. So when Dad approached a local eatery, the sign on the door advised patrons to open the door carefully due to high winds. But Dad opened it wide, brandishing a "Look at what I think of your sign!" grin–and the wind had its way with the contents of the interior. Napkins and flimsy menus tore from tables, racing around the restaurant like pixies on crack.

Breakfast was good, with an incredible view and a potion of coffee that did wonderful things to my nerve endings.

We eventually walked seven miles of the Lake Michigan shoreline. The last time I walked that far, a cab driver had kicked me out for misbehavior. We walked by and then long away from the John Hancock Center until it looked like a matchstick at arm's length. I had to admit long walks were refreshing–when caffeine was our fourth musketeer.

Time soon became an issue. But, as usual, none of us was wearing a watch and cellphones were not yet their replacement. Trains run on schedules, with some countries actually quite proud of their precision. America is less fussy about railway punctuality. Still, we thought we should return to Union Station. Sean and I could always blame lateness on Dad and his never-ending optimism of arriving on time but missing a train would be disappointing.

En route to the station, we detoured to see the 136 fragments, rocks and bricks embedded in the exterior lower levels of the Tribune Tower, home to the *Chicago*

Tribune newspaper. Artifacts from all over the world had been sought, brought back, and interred in the walls. Some were from the Taj Mahal, the Parthenon, the Great Pyramid, Notre-Dame, and Great Wall of China. The latest addition was a twisted piece of metal from the recently fallen Twin Towers. I reminded Dad of his concern that if everyone took a piece of places as a souvenir, there'd be nothing left. Dad looked at me and replied, "You just don't get it, do you?"

"Yeah, I think I do," I said.

Dad looked at me and replied, "You really just don't get it, do you?"

"If you aren't being rhetorical… yeah, I think I do."

Our train–the *California Zephyr*–was far different from what I had imagined. It was tall for a train–and this meant stairs. Two floors. Heavy luggage and a full bladder were not on the agenda at the *Zephyr's* design meetings. A steepish set of stairs brought us to our sleeping berths on the upper level. Everything was chrome and shiny and functional. The corridor went straight down the middle, dividing double quarters from single bedrooms. A conductress escorted me to my room, which was also Sean's. He grumbled when he saw me. He had caught a bag strap while ascending from the 'tall' to the 'venti' area.

"I had to cut my good business bag free when it got caught on the stairs," Sean said grumpily.

"You are now one of the free. Your bonds of business travel have been burned, and you are now a phoenix…."

"I call this bed-thing and that chair-thing, and I call that space for my stuff," he said, pointing out the best propositions.

"Oh, and what's left for me, Sean?"

"That bed-thing on top of my bed-thing. It's yours."

"That isn't a bed; it's a chair stuck up on the wall."

"Call it your 'quarters'."

The train slowly started moving; tracks sliced across tracks, red and blue signs swiveled, and switchers threw partial trains into spurs. Worried about the train's double decker height, I closed one eye in worry for any tunnels along the way. But we were to enjoy flatlands in the coming hours.

We had a split-level bed while immediately across the corridor Dad was on the opposing side, melding into what would be his room for a few days. He was determined that he could figure how to convert it from a dayroom to a night room. Without glancing at the do-it-yourself placard, he pressed and pulled, and soon the half-chair, half-bed creature chewed at his leg.

This train tackled the rail version of Route 66, which deserves a mention. It would cross Illinois, Nebraska, Kansas, Colorado, Nevada, and settle into California. The bucolic visuals of patriotic towns flying American flags gave way to stretches through forests and across fields. To repeat: I love America.

I stared at Sean. "Are you reading?"

"Yes. Carry on. I can multi-task."

"But this is what's called a conversation," I explained. "It needs two people."

"I've never met anyone who disagrees with himself more than you do. You'll see... keep talking. You don't need me."

"Be warned: If this is a non-smoking train, I'm getting off in Omaha. The trip is 51 hours and 20 minutes. It's a 2,422-mile run."

The railcar next to ours was, for lack of better words, the TV car. If you're crossing the country to experience what the brochure claims as "One of the Most Beautiful Train Trips," then you should be able to do without *Survivor* or *Friends* reruns for a few days, I thought. There were rows of overweight Americans watching TV screens under a Dome Car that let America slide by.

At the end of the hall a rancid odor made my eyes water and breathing difficult. I had found the smoking section. Grabbing the railing and climbing down the steep stairs, I saw a glass enclosure and, within it, 16 hard wall-mounted plastic seats and two overflowing ashtrays. Five people clustered together, talking in a haze before returning to their lives upstairs. Three people welcomed me upon my entrance–this was more social than my roomette. We intuitively knew each other, even if there was only one common thread: the slow and pointless suicide of smoking.

Smokers came and left. They were every age, weight, race, class, and creed. The room was a hub where a black man with *Death To Whitie* knuckle tattoos mingled with a woman of refinement whose bling should otherwise be securely stored in a safety deposit box. Another black man expertly gripped a cigarette with his bottom lip while reading *Anna Karenina*. Two women on drugs, evidenced by the way they frantically tried to out-talk one another about organic lettuce, needed long showers and not just to rid them of tobacco smells.

I listened to the conversations as Chicago receded. In time, I would be asked what I thought about abortion, if I could spare a cigarette, what class my carriage was, where I stood on the "Operation To Start An Endless War" in Afghanistan. Identities were suspended. On a train you could pretend you were someone else, your storyline could be retold, and your past could be what it wasn't. You could adopt a new personality, play into character, be your hero, or compromise everything you believed in–for the show.

Smoking is the key that gets you in the door, to make friends of people who you would, under normal circumstances, never have the occasion to meet. And here, your lies–your convincing stories of your life–compete with the lies of others.

Tony-Z was a black man who thought everything wrong in the world was the fault of white people and the Chinese. He embraced the Quakers, Jews, sweatshop workers, and visible-minority single mothers because, as he put it, "Every underdog needs a little Tony-Z".

Vicki said she was headed home to bury her father. After putting MIT on hold for a year to deal with the family's fallout, both emotional and financial, she was rushing to Wisconsin to salve the wounds. She was making this up as she went along, illustrated by missteps such as alternating "dad" with "mom," maybe because she'd never see any of us again. She was soliciting pity. I gave her some because she was kind of cute and had a Boston accent, but I knew she was on the wrong train for someone going to Wisconsin. The next day her story was that she was a model in New York and was going to the agency's headquarters in Los Angeles. She "couldn't reveal everything as it was pretty top secret," but let slip that she was a famous actress's body double. She was on the wrong train if she was going to LA.

Smoking on the train was reliably social. The peculiar fact that people are setting fire to dried plants and inhaling them into their lungs does not make a good defense of the activity, but it makes for new friends. Fellow smokers take you as you arrive, knowing you share a habitual, ritualistic addiction that calms, soothes, and, in the later stages, brings about dyspnea and that brass ring of inhaling carcinogens, –the Big C or Big E or even the Big L. Even the non-thinking smoker knows that if death doesn't get you first, chemo and radiation could interfere with the plans you have for your future. But you can't dismiss the Francis factor.

Francis was runway-model material. I saw her twice the first full day on the train, and she was always dressed in something that was fitting, pressed, clean and magazine-level stylish. She wasn't shy and that made me shy. Then I said hello. After a few minutes of introductions, I slipped self-consciously upstairs and into a battering ram of insults from my family, among them:

"You missed dinner," Sean said.

"Shit. I guess I get Melba toast...."

"Dinner is included in the price." Dad peered over his bifocals at me.

"You know, guys... Dad, Sean, it's your cynicism that reminds me we are back travelling together again. I don't get this anywhere else in the world. If I went to a sarcasm workshop, I don't think I'd feel humiliated anything close to–is anyone listening? This is *my* monologue."

"I think Dad's listening," Sean said.

Not much later the rumbling talk and rumbling train found us in our rooms. I picked up my book on quantum physics and climbed into my berth above Sean. I told him about Francis, the angel of the train, and what she looked like, how she smelled, how she spoke, how she smoked. I contemplated that arduous traverse across those carriages with Francis as my destination. Maybe it was best to wait until I could change into my finest clothes, the ones I'd worn the day before. They made a better me.

Iowa was overlooked in the night, and we seemingly went straight from Illinois into Nebraska. Omaha was brightly lit for our arrival at 2 a.m. or 3 a.m. or 4 a.m., depending on when you last noticed a new time zone. The grilled stairs of each car lowered and the few of us who weren't departing the train stood around cursing the wind chill. The others–those citizens of the Heartland who turned their acreages into bread, Honey-Nut Cheerios, and biofuels–left the station in the Ford F350 pickups that had come to greet them. We were ushered back onto the train, the grilled stairs pulled up and secured, and an "All Aboard!" hollered into a walkie-talkie by a woman dressed head to toe in engineer garb. I thought of Francis. The night sky returned and the stars came out from behind their curtains of darkness. Our train coursed through the plains of Nebraska.

The long train windows allowed the sharp sun to UV at least two wrinkles onto my face. Sean had folded his bed into the wall and was sitting up reading, halfway into his 700-page book. Blond wheat fields sped by, combed in fresh air. The distant dunes of soil were covered in cereals. We were now in Colorado–a split state with the best of both worlds: a prairie occupying its eastern half and the untamable Rocky Mountains dominating the western half. Every now and then, the top of a John Deere combine could be seen threading farmland. This was the land of wind-mills, homesteads, bull horns, Friday night football games, fences that ran to the horizon, cowboys and their cattle, front porch swings, dilapidated stagecoaches, defaced water towers, paint-stripped silos, and pieces of rusty farm machinery parked eternally beside leaning barns. Elsewhere, workers were building fences and driving their pickups with gun racks down a road, leaving trails of dust to hang in the still sky.

The train's public address system ordered passengers of each coach to the dining coach in sequence to minimize traffic.

The fourth chair at our table was not yet taken and I had hoped Francis would be on our carriage, would spot me and settle in beside me wearing amazingly elegant dress, a lazy top hat, and too much lipstick. Dad and Sean would go silent and poke at their breakfast meatloaf and grits. A guy can dream.

Russell came instead. A rather large man sporting a sweatshirt blessed with an oversized Jehovah's Witness crest, Russell sat himself down in our fourth chair. He was advertising the fact that he would bother us. Our meal arrived. Food, we thought, would save us from his encroaching enlightenment.

We were wrong.

"God has a plan for you," he said. It was as if he'd dropped a porn collection on the table. You don't just brush these things off.

"Well, let's hope it involves us arriving in San Francisco," Sean replied. "I don't want to die in the lonely half of Colorado."

"I mean a bigger plan," Russell said, undeterred. "God has a bigger plan for all of us."

I couldn't stop myself from blurting. "Why are there no exclamation marks in the Bible? I mean, if there's one book that could use them effectively, it'd be the Bible."

Russell looked as if another door had slammed in his face.

"Russell," I added, "I don't want to challenge you on the different blueprints that our lives will follow, but if God has a plan then what of the freewill He gave us?"

Russell itched his nose without using his fingers. He was in combat. His mind rifled in search of Bible passages that addressed this acute situation.

"For he that hath made a covenant unto the Lord Almigh–"

"Russell, scripture won't justify me, you, Sean or… Okay, my Dad is gone." (He'd up and left.) "I won't be pigeonholed by a fossilized quote. And if there is a God–and I know intuitively that there is a spiritual component to life–my God would beat up your God. I don't have the time to joust with a fundamentalist."

"I'm not a–"

"Yes, you are. A harmless one, but you are…" I said, trailing off. Train travels bring out truths, and my train trip had something else going on. Truth is, I'd had the sensation of depression in Chicago, something recurring and unwelcome in my life. Depressive cycles don't announce their arrival nor duration. But they are highly introspective and quizzical–a 10cc shot of spirituality could be useful when your questions have no answers. But Russell wasn't the 'religion-on-tap' for that job. The only good thing about depression is that when you realize you are depressed, you're already about halfway through it. I knew at an early age that I would be studying psychology from a couch.

Russell left the table and swayed away with the train's rocking. Being insulted wasn't in his vocabulary. But he knew the sound of a door that was going to stay shut.

"So what about the trip?" Sean asked me as the waiter topped up our coffee.

"You first."

"It's great. Funny we'd feel that crossing the country and anchoring a few free days at either end would seem short. In fact, this train is too fast already. Life is so much yarn, so little time to knit."

"Yeah, I guess. The roomette's layout is goofy and there's too much technology–buttons for everything! It's like a hospital room."

"Well, okay. On that note, I'm going to shower. It's great being on another trip with you, dude. Who knew we'd ever make the third Antonson voyage."

I skipped the shower and headed to the smoking car. Francis was there. Tony-Z was convincing an older white man that black people had invented the television and the white man's patent would run out in 2021. After that, it would be B-TV on every channel. The white man put out his cigarette and left, never returned.

Francis wore a conservative skirt cut at a playfully liberal length. We talked.

"What is a girl like you–beautiful, intelligent and possibly with innocence intact–doing on a train when she should be on the red-eye to California instead? I mean why would you pay to take the train and add four days to your trip?"

She smiled a smile within a smile. "The romance of travelling by train is overlooked by the business class in order to aspire to be something we are not. The world dictates time is money. We should cut corners that give us the edge and step on fingers climbing to the top. We become someone who doesn't look back at us from the mirror."

"I have to ask you if this 'romance' of train travel is your determination, your time to slow the clocks and enjoy the scenery, even Nebraska."

"It is. Romance isn't the rule. Sometimes trips are lonely or terrible, but...."

"But?"

"There are always fresh new friends you can borrow for a while." She smiled that smile within a smile again. I wept inside. Barely knowing anything about her, I had fallen in love.

When you meet someone on a train, there's an unspoken agreement: who you really are is the person who stood on the platform waiting to get on the train; once you step off, that's who you'll resume being. In between... I could've been anyone, and she could've been anyone. All we had in common were our endless packs of cigarettes and topics like killer bees at the border, crazy relatives, illicit drugs, and ghosts versus UFOs.

"I fall in love easily," she said. "Imagine the world before déjà-vu was part of the language."

"The world is held together by prayers, PIN numbers, passwords, and promises."

"You're a sweet guy."

"You're at the end of my rainbow."

"That's a sweet-guy thing to say."

When Francis was gone, she'd be gone. Train romance is the sweetest of relationships–there isn't enough time to lose face. The relationship was terminal.

With morning came too many photons for my eyelids to stay closed. I bounced into Dad and Sean's space, both reading in Dad's single room. Breakfast had given me the civil liberty of happiness and the pursuit of more of it. The coffee had been good and strong.

I showered the kind of public-use shower where although the door is locked, a dozen people will pull violently on the handle. And when you have been irritated enough and gotten dressed semi-wet with soapy residues, heavy in parts, you emerge to find no one waiting.

Dad and Sean had a caffeine reading of .08. They played chess using their knees to hold a board whose natural position was to be folded. I was headed downstairs in my finest clothes.

Francis wasn't there. Tony-Z still hadn't left.

"Mister Canada," he said by way of welcome. "My friend the draft-dodger… lend me a smoke, will ya? I'm getting a bunch at the next stop."

I obliged.

"Thanks," he said, rolling it between his fingers. "You hookin' up with that Francis Jell-O flavor of dee-light? Man, she is a spotlight. I don't know why her boy lets 'er outta his sight. Man, a brother would let his eyes bleed to protect that sapphire…. And that's what she be, no mistake about it man. She is a sapphire.'

"She has a boyfriend?" My heart dropped like an anchor in Heartbreak Cove at low tide.

"Fo' sure. She was carryin'on at that Shelley-Jane yesterday… Says he's at a bank, numbers… He's a numbers man. Adds 'em up and shit."

'Is he on the train?'

"Do I look like a fucking search engine? I just heard 'em talking. Ain't my business. Not that my business is skyrockets and fireworks. This is the driest train since Baton Rouge."

"Business… what kind of business?"

"Ha, the white brother wants to know what kind of business…. Ha!"

"Well, businesses tend to grow when the clientele know what the business is."

"Yeah, well the business is… let's put it this way—", Tony-Z started to say, before being shut down. Three stewards, one of whom was a sheriff, stood in a routine V takedown formation behind the glass doors. One pointed at Tony-Z and motioned with the same finger for him to approach. Tony-Z was a big man, heavy, and could have made a few minutes of loud, profane and difficult-to-handcuff memories. He could have trashed the white man, could have said the patent on handcuffs goes back to the black man in 1716 or he could have screamed that his business was going to cost him a few years in the red, a regional correction center type of red. Tony-Z, I later learned from a source who couldn't be trusted, was selling cocaine, crack and all manner of multi-colored pills. The only question I have is, why wasn't I propositioned? Hell, that could have made Nebraska palatable.

"Because you look so sweet and innocent," Francis said later when I asked her the same question. I don't think so. I look neither. I wanted to feign innocence in response but it takes time just to get to when I was innocent.

Even meek Jules had been asked (and had quietly declined). No one had cracked Jules. But I only concerned myself with Francis, who was back and wearing a semi-see-through dress and a charming straw hat. Her gold-plated hair was held back by her ears. The sparse bangs that escaped the brow of the hat looked like prison bars, holding back her felonious blue eyes. How is it that a wonderful relationship can start and end happily in a few days, while a relationship with the longevity of a fruitcake can turn into a lengthy battle between devils?

Colorado's peaks were coming into view, stretching across either side of the coach and bringing geographic challenges for the train closer. The days of travelling from Chicago had been smooth, with few dips or hills of consequence. But the Rocky Mountains were a horror of engineering, surveying, designing, and building. And with the Rockies came windows full of stunning scenery, steep ascents and switchbacks that let us look back and see our own train's tail. It also meant the end of the wheat fields, the coma of the Heartland. I had to battle this beauty of the Rockies, as well as Francis's interests and my own curiosities about us. I also had to douse the 'sweet and innocent' designation, especially since I was still at the 'peck on the cheek' level. As I sat, my arm around her neck, I decided to advance the situation. I like to set my heights high and back down a rung or two when appropriate.

"Well, Francis, we have a finite time on Earth. And our time on this train is unbearably finite. Is there a way we could make a **bolder statement** that we'd met?"

"Ahh…," she said, with her tongue poised in such a way it could be considered erotic–or exhausted. I figured either was good. As Denver loomed and the Rocky Mountains developed in sharp detail, Francis leaned in and gave me a peck on the cheek.

Denver was a busy station. We lost people there but picked up new ones. Tony-Z was led away in plastic cuffs (developed by a white man; patent number 3,408,699) but carried on, mixing-up important speeches by the reverends Martin Luther King Jr. and Al Sharpton. Changes in the crews–food staff, brake checkers, engine checkers, sanitation, water–ensured that the train was ready to roll into Rollins Pass.

Rollins Pass was a complicated path to traverse the Rocky Mountains. When it was being routed, substantial snowfalls, court judgements, and financing difficulties interfered with the plans many times, trampling railroad pioneer David Moffat's dream in the process. Upon his death, however, the project gained financing and court approval and came to bear his name for part. The Moffat Tunnel cut through 6.2 miles of snow-covered mountain and straddled the Great Divide at an elevation of about 9,000 feet.

On leaving the outskirts of Denver, our *California Zephyr* climbed the Rockies' east face, often clinging to the edges of canyons and switching back. The track ascended, sometimes leveling off, only to turn on itself and climb the steep incline. Dabs of snow in coves that never saw sunlight gave way to the spring runoff before we reached higher elevations. Soon the snowpack was permanent, giving notice that no matter how much sun and global warming you threw at it, the snow was here to stay. Large curling waves of thick snow were frozen and grafted by mountain gales, conveying that this inhospitable place was not meant for humans; only the insane would venture into such a sub-zero inferno.

Passing through the Moffat Tunnel took fifteen minutes. As we triumphantly exited on its west side, the large and busy ski resort hugging the mountain struck me as beautiful. Winter Park, an actual town, had built itself into the landscape. Imminent danger had turned into profit.

As the train climbed, Dad, Sean, and I hollered across the hallway at each other, saying so-and-so had just missed seeing a frolicking doe or a gorge had just swallowed a tree or that a crystal-clear waterfall had icicles in it. After days of little variation of geography to comment on, we had a few hours of abrupt scenery, sheer granite rock faces, potential avalanches, and excitingly narrow trusses. It was the kind of terrain that probably got a thumbs-down from the first pioneers but it was the most breathtaking stretch of our trip across America.

iiiiiiiiiiiiii

The train's smoking room was empty except for Jules. We hadn't spoken to one another in the four days since he'd boarded the train. His straight black hair was parted in the middle. It wasn't a style; rather, it was the least he could get away with and still appear in public. He looked nervous. Jules was thin and wore the same white knitted sweater and windbreaker every day on the train. When his wire glasses slid down his nose, he'd use two nervous fingers to push them back up. A strange pause hovered in the little room, a pause as thick as the smoke. Jules maintained his silence; it was clear something unpleasant was circling around and around in his head. He looked like he needed someone to talk to. And I just might be the wrong person.

"You're Jules, right?" I asked.

"Yep."

"Did you start out in Chicago with us?"

"Yep." He played with the zipper on his windbreaker, an irritating noise.

"Going home? Leaving home?"

"Going home," he said. This social injection wasn't going well.

"San Francisco?"

Jules inhaled sharply. I think in the animal kingdom that means, "Leave me alone." If we'd dropped the interaction at that, I'd never remember him and he'd never remember me. And a lot of train travel is meeting people you otherwise wouldn't.

"My parents live in Provo. I'll be getting off in Salt Lake," he said, ensuring the conversation would continue.

"Ah, Utah, the other side of these mountains."

"Yep."

"So this is your last day on the train. I bet you're looking forward to seeing your hometown and your parents," I said with a crowbar ending.

"Not really... not really," he said.

"Is it one of those... kind of... don't-want-to-go-home situations? I get them all the time. I would always rather be where I made it to than go back to where I started." I reworked that in my mind: it made sense if it wasn't used as advice.

"I'm really not comfortable going back. It isn't Provo..."

"Is this a Mormon thing? Because if it is, I'm not qualified to say anything because I don't know much, but that won't stop me from pretending I do. Is the Tabernacle Choir still on Utah's Top 40?"

Jules laughed, the first time he'd changed facial expressions in four states. "No, not everyone in Utah is Mormon. We're the most secular family in our secular suburbs."

"That's pretty 21st Century," I smiled. "You just don't want to be there."

"I'm...I have to...I don't think this is something I want to discuss with a stranger. No offence. I'm just not sure I even know what I'm in for."

"First, Jules, I am not a stranger. That guy with the eye patch, handlebar moustache, and the tattooed knuckles who left in Omaha? He was a stranger. I'm Canadian, and in my life I've met fewer than 10 Canadian strangers. All of them were in Toronto. And secondly, you've been tormenting yourself by sitting in that uncomfortable plastic seat for days shifting your eyes around like you just made the Most Wanted list."

"Yep. I'm just chronically nervous when..." He stopped. "OK. I'll tell you something. But you can't tell anyone else."

"You know the code–what happens on the lower deck in the smoking section on an Amtrak train stays on the lower deck on an Amtrak train."

He thought that through and then said, almost with hesitant freedom, "I'm gay."

"OK."

"I'm gay," he said again with an accented semi-smile.

"OK. Is that it?"

"That's it. I'm gay."

"Is that all? Tony-Z thought you were going to blow up an airport. Chantal thought you were getting married to your sister. All this time and you're just gay?"

"I expected a different response," he said. We both lit our cigarettes.

"I think the 'I'm Gay Threat Level' is at yellow now. Has been for years."

"I'm going home to tell my parents. They still think the threat level is red."

"It's a new world. Maybe Provo isn't in it yet, but closets are opening all over the place."

"Are you gay?" he asked with intensity in his eyes.

"No. But if I were gay, my family wouldn't bat an eye. The peak of the topic would be over before dessert. I'd likely have to remind them occasionally that I was gay."

"I'm not sure my parents will feel the same way."

"It's not like you're telling them that you're going to be a career poet. They'll come around. Send them websites. Do you know how many Americans died in Afghanistan today?"

"No."

"I don't either. It's been days since I saw a newspaper. But my point is, I'm sure your parents would rather hear that you're gay than find out you died in a roadside bomb attack outside Kabul."

"Hmm… my confidence is…" he said in a staggered voice. "I've wasted years worrying about this day. Wasted them."

Francis came down the stairs as Jules looked at me and smirked. Jules got up to leave as Francis came in.

"Hi," she said.

"I'm gay," he said with a proud smile, practicing, and ran up the stairs of his "freedom" train.

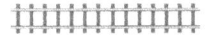

Our stop at Grand Junction gave us an hour to get off the train, wander, and get our land legs back. Francis and I got off three cars ahead of Dad and Sean. The temperature hit 100 degrees, the snow had melted, and birds roared overhead. Touristy stands and shops overran the station, selling all sorts of knick-knacks, T-shirts, and toys with "Grand Junction" etched into them. Francis and I walked to the lonely end of the platform. She didn't have a boyfriend; Tony-Z had it wrong, misinterpreting Francis's story about withdrawing funds at a bank to pay for her train ticket.

We boarded the train and headed to the back. Francis had a look in her eyes that I mistook for sex. She smiled when she talked, and the hugs and arm-around-the-shoulder initiatives were hers. I really knew nothing about her, and understood less. If I had to describe her life, I couldn't with any certainty. Train relationships are often half-truths and if she had told the full truth these last few days, surely she had squared circles, crossed a few i's and dotted a few t's. Who she really was and who she wanted me to think she was might have been completely opposite. And she might have detected that not all my bolts are screwed in tight. But those are things to build upon. Other people came into the smoking room but neither Francis nor I looked their way. The sun was setting along a dark ridge of the Rockies. I told Francis I had to make a dinner appearance, otherwise Dad and Sean would assume I'd been left behind in Grand Junction and start splitting my assets. I got up and left the smoky room, turning to smile at Francis before climbing the stairs. She did her tiny wave that said "I'll be here," like she always did. It was the last time I saw her.

When I awoke to the rattle of train noises the next morning, Sean had finished the last Harry Potter book–which means I could no longer hold the ending over his head by threatening to blurt it out. Dad had finished *To Kill a Mockingbird* and my reading on quantum physics was somewhere between pages xii and xiv. The landscape before us had changed dramatically. We'd come down the western side of the Rockies and stopped at Salt Lake City before continuing through the barren salt flats. Jules had left. The train trip had given him the courage to identify himself, a gift train travels often give to the insecure, the wonderers, and the wounded. That morning I was among the wounded. I wrestled with how–and where–Francis had left. Now that I was estranged from her, the smoking room was empty of people I wanted to know. I was the elder and I didn't have the energy to invest in the recent arrivals. I did what I did best: smoked and thought.

The last stretch of the journey was uncomfortable. Crossing the Nevada desert made me thankful trains don't break down like they used to. Being stuck in the desolate middle of nowhere in the pounding heat would be unbearable. Suddenly the train stopped in the desolate middle of nowhere in the pounding heat. Not a house, town or even road in sight. Everywhere I looked was a time-hardened, rattlesnake-infested nature where tumbleweeds rule and the wind is the law.

An announcement over the public distress system informed us that due to union regulations the engineers had hit their hourly limit and would not move the train another foot. A tumbleweed rolled by. The announcer gave the hundred passengers time to digest this news. Before I could yell, "Let's roll!" the announcer continued: "A crew from Reno is being driven here to replace the crew in the loco-motive. This shouldn't take more than a couple of hours."

"Let's roll," I called out in an effort to conscript other passengers. Another tumbleweed bounced by.

After a couple of hours, each one longer than the one before, a dusty haze appeared on the horizon. A Jeep was bouncing towards us in the desert. I was so dehydrated I couldn't even cry. Within 10 minutes, during which I hope someone landed a few good punches, the Jeep left and our train stammered up to speed.

I spent the last few hours with Dad and Sean, lamenting. For them, both of whom travel a lot for business, the train was a spa, a relaxing do-nothing, do-something, do-nothing-again trip. They hadn't missed me much. They'd talked endlessly and read, napped and gone to the bar car. But my train journey had been mine; the way I passed the time had been mine, and all of the people I made friends with–or even become infatuated with–had evaporated. They'd be near impossible to track down (except for Tony-Z, who was likely in custody and therefore accountable).

We rolled into Emeryville, California at dusk. As a trunk line for the *California Zephyr*, the Emeryville spur route is positioned as the train's arrival in San Fran-cisco, missing the emotional point by miles. Dad, Sean, and I took our luggage and backpacks down the platform, climbed onto an Amtrak bus and travelled into San Francisco proper pretending we were still on a train.

The following morning, we took breakfast in the wonderful surroundings of San Francisco's Palace Hotel, built in 1909. The marble columns, jade, and glass dome of the Garden Court restaurant granted the ambiance of a railway journey's desti-nation, which it represented to us. The court's ceiling reminded me of the Hotel Metropol's in Moscow, built a few years before the Palace, and in a similar "Style

Moderne" as the Russians would say, or Art Nouveau as my French teacher would call it. Having shared our travel yarns with attentive waiters, we strolled about the hotel lobby strategizing our trip's final day. We each had a flight home that evening, all leaving roughly an hour apart. That gave us the day. Dad opened a map of San Francisco, and touched a few spots, then slid his finger across the Golden Gate Bridge and snaked it down the road to Sausalito.

It was hot, the kind of hot that makes you want to be naked in a pool in the Arctic. We walked down Montgomery Street, leaving behind the financial district's forest of skyscrapers. Walking Columbus Street, which carries itself across the city diagonally, we cut away much of the clutter enroute to the Golden Gate.

I put up the first resistance: "They have transit for things like this. Hey! They have cable cars."

"OK, we'll take a cable car."

I felt like I'd sold myself out. If we took a cable car one block, I was committed to walking the rest of the way to Sausalito.

"It's going to go over 100 degrees today," Sean said. The city had been in a heat wave for the better part of a week. It was Los Angeles weather up in the part of California where the ocean usually cools down any serious heat before it becomes Hell. But there was no wind off the Pacific yet–the day was a blanket of stale heat.

We rode the cable car for a block, but it turned and we got off. The early hour meant our planned stops (Starbucks, Seattle's Best, Starbucks, Coit Tower, City Lights, Starbucks—I chose this way to underline how poor train coffee is.) still closed. This expedited our approach to the Golden Gate Bridge. I took a big hug from the Transamerica Building–a white pyramid that has punctuated the San Francisco skyline since 1972.

I could sense Sean or Dad about to say something sarcastic.

"Don't–it was my hug, leave it there."

It's been said the Golden Gate Bridge is more famous than San Francisco. You have to walk across the bridge to appreciate its scale. The workmanship and enormity of the project is powerful; and anyone with a heart will give the workers of long ago respect. The ocean wind felt warm and fierce, usurping the dead climate and spreading out into the bay where it became a whisper of cooling comfort. At the north end of the bridge Highway 101 shoots off into a lonely hillside tunnel. On the long walk after the exit to Sausalito, the heat played us, the shoulder of the road twisted our ankles, and passing cars left dust in our eyes. Our feet shuffled. Our conversation lost its strength.

"Can you use *America* as a verb?" I asked.

"A verb?" Dad asked. "As in, *to America*?"

"In the infinitive, yeah. Like, in 'I want *to America* that tree, or Maybe we should *America* that yacht."

"I don't know where you're going with this." Dad shook his head.

"To America."

"Yeah, I don't know."

"It means the action of all that America is," I said. "How else do words get invented? I'm sure I can do this."

"America me," Sean said.

Dad stopped. He was covered in sweat and took off his shirt, wrapping it around his head like a hot extremist. He looked over his sunglasses at the road we'd travelled.

"Do you guys know where we are?"

"No," I said.

"I think that fork in the road went to Sausalito and this one is the less travelled, and that has made all the difference," Sean said. "We'd be in Sausalito now if we'd taken the road with two lanes."

I nodded. "I think we've been America'd."

FOURTH JOURNEY ~ Beijing-Pyongyang-Beijing

INTO NORTH KOREA

W e had choices. We had travelled on three of the longest train travels in the world. We decided against Australia because it seemed too first-world and safe. So we had to find an epic destination for our fourth major train trip.

"*North* Korea?"

Dad was responding to Sean's suggestion for our next train trip. "North? DPRK? Are we even allowed to go there?"

Our Greek friend and Neighbours Restaurant owner George was adamant: "No. You can't get into North Korea. And even if you could go, don't. It is far too dangerous. You may not get back out again."

I pushed away from the table, my dinner finished, and thought long and hard about his warning. "But, if we could get in... and get out. It would be awesome."

"In?" asked Sean. "In," said Dad. "In," I said. George shook his head. "Those who go away... well, just come back safely."

George recognized we were maturing travellers and growing in our personal lives as well. In the three years since our last journey, we'd passed some pretty meaningful personal mileposts. Sean and Hilary married. He had found exactly the right person to be my sister-in-law. While I did choke on the inevitable life shifts that Hilary brought into the family dynamic—you-stole-my-best-friend syndrome. She was beautiful, enthusiastic, intelligent, and a proven hard-traveller. Dad's wife

Janice had accepted a vice-president role with a team building a new airport in the Bahamas, adding new enchantments as she and Dad committed to meeting up once a month somewhere in the world. After returning from teaching English in Voronezh, I began writing a book about the experiences, which was eventually published as *Of Russia; A Year Inside*. I hadn't given up on teaching but I did get dragged into a financial vortex that kept me at home, working jobs I'd never look back on and laugh. Though I was domesticated enough to have a storage locker, I was 180 pounds of pure wanderlust.

I read all I could find on North Korea, and the 833-mile (1,340-kilometer) train trip from Beijing to its capital city Pyongyang. As our North Korean adventure took shape, the risks became more real.

Sean and I planned a pre-trip from the bottom of China to the top of the country in order to get to the start of our fourth train journey with Dad. Before meeting Dad, we flew to Hong Kong and railed our way across China's eastern side up to the capital. Hilary and Sean had spent 11 recent months travelling Europe and then living a year in Scotland. She was family now and determined to come along for the Hong Kong to Beijing escapade. Dad met us in Beijing. Two days later Hilary left China, and Dad, Sean, and I headed into the least understood country on the planet.

Sean, Hilary, and I rendezvoused with Dad at Beijing's Sheraton Hotel, making the lobby loud with hugs and missed-trajectory knuckle bumps. Dad had arrived directly from a business trip in Bhutan. Other than having endured aviation gymnastics, looking haggard, acting dozy, and feeling as if he was perpetually moving at 550 miles per hour, Dad was pretty normal.

"So…" he said. "North Korea. This is a big one, guys. Few countries in the world have this status."

"Axis of Evil? Totalitarian dictatorship? Dead man as president?" Sean's questions were a list of reasons why he thought we wouldn't get in. "Everything I've read says it's nigh on impossible. And here we have a week booked into the most reclusive country in the world, the winner of Amnesty International's coveted 'Absolutely NO Human Rights' trophy. If we pull this off…"

"Our visas are about to be endorsed," I interjected. "They had their chance. We'll get in. Maybe not *each* of us, but most of us."

"Well, I'm clean,' Sean said. "I am so squeaky clean, I bet they shake my hand and say 'squeaky-clean' in Korean. If Brent gets in, it means North Korea doesn't have the password to get into Interpol's site."

"So many people..." Dad held the moment with a frozen gesticulation–"get turned away at the border even with visas. And without explanation. Do you know that fewer than three hundred Westerners get into North Korea every year?"

"That's my reason for feeling like I do," I explained.

Dad leaned in. "I'm excited. Even if we get turned around at the border, we'll have touched North Korean soil, sat in a bright room without sleep, and lost our luggage to the regime. Then we'll have a week back here in China."

"Well, our 'meeting' with the travel company is in..." I looked at my wrist for a watch I'd never worn; luckily there was a clock on the wall..."90 minutes. We should head over. Don't forget your passport. It's time to have each other's backs, cover, go dark, watch, lend money."

"You hinting you're out of money?" Sean asked.

"Not in the North Korean sense," I said.

If you are caught swimming in the river that divides China and North Korea, your body will be riddled with bullets fired from either side—or both. But a sacred North Korean visa–the aforementioned coveted rare one permitting entry of only 300 Westerners the previous year–would get us on a train over the river and into the country and, all being well a week later, get us back over the river and safely out.

Over the Internet, I'd tracked down two British men living in Beijing. They said they could help get us into North Korea, but there were no guarantees. In fact, there was little in the way of normal travel arrangement protocols to give us confidence. We decided to try anyway, trusting in their British-ness—and having inserted our traveller self-images into the risk equation. Ten weeks prior we'd sent them copies of our passports, a whole lot of personal detail, and a down payment on their fee. With this in hand, they later reported they'd obtained provisional clearance that North Korea intended to issue all three of us visas. They promised to meet up with us once we were in Beijing, take our passports to the North Korean embassy, and return them a day later with the necessary travel visa implanted.

We met them in a bar.

Over the years, these two young men had earned the respect of North Korea's anti-tourism bureau and helped hundreds of foreigners make their way into North Korea. As we sipped beers, they asked for our documents and confirmed their strategy. I felt a rush of bad judgment as I handed over my passport, but this meeting had the aura of how such business—however clandestine—was conducted. As they left us sitting there nursing our second beers and apprehensions, the taller one handed us their travel company's business card, and told us to meet them at their office the following day at noon.

To sit in a Chinese bar and give up my passport felt like a punch line I didn't want to hear. In exchange we'd been given sheets of paper covering the rules, expectations and mandatory conduct while we were in North Korea. None of it was negotiable. We were also told to refrain from using "North" as a designator; it indicated that one didn't respect or understand the nation's pride in being the true Korea. Alternatively, we could refer to it as "the DPRK," the Democratic People's Republic of Korea.

We were to visit a country dominated by famine yet one that bragged about its nuclear potential. It was hostile and aggressive, had the world's fourth-largest standing army and hated America far more than America hated it. "America" sat in South Korea looking north.

One of the travel company reps pointed to the pages of rules and said we needed to commit them to memory; a minor slip would have us shot back to Beijing… or worse. Upon our arrival in North Korea, we would have two government minders and a driver–any deviation from their wishes, any activity listed as forbidden, or any remarks about the country being fucked up would not only get us expelled from the DPRK but would also affect the government minders. If something went terribly wrong because of our actions, if we decided to venture off alone, to lose our minders, or try to push them into something that made them uncomfortable, they could lose their privileged positions as trusted state representatives allowed to interact with foreigners, and their lives would be torn apart. If we did something worse, our minders and their families might be sent to a labour or "re-education" camp. In other words, it would not just be we foreigners who would suffer.

We had 48 hours left to adjust our mindset before we departed on the twice a week Beijing-Pyongyang train that shunted diplomats, trade delegations, and trusted officials back and forth.

Beijing is encumbered by history, by a thousand generations of architectural legacies, and by its vast girth. It's embodied with far more history than aesthetic appeal. And the traffic is often the worst part of one's waking day. Speak all you want about the Chinese approach to life—serenity, Confucius, and green tea—if you put a steering wheel in a Chinese person's hands, the nation's life expectancy drops. Gridlock is from 5 a.m. to 11 p.m. The night's arrival was difficult to determine, as Beijing's lights fired up the Gobi dust storm as much as the Sun had. And Beijing is not a walking city; it's a taxi city.

Leaving the bar absent our passports, we ambled back to our hotel full of mixed expectations about the journey that lay ahead. I was rooming with Dad and after a few drinks in the lounge I left for our room, propped up my pillows and started to read the North Korean rules. They were sacred; saying or doing the wrong thing would end our trip. We had to remember that we were guests, and our minders would not welcome revelations about our life experiences, the way we lived, or political suggestions—nor would they be tolerated. Their limited exposure to the outside world, if any, would have been to border bound towns in China and not even to cosmopolitan Beijing. Their leader, Kim Jong Il, was their source of information about the world. They adored, loved and believed him. We must—despite our feelings that he should be drugged and abandoned on an ice floe off the coast of Greenland—respect the country and culture of the DPRK.

These were the rules:

1. No contact is to be made with DPRK citizens.

2. No contact is to be made with DPRK currency.

3. Any photography must first be approved by the minder. Images of any government installations, soldiers, poverty, or anything likely to cast the current regime in a negative light are forbidden.

4. Cell phones may NOT be brought into the DPRK.

5. Laptops may NOT be brought into the DPRK.

6. Travel anywhere outside of the hotel MUST be approved by, and accompanied by, the minder.

7. Leaving the hotel without permission is forbidden. The grounds may only be walked with a minder and without a camera.

8. The first stop inside the DPRK is a 20-meter bronze statue of Kim Il Sung; a bouquet of flowers should be bought and placed at the feet of the statue, and a bow of respect is essential in bonding with your minders. Should you feel uncomfortable in following this procedure or in feigning admiration and grief, the DPRK is not for you.

9. Do not criticize Kim Il Sung, Kim Jong Il, the government, its policies, food shortages, the lack of a McDonald's, or the shortage of ATMs; or query if they actually have a mandated dress code; or propose, even philosophically, that they could turn their country around with one bullet. North Koreans believe they live in the best country in the world and trying to convince them that they live in the worst of all possible worlds will not make your visit a happy one.

10. The DPRK is a socialist republic and, despite the D for Democratic, the republic is recognized as a family-owned Stalinist totalitarian dictatorship.

11. Do not bring these pages with you into the DPRK. Please leave them with your belongings in China. Again, please don't bring these with you.

I fell asleep at Point 11, my dreams filled with curiosity, statistics, and the fear that an entire family could take the rap for my actions. That I was the only one in my family to read these sacred pages would become apparent soon enough.

At the small travel office the following day, we were led upstairs to a restaurant. Also present was a group of 20 people who would be entering the DPRK at the same time as us. They were all British, made up of a group planning to see old steam locomotive trains still in use, as well as three couples and two individual travellers. Among them were three women. Through a calling out of our names, each passport was placed in the hands of its owner. And each recipient's face held a similar squint of disbelief. The indicator for North Korea's "visa" was a small sliced square of yellow paper with dates on it. It sat loose in the passport.

Our travel organizer (entry visas, transport coordination, lodging and such) did not hesitate to warn us: "Your hotel is on an island in the middle of the Taedong River. It has a nice walking area but do not attempt to leave the confines of the hotel without your government minder, do not attempt to cross the bridge to the mainland, and do not think you have an excuse that will work. No one misses a Frisbee by 200 yards."

Sean, Dad, and I were going on a 23-hour journey by train. The 20 other travellers in the room were flying to Pyongyang on a salvaged 1960s Soviet Tupolev jet. Both modes of travel felt equally exciting and dangerous.

Late the following day we were set to depart. The Beijing rail station feels to house 10 per cent of China's population at any one time. Some people are there to run around and bump into your backpack; others stream by while the rest of us are surrounded by far too many bags of fake Levis and DVDs. The nearest person who speaks English is in a Swedish office a mile away. While we figured out where the trains departed, we were still trying to work over the specifics of our particular train. The signs in fractured English were misleading: "Train exit this way", "Train exit that way", "Train exit a ways away." It was only with sign language help decoding our tickets and discovering the level of importance of various numbers thereon that we located our train, platform, and couchette.

A long, forest-green train affixed with Peking-Pyongyang (Korea still referred to Beijing as Peking) signs sat at platform four. The Chinese operated it. The carriage attendant thoroughly examined our documentation, checked our DPRK visas, and allowed us into his wagon. Excited by the start of another train trip, we parked our happiness when a fellow passenger stood at our roomette's doorway. He was Japanese, and in his later 30s. Together, we glanced at his ticket and then the room number, and finally calculated that he was our cabin's fourth occupant. This threw everything into disarray. I'd already lost rock-paper-scissors and had a top bunk; he owned my bottom bunk. Even though he looked friendly enough, my imagination hovered over a question: was he a spy? Would we have to self-edit our family conversations (which were normally as unrestricted as an X-rated movie, and politically cavalier) or risk being turned into the authorities at the border?

Imaginations can sometimes be just that: imaginings. In broken English, the intruder introduced himself as Yokada, a Japanese engineer headed to Pyongyang and then moving on to another area to oversee a construction project. It was not his first trip to the country. He didn't elaborate. He was more interested in us, and our visit–which did seem of more interest to all four of us. Sharing our room with

Yokada provided a contradiction. First of all, he was from a nation hated by Korea after its 1910 invasion and subsequent 25-year occupation of the peninsula. And he was full of information on the DPRK: we had our own anti-propaganda machine on the lower bunk. Yokada would struggle for English words, then drop to a whisper and regale us with how bad things really were "inside". He warned us to expect little or no Western comforts.

The train lurched, and the couplers clasped as the four of us peered out the windows in the hallway. Beijing's gargantuous station and the miles of track crossings and rolling stock dragged past my window for a half hour. Then heavy industry sided the tracks, belching unfettered pollution and carbon dust into the Gobi-dust-soaked air. *Screw the Kyoto Accord*, screamed the chimneys.

We talked away and looked for hidden microphones in the wall. I had secured my smoking area at the rear vestibule and frequented it often. Dad and Yokada headed to the restaurant car for something to eat but found most offerings inedible. Instead they enjoyed Soju, Korea's contribution to alcoholism. Yokada returned without Dad. Yokada knew he'd had enough. Dad, always a moderate drinker with an asterisk, cashed in that asterisk and further enjoyed the Soju. When he returned, he was loud and happy. He broke into song three times and took his shirt off.

Dad has dealt with me under similar circumstances and I felt obligated to help Sean minimize the attention the tallest person on the train was drawing to himself. The train was full and people passed our doorway constantly as they headed to the restaurant car. Dad hugged one of them, a small woman who looked like she was next up on the list of oldest surviving humans. Soju had made this woman a super-model in Dad's eyes and he asked for (and got) her phone number. With persuasive lies about her husband coming to beat him up, Dad was encouraged to lie down in silence, given a book to read, and then shushed again after trying to finish his song. He looked at Sean and me like a cow that had a secret. Then he slept.

The windows in the hallway wouldn't open without a key from the carriage attendant. This triangle-shaped device was the ultimate rail tool or souvenir; it unlocked everything on all sorts of Chinese trains across Asia and Europe. I went to the carriage attendant's room, where he was playing cards with a younger man. When he saw me and I saw his open bottle of 12 per cent beer, our friendship was immediate. I made signs and gestures indicating that the windows were locked and it was 40°C inside the rooms, slowly wiping my brow for effect. Ming, the attendant, was not about to get up but understood that the heat had gotten to an uncomfortable point. He leaned over to one side, searched his pockets, produced the triangle key, and handed it to me. A chill ran down the length of my spine. I could now disassemble the entire rail car in two hours.

I ran back, showed the key to Dad and Sean, and then unlocked every window in the hallway. I went to the vestibule and unlocked a panel that had a gauge in it, then opened the side door, leaned out, and hollered long vowels. I was standing at the edge of an international incident. I locked the door and returned to Ming. He didn't really want the key back but instead thought it funny to give me his hat and armband. His jacket was too small for me but I did manage to look like I worked for the Chinese railway system. I locked bathrooms, asked for tickets, and told people I was kidding. Ming seemed to think I was such a neat Caucasian that he called his daughter on his cell phone and tried to get us acquainted. She spoke English and we traded e-mails, beginning a friendship that, as unlikely as it sounds, would last for years.

▯▮▯▮▯▮▯▮▯▮▯▮▯▮

We stirred as Ming opened our doors to announce we were now entering Dandong. We didn't know it yet, but this metropolis was our last chance to buy almost anything we'd come to take for granted in our daily lives–Pepsi, chocolates, candy, beef jerky, lighters, bread, cheese, and bottled water. But who needs a last chance, we thought, when we would be able to survive with the equivalent North Korean products? In our we-want-to-experience-a-country-the-way-people-who-live-there-experience-it enthusiasm, we forgot Yokada's warning.

The train crossed the Sino-Korea Friendship Bridge, parallel to a train bridge that abruptly ended in the middle of the river. The Americans had bombed this "Broken Bridge" (as it's sometimes known) in 1950 during the Korean War, and it had been repurposed as a tourist destination; many people walk to the end to catch a glimpse of the DPRK through telescopes. But we were slowing down to ultimately make our stop in the country itself. To our left was an attempt at a children's park, featuring a timeworn Ferris wheel. On the right was a large building with Kim Il Sung's beguiling smile posted dead center at the very top.

A train guard stopped at our roomette's door and–without displaying curiosity, suspicion or contempt–collected our passports. Then came an older gentleman, dressed in a color that defines North Korea: greenish-grey that is dyed into most of the military and political personnel. This guard was a little too curious, suspicious and full of contempt. He first went through my backpack, splaying the books to see if anything was hidden among them and unwrapping bunches of socks (the main thing I change when travelling) before moving on to Dad. Though Dad was clean, Sean's backpack became worthy of further evaluation. Sean had magazines whose purpose was the conventional: relief from boredom and, possibly, some education –*Vanity Fair, The New Yorker, Maclean's*. The guard took a magazine and left, informing another guard to carry on with checking Yokada.

The whole Japanese-North Korea history could be felt in the room; Yokada had said it would be awkward. Well, Yokada furthered this awkwardness and fueled suspicion by bringing a cell phone into the country (we'd left ours stored at the Beijing hotel). This was, as he knew, forbidden. Often people smuggle in cell phones and have North Koreans meet near the river so they can speak to their loved ones who had fled the North. North Korea has little contact with the outside world–both international and domestic phones are tapped–so the 21st Century is a threat to a reclusive nation that wants its people to know little of anything occurring outside its borders. Hence Yokada's cell phone was taken away–no words, no protest.

Sean, summoned by a guard, gave us a fearful look of goodbye. I waved.

"I want his TV and computer," I said.

"That's a horrible thing to say," Dad protested. "However, in light of this, it would be fitting that I inherit his flag collection."

Sean returned to our coach whiter than the average winter. He'd been gone two hours, and was the reason for the train's stall. His *Maclean's* magazine featured a picture of Kim Jong Il in a collage of nine people, one of whom was Britney Spears. This was considered contraband and therefore confiscated. Though it's uncertain whether the guard could read the English-language article that accompanied the photo of Kim Jong Il, at least he had a picture of Britney to pin up in his locker.

Soon Yokada's cell phone was returned to him. It'd been secured in so much bubble wrap that it was the size of a roll of paper towels, It had been stamped repeatedly with DPRK seals. Yokada was to leave the country with it in the same condition; it was not to be opened and the seal was not to be broken. I reached over and popped a bubble. Then we slept.

Our train didn't have a lot of speed and crossing the remaining distance to Pyongyang took all day. The site was of identical villages consisting of small dwellings and the occasional person on a bike or a horse and cart. There were endless acres of famine rich land being farmed with rakes and men following ox driven plows. With the fear of God instilled in us, we didn't take pictures. North Koreans on the train were to notify the authorities if non-Koreans took any pictures and it was not improbable that our digital cameras would be rifled through over the coming week. Violating procedure was now tantamount to spitting in the country's eye. In a culture of respect, disrespect was treason.

It was dark when Pyongyang finally came into view; in fact, Pyongyang itself was dark. We crept from the countryside into the urban setting with darkness the common attribute. It is a large city, but only a few tall buildings had lights on, and those would be single lights—one or two within each building. Were it not for the immense railway station, the many people and–we hoped–our government minders, it would have been hard to tell we'd arrived in a huge city.

A mesmerizing piece of music flowed throughout the station and through the moment; it was a channeling of the magic and wonder of Korean intimacy, political and otherwise. The welcoming song played loudly over the platform. The music, both eerie and transcendent, broke through our prejudices and their rules, disarming us. The singer's voice glided along beautiful notes and was only familiar in a foreign sense of new music to old ears. Steam spit from the train's brakes and the carriage doors creaked open. A woman of about 30 stepped forward, introducing herself as Kim Liew, and her government-minder peer as Mr. Li. Both wore modest business attire and sported a red pin on their left breast pockets. The red pin had a face. It was Kim Il Sung, smiling at us.

"Welcome to Pyongyang, Korea!" Kim Liew took my hand, giving it a shallow shake. Mr. Li proffered the same soft handshake. He was a small, thin man of about 25 and peered at us through thick eyeglasses.

"Is this your first time to Korea," Kim View offered. He smiled with ample knowledge that indeed it was. I don't know what the repeat visitors rate is, but I suspect most people who visit North Korea do so only once. Because twice is suspicious on so many levels.

"Yes, Mrs. Liew, it is our first visit. We have wanted to visit Korea for a long time. I've seen pictures of beautiful landmarks, the striking legacy of your country's artistic talents, and the rugged mountains and scenic forest in the north."

"Please, you must call me Kim!"

We had become informal in a short time. Mr. Li, however, remained Mr. Li. A silent but ever-watchful "Mr. Li", as he preferred to be called, allegedly didn't speak a word of English and would remain on the outside of the inside of our journey.

As we chatted, I noticed that both were wearing the same Kim Il Sung lapel pin. We pulled our luggage onto the waiting minibus and were soon introduced to Chook, our new driver. Chook had the same name as our driver in Mongolia–nine years prior. He too had the lapel pin. Chook was about 60 and smoked. He seemed tired of life as well as having a head full of secrets. When he looked at you, he was reading you. But a smile meant he liked what he read. And he smiled at us a lot.

Chook drove us along the dark and eerily empty streets to our hotel. Huge, illuminated signs portraying North Koreans with either semi-automatic rifles or large red stars dominated two buildings. It was a confusing drive and disorienting to someone like me who claims he can sense directions. The lack of streetlights coupled with the bending roads messed with my internal compass. We arrived at the Yanggakdo Hotel, situated on an island in the Taedong River. Kim conducted check-in on our behalf. The ceiling over the foyer slanted and rose to meet with the hotel proper. Russian rubles had funded a lot of the DPRK's efforts to farm and build libraries and hotels. Thankfully the Yanggakdo Hotel had edged beyond the Soviet blueprints in order to exploit the lovely Korean styles of slants and glass. It reflected a complicatedly beautiful country punctuate with Soviet influence.

Kim told us to take our luggage to our rooms and then meet her in the restaurant. Sean and I were to share a suite. Kim had been assigned a room down the hall. Our room was a clean two-star experience, with certain three-star attempts. The decor looked like one of those white-collar prisons that prisoners walk away from. After settling in, we met Dad in the hallway and headed down to the restaurant. Our rooms were on the twelfth floor and when we got in the elevator, Dad accidentally hit the button for the seventh floor. The doors opened to darkness so black that Stevie Wonder would have felt uncomfortable. This floor, like so many others, was unoccupied. The hotel strove to maintain a façade of being a bustling high-occupancy base for the adventures outside its doors but I surmised most guests were on one or two floors, and the rest of the hotel was dark and empty.

In a country where famine is a cruel truth, we were unsure about the quality and quantity of the food we would be offered. Kim did not appear so we entered the restaurant alone, picked three seats in the empty dining room and waited. A Korean woman emerged from the gloom, arrived at our table, confirmed our names and left for the kitchen. She quickly returned placing a plate on our table and uttering words that I supposed wished us a good meal.

"I've seen Discovery Channel," Sean said. "These are squid. It's called a pod."

"That *is* squid," I nodded. "Six uncooked squid for dinner." It dawned on me that I might be on an all-rice diet for the rest of the week. If rice was available.

As Dad threw his trademark optimism at us, he picked up his chopsticks. "Maybe they're good. Maybe they…"

"And?" I asked as Dad struggled to get the slippery thing God-meant-for-looking-at-and-not-as-food into his mouth. Dad's palate can handle a half-cup of camel milk with a Sahara sand chaser, but he couldn't eat the squid. The woman in the kitchen closed the restaurant on us. Our train had arrived two hours late, but we had a contract for things like a full dinner–and six squid were not adequate–even if we loved squid, which we didn't.

"Well, what can we do?" Sean asked.

"It's too late to throw them back," I said. "I say we put them under the table. They'll stick to the bottom like bubble gum."

"If we don't spend this squid budget," Dad said, using a complex metaphor, "we won't get this much food served next time. Simple global economics."

"OK," I said. "We have to get rid of the squid so that it looks like we ate them. Is that it?"

Dad gave in. "Get rid of the proof and in the morning we'll tell Kim that extreme seafood isn't our type of adventure."

I couldn't have taken any wisdom from the dichotomy of being a "have" in a country of "have-nots". I didn't like being treated as overwhelmingly rich and well travelled when everyone around me was poor and local.

A table across the room held remnants of a dinner that'd been enjoyed earlier. In the midst of transferring five of the squid–and the reputation of being undeserving diners–to that table, Kim came in.

"Hi," I said.

"Hello," Kim said without showing concern.

"I was cleaning up our table and decided to put our plates over here."

"Tomorrow morning, eight o'clock, we meet in lobby, yes," she replied.

"Great," said Dad. "And that would mean we should get a wake-up call…"

"Wake-up call is seven o'clock. For whole hotel. We meet in lobby at eight o'clock, yes?"

"Yes," we agreed. The shorter the dialogue, the better our conversations moved along.

Kim, Chook, and Mr. Li were staying in the same hotel. They would be away from their families for the duration of our stay. It would have been nice to dismiss them, grab a road map, and take the minivan for a few days. But I could see in Kim's eyes that we would not stray so much as a hair's width from our itinerary. She was built for this job.

At seven o'clock sharp, the phone rang at a volume that would make most people wet their beds. I was fortunate and had already been up for an hour. The choppy Korean voice on the other end of the line was brisk. I was sure it said, "Korean wake-up call. Did you wet bed? Xa-xa…(click)."

The view from our room, facing west, encompassed an enormous part of Pyongyang's shorter buildings. We could see trees and streets and people walking rigidly or riding old-fashioned bikes. The river crept by. While Sean showered, I fiddled with the five buttons on the radio. One station was belting out Korean squid recipes while the other four were broadcasting static.

The lobby housed other foreigners, some of whom I recognized as the tour group members in Beijing. Before we could engage them in conversation, Kim appeared with Mr. Li a few steps behind her and asked how we'd slept. As we all answered in the affirmative, she broke in and laid out the start of our itinerary. "First, we go to the statue of Kim Il Sung before anyone else gets there today." This required us getting to the minivan, greeting Chook, and departing before coffee could be proposed. He was propped beside our 12-passenger van, to be used only by the six of us. Chook looked tired, as if he'd spent the night watching adult pay-per-view and raiding the minibar. Mr. Li seemed to be responsible for ensuring the lights were green and that the forthcoming attraction was devoid of any Koreans who might try to make contact with us or us with them. This is a peculiar rule Kim explained: "It is against the law for a North Korean to establish verbal contact with a foreigner without applying for authorization through government channels." Thus, I expected, they'd flee in our presence.

Chook drove us through quiet streets to the base of a long set of steps leading to the Kim Il Sung statue. A woman stood by a table holding small, medium, large and "omigod-I-can't-believe-he's-dead" extra-large bouquets of fresh flowers. Using our US currency, we bought a medium bouquet–visitor-size–and walked up the steps.

A note on leadership names in our North Korea saga and why they sound confusingly similar. The Kim Dynasty is a multi-generational family of leaders in North Korea, descending from the country's first Supreme Leader, Kim Il Sung. Russia's Stalin put him in control after World War Two when Japanese rule came to an end and the Korean Peninsula split in two along ideological lines. That split was reinforced when the Korean War, circa 1950, left territorial matters unresolved. His son Kim Jong-Il who took over upon the elder's death in 1994 enhanced the country's personality cult. Kim Jong-Il was in charge when we visited his country. (In the wings for control of the cultish clan in later years was the great leader's grandson Kim Jong-un, seen as 'the Great Successor'.)

Kim Il Sung's presence was huge. And he looked bronze. His arm stretched in a kind way, to show what had come of his path and indicating history would never forget it. I carried on walking to the statue's base as the rest of our entourage waited. Laying the flowers beside other bouquets and wreaths, I stepped back and bowed–partly to acknowledge Kim Il Sung's transformation of the northern half of the Korean peninsula (admittedly, a disaster) and partly because I wanted to earn Mrs. Liew's respect, and leverage for ordering my own food.

Chook stood smoking beside our van as we descended the stairs. We had been left alone on our visit to the monument–just the five of us and Kim Il Sun–but as we rounded out of the lot, a tour bus rolled in behind us, packed with Koreans. We left just in time and Chook drove us through the city. Pyongyang had Soviet hangovers–largely in buildings–but the streets were wide, the sidewalks were vast, and at 10:00 in the morning, neither were being used much. Few vehicles were on the road. The cars were business-class Mercedes and Audis, with an occasional Japanese right-hand-drive car or van. Cars were rare because of their cost and traffic is sparse because of a severe petrol shortage.

Electricity was also in short supply. Though traffic lights governed intersections at night, traffic girls ruled the day. These young, uniformed women stood in a circle in the center of the intersection and mimicked with flags what lights would otherwise do. But the duty wasn't a wave-through of the few existing vehicles; it was a sophisticated and precise execution of stomping, marching, and swiveling to direct whatever was coming at them. Striped truncheons gracefully flew up and directed to the left then lowered as the traffic girls swiveled towards us. Now Chook's signal was on, an indication for the girl to stop the cross-traffic and guide us right with her truncheon. It was a beautiful sight; the lack of electricity had produced a creative and stunning solution. And to a person, the women were notably attractive.

Leaving Pyongyang for the countryside, we arrived at Mangyongdae village, best known as the birthplace of Kim Il Sung. Since this small village had no other visitors, we were left in the hands of a guide specifically assigned to the site and to us. She rifled off a long string of fanciful facts and spurious stats—concerning his birth beneath a Christ-like star, his prodigious book writing at a young age, and his invention of a musical instrument—as fast as her English allowed her. I desperately needed a coffee and Kim Il Sung–dead though he might be–was preventing that. Having a time sensitive itinerary and protocol politeness was aggravating. North Korea was twisted but sacred ground for a traveller, yet the need to learn minute details of mythical legacies wasn't making for the ideal journey.

Dad is an extrovert to the power of 10 when we're travelling. At the beginning, his outgoing attitude was a little much for Kim and she often stared at him with a look that said "Robin Williams had half this energy when he visited." But she was warming up to us on our little shuttles around Pyongyang. As she slowly lost her robotic and rehearsed monologue, she would smile a smile that I was sure rarely got used. It was genuine. Dad broke the ice among the entourage. He said he wanted four things and told Kim to prepare herself. Kim put up her shield–visitors don't ask. "Visitors know better than to ask."

Oblivious to her caution, Dad held up four fingers.

"I want to ride a bike in Korea," he said.

Kim blinked, taking in the request. He wouldn't get it.

"Secondly, I want to ride a horse."

Kim didn't want to tell him that due to the food shortage, horses were not on the hoof but on the menu.

"Third, we'd like to get haircuts. I like to get one when I go to a new country."

Kim swooned at the impossibility. Mr. Li grinned as he was yet to be informed.

"And fourth, Sean collects flags from the countries he visits. Is it possible to get one of yours?"

As Kim thought through one to four, Mr. Li guessed at her dilemma. He looked at us. Dad had just complicated the simplicity of Mr. Li's life and rewritten DPRK-by-the-book. Mr. Li's state-funded mind was focused on computing times and destinations; counting Dad's fingers was beyond him.

Chook pulled alongside the riverbank. Across from us rose the Juche Tower. Juche means self-reliance and it encapsulates the country's philosophy. I read it as a government edict indicating "You're on your own" but apparently it's a different color of alone. The Juche Tower was 560 feet (170 meters) of granite, topped with a metal red flame that glowed at night. Our immediate focus, though, was a boat moored to the dock. An old white paddle-wheeler was the setting for lunch, and we'd arrived just after the English tour group had gotten there and taken the best seats.

Near by us, scores of Koreans were enjoying the river walk and sitting in the trees' shade. No one was casual; no street-corner chats, knee slapping or gesticulating to emphasize or animate; no laughter; no first-love kisses. Everyone was following a trajectory to get somewhere, travelling at speed. Even interactions between North Koreans seemed to require government approval. Maybe it was the feeling of living in Orwell's *1984*: no one could be trusted because you didn't know who worked for whom. They lived most of their lives in their own minds.

Lunch was a series of plates filled with things I wouldn't try even if I had wanted to be adventurous and polite. In my small Korean dictionary, *gag reflex* didn't appear under *food*. I began something I would do throughout my time in North Korea. A large bowl of brown broth formed the centerpiece of our plates. A dozen copper bowls surrounded it. Dad liked to imagine he knew what was being served. My imagination took me to dark places so I stuck to rice. Everything else I covertly plopped into the ubiquitous *kimchi* broth, making it look like I'd sampled, possibly enjoyed, every plate. When the broth rose to the brim, it felt a good time to look over at Chook, grab my cigarettes, and nod. Chook and I had no common language but the cigarette. We'd try hard to convey ideas, and often we'd laugh together at something neither of us knew the reason for. We'd shake hands, sometimes exchange a quick hug of understanding, By the time we returned, our table was cleared.

Next, Chook drove us to what Kim said was "A park." Dad was excited that we might see nature–while avoiding North Korea's land-mined wilderness. But it wasn't that type of park. The park was filled with thousands of schoolchildren rehearsing for Arirang, the Mass Games in August, North Korea's shining example of communism. If there is one juggler, one fire-breather or one man on stilts in any North Korean event, there are 50 jugglers, 50 fire-breathers, and 50 men on stilts; such is the need for imperative community involvement. Everything was to sow the belief that if you weren't important enough to watch and you weren't outstanding in your field of talent, you'd return to the farm and find yourself standing in a field of dirt. Acres of land before us were filled with children repeating the same moves over and over. The choreography was fantastic, the alignment flawless. In one area, a synchronized group of a hundred grade-school girls rolled red balls along their slender outstretched arms. In North Korea, looking good for the brass is your shot at the gold.

We moved along to a stage fronting a thousand seats, all filled. The two women on the stage wore the hanbok, the traditional Korean dress with a wide colorful band that wraps across the chest area, reminding me of the way my grandfather used to hike up his jeans. His belt often went right across his nipples, too. The ceremony, during which songs were sung and speeches were read, was at least an hour long. Kim and Mr. Li were greatly entertained but Dad, Sean, and I traded glances for the last 45 minutes. We could hear the screams of carnival rides coming from beyond a stand of large trees with fresh April leaves and, bored by the ceremony, grew intrigued by the prospect of enjoying a local carnival.

The carnival rides were few and the queues were lengthy. There were bumper cars, a shooting gallery, a roller coaster, and electrical thing that either propelled you into the air or hit you with enough electricity that you spasmed and launched yourself into the air. Dad wanted to ride the bumper cars. He was toying with our minders, who clearly thought it inappropriate behaviour for visitors. Dad pressed Kim, who told Mr. Li who used a red pen to write something in his notepad as he walked toward the ticket booth. He returned with tickets for Dad, Sean and me. We'd noticed that their version of bumper cars was to drive counter-clockwise and avoid any contact with all other cars. The three of us brought the storms of hell to bumper-car heaven. There was no counter-clockwise in our game; and every single Korean got a dose of Western bumper-car diplomacy. Our banging, knocking, ganging up on and reversing into each other's bumper cars created carnival chaos no North Korean had known. It was shock and awe. I wondered how many demanded their money back.

Kim and Mr. Li at first shied away from the idea we all ride the roller coaster. Kim admitted they'd never been on one, but Mr. Li said something suitably reassuring and she agreed to join us. Either Mr. Li had a persuasive nature or he was flashing his government minder badge around; whatever the case, we were brought to the front of an hour-long line-up, and boarded for our ride. The roller coaster climbed, as would a roller coaster in the free world. But karma was swift. The cars' squeaky little wheels turned at 60 miles per hour, only to be ripped at a 90-degree in a sharp second. No one had thought to bank the corners. Never was Kim so close to me as then. My face meshed so much with Kim's at the corner that I took half her make-up onto my cheek. When it was over, Kim and Mr. Li looked liberated.

Dad looked at us as Kim and Mr. Li followed at 20 paces. "Do you know where you are," he said in a low voice.

"*North*... Korea," smiled Sean.

Dinner was again in the squid restaurant but this time there was a menu. I chose rice. Kim met us after dinner and took us on a stroll through a catacomb of shops beneath the hotel. The steps off the lobby led to a cavern of low ceilings and strange rises that boasted souvenir stores and a bar. I was looking for a soda, the replacement for my now beer-less life. (Now I always remember what I'd done the night before, and whether I regretted it.) All the cave-stores had little glass bottles of Sprite.

Back in our room, Sean and I got ready to sleep in hopes of beating the wake-up call the next morning. I looked out the big window at the city on a moonless night. The entire area below me and out to the horizon–a fifth of the city–was completely and utterly dark, except for 21 lights. (I counted them twice.)

Kim was waiting in the lobby the next morning, and Mr. Li held his clipboard close to his chest in hopes the day would go according to his plan. Ha, such optimism.

Chook drove us to the monstrous Grand People's Study House, which sits on the brow of a hill overlooking Kim Il Sung Square. Here the nation's leaders and eligible spectators glimpse the country's might when its intercontinental ballistic missiles (ICBMs), cannons, and military are paraded on 75,000 square meters of granite.

Opposite the Study House and Kim Il Sung Square stands the mighty Juche Tower.

Arriving at the foot of Juche Tower, Chook pulled over and slid open our door.

The tower is on the east bank of the River Taedong, directly opposite Kim Il Sung Square. Created to commemorate Kim Il Sung's 70th birthday, it is a tapering spire that is built with 25,550 blocks (one for each of Kim Il Sung's days on earth) and capped with a 45-ton illuminated metal torch that never dims. Modeled on the Washington Monument, it throws shade on its American counterpart by being almost a meter taller.

We squeezed into a small elevator that took us to the top of this granite and white stone tower for a 360-degree view of the city. It was a rare sight–the Taesong River at our feet, butted against a wide esplanade of Koreans and Kim stressed that we had the view to ourselves for as long as we wanted. Given the glamour before us, we were in no hurry. Below was the Grand People's Study House glorified traditional Korean architecture, another 70th birthday present then given for *our wonderful and articulate grand leader*. A fountain in the river shot to life, and just beyond, we could see the unhealthy state of the unfinished pyramid known as the Ryugyong Hotel–once destined to be the world's largest hotel. Even unfinished, it was the 24th tallest building in the world. Its construction had stalled as funding dwindled and the carcass sat dormant, awaiting a new USSR to revive it. Off to the north was the May Day Stadium, where Arirang–the mass games–would be held. It was the largest stadium in the world, and on May Day holds 150,000 people.

Arirang itself would involve more than 100,000 performers on the field, entertaining with dance, gymnastics and other choreographed routines in celebration of North Korea's history and the Workers' Party Revolution.

The monuments and towers we were seeing were matters of great pride, significance, and achievement for Kim and Mr. Li and Chook. (Chook held an external wisdom in his eyes. He may have spoken English for all we know. He seemed the guy who could get things done, things we needed or things his neighbours feared. He had a confident air. Chook rarely participated in our exploits, but I wondered if he was smuggling radios from China or laundering euros on the side. I don't say that facetiously, I say it with intent: within North Korea there are those who stretch the law with impunity, and often do so under the guise of common lifestyles. Was Chook one of them I wondered.) All these structures and symbols, given to the people during Kim Il Sung's lengthy reign, empowered the North Korean psyche with grandiose buildings filled with history, books, and culture. They were of a stature and style competitive with—at times more grandiose than—those experienced when walking around Washington, DC.

▓▓▓▓▓▓▓▓▓▓▓▓

With Chook at the wheel, and having negotiated around several of the dancing traffic girls, we cruised by Great Leader Kim Il Sung's mausoleum. Even dead, he remained the Eternal Leader and president and liked to be visited. Kim pointed this out as we passed.

"Can we go in?" I asked. I'd seen a dead Lenin and there aren't too many other chances to see dead Communist leaders these days.

"It is closed," Kim said.

"But there are people, lots of peo–"

"It is closed."

"Can Mr. Li get it open for us?"

'No, I am afraid you came at the wrong time."

"Did he wake up?"

Dad swatted at me.

We continued driving through the carless streets to the 60-meter Arch of Triumph, designed to be similar to–but, you guessed it, larger than–the one in Paris, a fact that pleased Kim immensely. It is dedicated to the return of the Great

Leader Kim Il Sung, revered as single-handedly responsible for liberating Korea from Japanese colonialism.

A short drive away was the deepest artistic impression of North Korea–the Workers' Monument–three pillars supporting monumental stone sculptures of hands: one holding a hammer, another a sickle, and the third a writing brush; in North Korea you are one of those three archetypes. That symbolized an idealized worker, a peasant, and a 'working intellectual,' respectively. This epitome of North Korean popular thought drew its inspiration from an ideology that seeks to put skills where they belong, drawing lines between classes of people.

Having had enough ideology for the time being, Dad asked Kim to show us the subway. "Foreigners cannot see it–it is forbidden territory," she told us. Though she didn't use the word forbidden. Rather, she simply said, "No." I knew that foreigners before us had actually seen it but realized that it might screw up her itinerary. Kim spoke in a low voice to Mr. Li, who pursed his lips and stalked off in search of a phone. None of us wanted to embarrass Kim or Mr. Li or Chook–especially Kim, who had bonded with us. We still considered Mr. Li an outsider. Chook, though rarely visible, was our favorite. However, Dad pressed our intentions, and soon we were on a down escalator.

Pyongyang's metro is the deepest in the world, approximately 110 meters underground. There are 20 stops on two lines that cross each other. Stations are splendid, with platforms wide enough to hold thousands of people. The subway is a testament to both Kim Il Sung's pride in himself and the happiness he always seemed to radiate in portraits. He played the main character in the station's large, happy murals and mosaics. Kim Il Sung watches everyone wherever they are. Through pins, posters, murals, pictures and portraits adorning building fronts, Kim Il Sung was a precursor to today's surveillance systems. His mere image guided a country with a near-zero crime rate.

An old German subway train, perhaps from the 1950s, pulled into the station. We boarded a car not unlike many in the world but two distinct features were immediately apparent: the use of real wood for furnishings and accents, and no advertising. It was a carriage, much like a whiskey cask on rails. Neither consumer nor government propaganda distracted commuters. We emerged two stops later into a clone of the first station. These stations–just like Moscow's–are meant to serve as bomb shelters during a war, so entering or leaving them involved an escalator ride that took a full two or three minutes.

Out on the street, Dad pointed at the TV Tower: "What in the world is that?" Kim made the mistake of saying; "There's an elevator and a restaurant at the top." Dad can be impulsive at times, particularly if he senses someone doesn't want to take him where he wants to go. "I really want to see that restaurant." Mr. Li did not want to call State Control of Visitors twice in one day. Kim said, "It's not a proper day to go there. So we won't." Dad's not the kind of man you want to war with, even in a country that often postures about war. He cannily absorbs every detail you leak and cleverly turns it against you. Our minders surrendered.

The view from the TV Tower on this clear April day was stunning. Lower Pyongyang sprung to life in spring's wake. We were in the tower restaurant and even Chook accepted our offer to treat lunch. When we ordered I pointed at two things randomly and then said "Rice. Lots of rice." I apparently ordered a burned fish with a hairball and everything intact. Hiding a complete fish in my broth presented a challenge. Kim asked if I liked rice because I had three copper bowls of it.

"No," I replied, 'A month ago I did."

I enjoyed the green and red parts of my salad, but the rest looked suspicious. I whittled away at the fish, tearing off parts, intent on leaving only a skeleton. Kim told me that in Korea it was good manners to pick up the whole fish and nibble on it. *Thank you, Kim.* I picked it up by its eyes and tail and set it into my soup. I was done.

Chook, who had been adding nothing to the conversation, was drinking a beer. He sat at a table next to ours with his back to Kim and Mr. Li. Periodically, he ordered more beer. Well then, I guessed, this is the end of the day. We'll wander back from here. A DWI in North Korea cannot fail to deliver anything less than a relationship with a sledgehammer. Yet he remained our driver.

As we took the elevator down from the restaurant, Kim told us we were off to visit USS *Pueblo*–the American 'spy boat'. Dad, Sean, nor I cared not to see an ally's captive hardware on show as a trophy. We all have our reasons for loving America and, conversely, hating it. But America is family to Canada and though we were in the Axis of Evil, I didn't want to join their ambitious project to hate Americans. And I didn't want to hear the United States get whittled down to size by a country that believed storks carried Kim Il Sung's body away. This may have been the closest we came to their attempted "brainwashing" in the DPRK. From this point on, we were constantly reminded by Kim of how horrible Americans are, how cold the American heart is, and how ignorant they are to confront (North) Korea.

Having surrendered on the impromptu trip up the TV Tower, Kim and Mr. Li were adamant about regaining control of our itinerary, and that include them forcing us to visit the *Pueblo*. We walked down the gangplank and stepped onto the ship, where a guard ushered us inside to watch a movie about the boat's capture and the POWs' admissions of spying (coerced, we knew). As the movie reel ended and the projector went flap, flap, flap, the three of us stood outside on the deck, each in our own American mindset. When I could no longer stand Kim reveling in her country's antique glory, I asked her what was next.

"We relax," she said with a tight smile.

"Just kick back?"

Kim tried assimilating. "Yes. I am kick back."

"I am 'kicking back,'" I corrected her.

"What is 'kicking back?'"

Chook was smoking beside the van, slowly touching his nose again and again with his palm rebounding his breath. His self-administered breathalyzer told him it was OK to drive. Mr. Li said, "You are free to walk short distance to your hotel. We will watch from here. You must call us if you wish to leave." Instead, Dad invited them to the pub in the hotel's cavern where he'd seen a pool table.

Kim and Mr. Li had never played pool; they spent nights watching foreigners play but had never been asked. We set up teams. The table was warped. The old rules didn't work on the well-worn felt. As well, my partner Kim had a handicap– the cue was a giant chopstick to her. When the shot was lined up so that she couldn't miss, she sent the cue ball into the bar seating. Mr. Li sank two balls perfectly but both were black. The game became for fun instead of for honor, itinerary changes, or driving privileges.

Kim met us in the lobby the next morning, quite happy it was the first of May. Was it a leader's birthday? A dead leader's birthday? The birthday of a living leader who should be dead? No, she said with dramatics, it was May Day!

"Aren't there 31 May days?" I asked. "Wasn't April Day yesterday?"

Kim looked puzzled.

Western countries give their workforces a celebratory day of rest every Labor Day in September but International Workers' Day on May 1 is a sacred North Korean holiday. The stadium we'd seen was named the May Day Stadium. It was important enough for Kim and Mr. Li to pull the widest smiles to-date. Chook wasn't smiling but seemed preoccupied. (Again my imagination credited this wise man with nefarious projects; perhaps he was adding up the costs of shipping a cell phone tower he'd acquired through channels who had bought it off Craigslist.)

We drove into a busy street lined with hundreds of North Koreans. We had arrived at Moranbong Hill, with steps that ascended beyond view. My New Year's resolution every year is not to break more sweat than the year before. But my family and Mr. Li were climbing happily, like North Korean soccer moms between the state brainwashing finals and piano lessons. Kim was not about to let me out of her sight. She said there were old pavilions to see, sentinel towers, and gates that date back to the 5th century.

Kim had lost much of her well-learned dimness, and now talked and laughed uninhibitedly and often. She began off-topic conversations, saying things that Mr. Li couldn't understand and that Chook couldn't have cared less about. She told us of her home life, the troubles of raising a teenager who didn't do his homework, and a husband who seemed to have lost his passion for life. She'd become human. Her candor was of her own making, and not in response to anything we'd said. I hadn't told her of the world beyond her borders. I hadn't told her that she lived in the country people point to when they think of most messed up and I didn't tell her that everything she knew, had studied, had prepared for–all her life–was completely untrue, and that when the line between the Koreas was erased, she would cry for weeks at the realization of everything Kim Jong-Il had withheld from his people, all while freely enjoying it himself.

All over Moranbong Hill ordinary people seemed to be picnicking in the forested areas, on the little patches of spring grass. It was the one occasion travellers like us would ever have to encounter North Koreans one on one. From within a thousand picnickers, a woman in her sixties, standing with six or seven friends, broke into song. The Korean lyrics carried on in murmurs from others, then one person and then another accompanied her. They were drinking bottles of May Day beer and some had begun to work their way through the first week of May rather quickly. This woman, whose voice could carry better than FM radio, came towards me doing a swan maneuver with her arms. She grabbed my hand. In my paranoia about North Korea, I feared numerous laws were being broken. As the British guys in Beijing had amply warned us, harsh punishment for the likes of Mrs. Liew in such an instance could be severe. It would not be us who could pay the price; it could be her. Yes, I could be sent back to China, but her family and extended family could suffer.

Yet, we danced. What else could I do? If Kim Jong-Il asked me directly why I had danced with that woman, I would have told him that, although she was happy for a day free from her job granted her by the state, she was also happy because a stranger befriended her lyrical voice and danced a dance neither of them would ever forget.

Kim didn't fetch the dance police. Instead she said it was ironic that this was the one day a year you would catch Koreans behaving like this.

"In their natural partying habitat?" I asked. '*Northus Koreanovis*.'

The five of us continued to walk up Moran Bong Hill on this sunny spring day. Hundreds of North Koreans milled around us. "Yes," she said. "And we are to prevent you three from meeting locals; it's a law. And we...where is Dad?"

Kim had taken to calling Dad 'Dad' after he refused to answer to Rick. Her question stood: *Where was Dad?*

Mr. Li fumbled with his clipboard and launched into a frantic exchange in Korean with Kim. Obviously, espionage was on their minds. Yes, a six-foot Caucasian who towered over the rest of the population was going to slip around unnoticed and steal plans for missiles that kept falling into the sea. Just then, the mass of Koreans parted, and from within emerged Dad riding a bicycle. He steered a figure eight around Kim and Mr. Li, then an oval around Sean and me. Smiling and finally passing off a wave, he disappeared from sight, enveloped by joyous North Koreans singing and dancing.

Kim spoke low while Mr. Li bounced his pen off his lips in thought. They decided it best to act as if this had never happened. Mr. Li looked poised for either a stroke (a national pastime) or a breakdown. His career was at stake and the man whose actions could leave Mr. Li employed in a metal shop at a drill press on nightshift was before him now, smiling and saying "I rode a bike in North Korea," and relentlessly reminding Mr. Li, "I want to ride a horse."

Over on a grassy knoll, a large group of women in hanboks were performing a traditional dance and clapping, singing and clapping again. When they saw Dad, Sean, and me, the musical score changed. The women circled close enough to touch noses. To have foreigners so near—those seldom-seen creatures—was a treat. And since it was apparent that we weren't American, Israeli or South Korean (all of whom have terrible times trying to gain entry to the DPRK), we were therefore good people. But were we good people who danced? Aha. The natural curiosity of our being white guys, and obviously having no rhythm whatsoever, drew a crowd of onlookers the moment Sean and Dad accommodated jive with the women.

I navigated safe passage through a forest of legs and found myself at a refreshment stand. Looking over the items for sale and not finding what I wanted, I moved to the next stand looking for an impossible under-this-regime Pepsi. I settled on a predictable Sprite. Behind me, 500 people crammed around Dad and Sean, who were dancing wildly with the ladies. I took pictures. *Sure glad I'm not a part of that,* I thought. We'd lost Kim and Mr. Li; they were probably pacing somewhere, wondering whether they should give us until curfew to return.

The crowd was loud and coerced Dad and Sean into encores. I could see exasperation on my father and brother's faces. I knew from experience when an Antonson was being diplomatic, smiling at a barking dog while looking for a stick. They needed an out. I parked my empty Sprite bottle, delved into the crowd and took pictures like a bulletproof-vested war correspondent before offering assistance. I took over for Dad, then pulled a high school basketball move and lost the first woman to confusion. Sean's shirt dripped with sweat as I cordially bowed, asking his partner if I could have this dance. Another slick basketball move and Dad, Sean, and I were buying Sprites while the women danced with each other. Kim and Mr. Li found us soon after.

"If you only knew," Kim said, "how few visitors actually ever get to meet a citizen, you'd be surprised. What you did today, no foreigner has done."

"Well, let's celebrate," I replied.

"We are late for the War Museum," Kim said. "Our timing may put us there with a school field trip."

Mr. Li's schedule, his purpose, had been threatened three times in one hour. He would not let go of our itinerary.

Off to the War Museum where we were to encounter the North Korean version of why it was split from South Korea, the blame resting squarely on America. Korea was a land of opportunity until the Japanese annexed the Korean Peninsula in 1910. The Japanese were defeated in 1945 as the Second World War ended. The

Allies divided the peninsula along the 38th parallel, with the Soviet Union control-ling the North and the Americans holding the South, all the while coveting control of the North as well. The Soviets acknowledged Kim Il Sung should rightly be in power. In 1950, the North advanced into the South, honorably seeking to reunite the divided country. United Nations forces, which included Canada, supported South Korea. Americans led them, and the North Korean explanation is that the war was actually provoked by Americans wishing to oust communism from the North. Thus reunification efforts had to be undertaken by the North. The North's single biggest stated ambition remains that of reunification, though under their aegis. War pushed back and forth across the 38th parallel for a few years. After three million lives had been lost, an armistice was drawn up that North Korea, China and the UN agreed to in 1953, with the border reverting to pretty much as it had been post World War Two. But South Korea refused to sign the acknowledge-ment. There was no formal declaration the war had ended. In continuation, Kim Il Sung ruled as dictator of North Korea until a heart attack, and died in 1994. His son, Kim Jong-Il, had been groomed for leading an unsteady and unstable country where war constantly seemed imminent. Responsibly for its defense, he worked on developing nuclear, chemical, and biological weaponery–as well as motivating massive conventional and robotic armed forces. At the time of our visit, a million North Korean men sat at or near the 38th parallel, while 50,000 American and South Korean forces defended the South.

In North Korea, America has been the wolf at the door for more than 50 years "raping, pillaging, and bayoneting pregnant mothers with their triumphant cries." And this feeling, freely displayed by guides at the museum, is fresh, as if it all started yesterday. It seemed overly artistic and implausible, but the guide had statistics and a large map showing where invaders bayoneted the pregnant moth-ers. The lengthy tour around the upper floor stoked a hate machine with dioramas of North Korea winning battles, and propaganda films showing victorious endeav-ors, and displays of American warplanes shot down during the war. As long as North Korean schoolchildren are dragged here on field trips, the country will always have a line-up of young people signing up for the military. And North Korea will remain a bear in a cage, poking everyone that walks by.

The next morning Mr. Li banged on our hotel room's door to make sure we were up and ready. His grunts in Korean conveyed there was no room for error in today's itinerary given the specialness of our mission. The five of us herded in the lobby and headed outside. Chook slid open the door, nodding hello. We were on our way to the Joint Security Area of the Korean Demilitarized Zone (DMZ)–otherwise known as Panmunjom–the most hostile border in the world.

Soon we were on the six-lane Reunification Highway heading 125 miles (215 kilometers) south to the border. Hours passed; cars did not. It is three lanes in each direction, with no overpasses; in three hours I counted five vehicles heading towards Pyongyang. If North Korean fighter planes needed alternative landing and take off platforms in case of an American invasion from South Korea; this highway was designed for that function.

Nearing the passive city of Kaesong, Sean noticed a sign reading 70 km. "Is that the distance to the DMZ?"

"No," said Kim. "That is to Seoul."

We let the presumptuousness sit alongside the implausibility of passage. Between where we drove and Seoul lay an entrenched military build up on both sides of the border, with enough power to obliterate the population of both countries.

Chook turned onto a dusty road. Ten minutes later we reached the crest of a hill where he pulled the emergency brake as part of his stopping maneuver. We walked onto a concrete patio with a concrete railing. A young guard whose hat kept sliding over his eyes started his recitation in halting English. He didn't look cut out for war. He forgot figures during his presentation, stumbled over facts, and lacked the overall robotic comportment of other guides. Insecure? Scared? *He's still part human*, I thought.

We looked out across minefields and tank traps, barbed-wire and trip-cords separating us from South Korea. Two sophisticated binoculars were set up on tripods to allow us to focus in on military installations five miles across the strip of horrific real estate.

"Sometimes across there you can see people. They raise flags or paint graffiti like 'Democracy and Freedom,'" Kim told us. "But today there is nothing."

"Maybe they're hung over from May Day," I offered.

Carefully scanning the opposite side, the guard nodded towards a wall on the

South Korean side, and noted that trees made it difficult to judge its distance. He told us North Koreans had tunneled under the wall.

After our visit at the DMZ in the Chanam-dong district of Kaesong, we retreated to Minsok, an authentic Korean folk hotel nearby. It was both a treat and touristy. We waited at the van while Kim retrieved a key, then stood behind her as she twisted the key inside a large wooden lock on a large wooden door. The door creaked open to a cobblestone courtyard. There were a few cabins which had no doors, just large roof overhangs should it rain. On the floors were woven mats that would serve as our beds.

Kim explained who was to stay where, and how to operate the showers. Every feature of the hotel had a traditional slant and rightly ignored Western sensibilities when it came to hotel amenities. The setting was a beautiful tapestry designed to show that Korea was not without its splendors.

After claiming mats and unloading our toiletry bags, the three of us walked out through the large gate. Kim was there, ready to lock it behind us. She rubbed her hands with excitement–it was time to take us for traditional cuisine. I dreamt of the little store in Dandong, China that had everything I wanted: Pepsi, nacho chips, a grilled chicken burger. Alas, I soon found myself sitting cross-legged on the floor and presented with a large tray of everything I didn't want–and that everyone starving within a few hundred miles did.

Dad, Sean, and I were eating alone–which was convenient because my secret-broth 'Plan A' was easier when I wasn't being watched. The meal included fifteen tiny courses served in little brass bowls, this in a country of famine. Not one of the offerings was identifiable, and that made them all suspect. Dog, horse, cat. I looked at my white rice and ate it, savoring its blandness. My broth bowl was filled higher than normal, thus forcing me to switch to Plan B. I poured the broth into the empty rice cup, and—

"Brent, what are you doing?" Dad asked.

"I'm making a Korean delicacy called 'Shut Up and Watch.'"

I carefully made room for a bowl of layered black vegetables and poured broth into it, replacing enough black things to cover the broth. Soon, it looked as though I'd enjoyed myself. The staff had been entering by a side door and then stopped coming. I had mixed two ingredients that had apparently started a chain reaction.

I took off my slippers at the sliding door, put on my shoes, tied Dad's and Sean's laces together and headed around the corner for a cigarette. Kim, who had a mental GPS for those in her care, found me smoking beside a sign, and sharply informed me that 위험 means DANGER and 가솔린 means PETROL. I thanked her and moved to the edge of a creek that flowed between the restaurant and the fortified courtyards. As darkness silently descended on the compound and the silhouettes of dark confiners held the perimeter, I truly felt as if I were in Korea. Not North or South politically, but the Korea of legends and the Korea of long ago.

I returned inside the restaurant. The tables had been cleared. Kim came in and metaphorically let her shoulder-length hair down: She proposed we take a bottle of wine and sit in our courtyard beneath the stars. I paid for a few heavily overpriced bottles of Sprite, wondering how this sole Coca-Cola product had made its way into and then through the entire republic. Mr. Li was present and no one felt any pressure to be anything but friends. Kim's demeanor changed. She was off-duty until one of us ran away. Mr. Li, too, was losing his anxiety. He tried to tell stories about other tours that had gone wrong, with Kim brokering our understanding. They laughed at their inside jokes between them. Occasionally Kim would say something to make him reconsider a particular story as if reminding him that the story wasn't really funny. I thought this was possibly where someone was shot, interrogated or water-boarded.

In a lazy after-dinner walk back to the cabins, Kim said her favorite movie was The Sound of Music and that she knew all the lyrics to the songs. We were startled at this admission regarding Western culture, but she said, "It is one of few such movies we've been allowed to watch." The word "allowed" struck us as uncommon candour. Kim was comfortable around us, perhaps trusting in an untrusting environment. She said, "Other trips are routine people. Some business people come, see, leave." She'd had "A few silly travellers who wanted to hike mountains or swim in bullet-infested waters." She confessed she'd never enjoyed a tour group like "the three of you not commons." Our walk of openness over, we settled onto the bamboo-carpeted balconies of our rooms, legs dangling, facing the courtyard.

Chook entered the center of attention from left stage shuffling his feet and humming. His arms were raised, one holding a water bottle. He was mesmerizingly happy for a 60-year-old driver; he'd shed some official skin and began to sing a folk song. My mind shifted into suspicious mode: maybe the EU had unfrozen his accounts in Switzerland, or possibly a rival had fallen on a pitchfork or maybe, just maybe, his bottle of clear liquid wasn't entirely two hydrogen atoms fused with one oxygen. Chook sipped again from the water bottle. He was drunk.

Chook sang a slow Korean song that made Kim and Mr. Li pause. Kim wiped the corner of her eye. The lilt of Chook's singing was as beautiful as the Korean lettering Kim later wrote down to explain the song for us.

하늘높이 날고
한마리 흰새는
자유를 노래부르며

When Chook paused both his shuffle and his singing, Kim sang wistfully for us an English interpretation.

One white bird
Flew and flew high up in the sky
Singing of freedom
Brought a windstorm
Its wings broke
The white bird fell
Fell to the earth

We'd learned that with Kim there was always more, if we were patient. Chook shrugged, shuffled, and sang more of the Korean, and she sang an English echo one beat or two behind his words.

Though its body was dead and buried
One white bird
Was in the arms it missed
Granted eternal life...

Chook and Kim finished and Kim smiled awkwardly like she had to collect herself after a childish moment. She sat down and moved her purse to her lap for comfort.

I approached Chook to say goodnight, and he held my shoulders and started to dance. We swayed but a few seconds and I swirled him over to an unsuspecting

Dad. Dad and Chook danced in the sickle of moonlight, Chook emptying his water bottle by the third song.

Then Chook crossed into a Korean opera remix. This started him both singing and step-dancing to his repertoire. The night now belonged to Chook. We were all just people without nationalities, and Chook's intrusion made the night beautiful.

Eventually, one by one, we left for bed. Even as I lay on my woven mattress, I could hear Chook a camp away… singing what his heart had to say.

︱︱︱︱︱︱︱︱︱︱︱︱

The DMZ is the celebrity site of any visit to the DPRK. After passing the surreal highway sign announcing "Seoul–70 km" —as if crossing the border to South Korea's capital was simply a matter of time and distance—checkpoint guards closely examined our documents. They found Kim's pass had expired, and she was not allowed to proceed. She was escorted away to await our return. When your guide is denied access, it is prudent to consider your privileges of passage.

Chook pulled up to a series of buildings and Mr. Li encouraged us inside with wide arms, as though he were trying to herd chickens. Standing in front of a large relief map, a guard was using his yardstick to wrap up the story of the Korean War. Before him was the tour group that jostled around our itinerary since Beijing. We came in at the part where the guard was explaining his disgust for America.

We were guided onto a tour bus that would take us the final few miles to Panmunjom, where the Korean Armistice Agreement was signed in 1953. As we pulled away, following a shiny black car of importance, the Reunification Highway's six lanes narrowed to the width of a large tour bus. On either side of the road were granite cubes 10 feet by 10 feet by 10 feet, perched on ledges, ready to be dropped onto the road should tanks try to invade. Both sides of the two and a half mile wide strip of land between the Koreas were heavily armed with pillboxes, tank barricades, barbed wire, and land mines.

Panmunjom posed not a whole lot of danger or threat to us. The tour's focus was a building that housed the red booklet that outlined the terms of the 1953 Armistice Agreement. Again we listened to the story of US stupidity and arrogance. I decided to step outside where a few fellow travellers stood on the pavement talking. It was a close-knit feeling, not to know someone but to be sharing an incomparable moment. I overheard one man telling others that North Korea was the 192nd country he'd visited. My ears perked up on hearing that amazing number; he had fewer than ten countries to go and he'd have been to everyone on the map. Someone asked him about his favorites and least-favorites. He plummeted in my eyes with each answer. He belittled countries and cultures unlike his own, as if they were hobbies rather than societies. He looked down on those of us who'd barely seen the world he had. He denied himself when he spoke.

"India would be among my favorites if there weren't so many Indians there," he laughed as if that were a funny statement. "There are places in the world you don't need to see. There's nothing there to learn. For much of the world it's worth paying for a sightseeing bus tour, seeing the opulent key sites, and getting out. You can do Paris in three hours, Tokyo in two, and Moscow in an afternoon, but that's because of the traffic. Seeing the reality that every country hides isn't worth the cab fare." His arrogance was palpable. His commentary was disappointing, simplistic, and judgmental. None of the lessons of true travel had washed over him. "All destitute people have the same things in common. They will do anything to get your wallet...."

I walked away. He was a racist and bigot who viewed his wide world through narrow lenses. From what I'd heard regarding how he travelled, I had experienced far more in fewer countries. So had most other travellers I'd met. What counted weren't the number of countries they'd travelled, but the encounters with people different than themselves. Two days later, I saw him standing alone on the train platform. None of his tour group was pressing him for stories.

A large man in a T-shirt, with long grey hair and glasses, asked me how I liked North Korea. He looked like he'd either been kicked out of a biker gang or had designed a computer virus to steal credit card numbers.

"I like it," I said. "I mean... well, I've thought about this hard, and after seeing the way it all works like a giant socialist machine, it is—although sad beyond measure—the greatest geopolitical, socio-economic science fair project in the world."

"I can see how you would come to feel that," he said. "This is my third time here, and I feel the cracks are showing."

"Third time? What would make you come back a third time? Don't tell me it's the cuisine."

He looked at me and whispered, "I'm smuggling in Bibles" with the need to witness his faith. The penalty for possessing a Bible was death by firing squad.

Even if Bill Clinton tried to intervene, it was a crime North Korea couldn't overlook. That man's secret never left my lips until we were safely out of the country.

"Everybody on the bus," someone yelled. Following our indoctrination presentation, the next stop was the Joint Security Area where a paved road led down to a series of white buildings that crossed the 38th parallel. North Korean guards stood at our side while, 20 feet of gravel away, the South Korean guards stonily stared back at them.

Facing off the South Korean guards, when you could see the whites of their eyes, was tense. The drama was not for show. Well, in a way it was. If you drag out a war for more than 50 years but nobody moves a pawn, it provides an opening for tour companies to drive in people (a few on the north side, hordes on the south side) who want to wave at each other from across the border. Yet it's also a tinderbox. A single order could turn a gesture into a flashpoint, turning back the clock to 1950 all over again.

A guy from the bus shouted, "Smile!" Then he said calmly, "Within 30 seconds, computerized imaging from the South Korean side will have identified everyone who got off this bus in North Korea. Forty feet from a country where they still sharpen pencils before their day begins, millions of dollars' worth of technology are discerning who we are and tossing that over to Interpol."

⫙⫙⫙⫙⫙⫙⫙⫙⫙

Dad never gave up on trying to convince Mr. Li to get us access to places where other foreigners didn't go. First he had to gain Mrs. Liew's willingness to interpret. Emboldened by winning us lunch at the TV Tower, he knew he could keep pushing, and on the trip back from the DMZ he chided away. "Kim, what is the most unlikely thing for a foreigner to visit? We want to go there."

Shortly after we were back in Pyongyang, Kim broke the news to us. "You will be visiting Korea's film studio." At the time I was working at a film studio back home and liked this idea.

Chook's role was to get us to studio parking lot E. From there a Korean woman with near-perfect English led us on a walk around the million-square-yard studio set up. Street scenes from American Western movies morphed into city street of a town besieged in war and that flowed to a stage setting of a small Korean village built around a palace. Koreans never see this side of their film industry's magic.

Because it is intended to remain as magic, not understood. Koreans love their films and here was the theater and the stage.

"You should now change," said Kim. We were made to dress up in movie costumes as ancient Koreans, for the entertainment of our hosts. Dad reappeared as a Korean warrior; Sean as a royal butler, me as a cook. I thought perhaps they were filming outtakes for use in future films where they needed Western victims.

Mr. Li made a phone call as we returned to the van. He was beaming. He whispered in Korean to Kim and then Chook. Kim shared the same smirk. They said nothing to us. Chook drove us 10 miles back to the city and parked on North Korea's most famous patch of land. Kim Il Sung Square was empty, yet the ghosts of years of military parades hovered. We crossed the square towards Taedong's shore. Our three serious minders walked with us, smothering chuckles. With a bow and flourish of his hands, Mr. Li swept our attention to the near horizon. On the edge of the square stood a tall wooden horse, 18 hands high. "Dad," said Mr. Li. This plywood steed was his alternative to one man's wish to sit atop a real Korean horse. Dad climbed onto the horse.

It was our last night at the hotel, and the lobby belonged to us. Kim asked us not to leave the hotel because she wanted to retire home early without security calling on her. Chook was dismissed for the night. Mr. Li went to his room. Dad, Sean, and I did our ritual at the restaurant; and I even tried the black stuff, but immediately spat it into my napkin. I don't identify with food and I don't know what was on the plates except beets and cabbage... and a bowl of kimchi. I hate my inability to stomach the food that travellers claim is the best part of travelling. It's not just a curse, it's inconvenient.

⊞⊞⊞⊞⊞⊞⊞⊞⊞⊞

Sean and I were freshly awake before the wake-up call on our last morning in North Korea. Kim was refreshed. I told her I'd taken a cab to Kim Il Sung's mausoleum sometime after midnight, but it was closed. She went pale then quickly wizened before her attempt at a cynical laugh turned into awkward throat-clearing instead. Chook seemed cautious as he slid open the door, then continued looking over his shoulder and glancing into passing cars as we drove.

Only the person in charge of the itinerary knew why the Pyongyang School-children's Palace deserved any part of our itinerary. It felt like further propaganda propping up the regime's self image of openness. Kim painstakingly translated the guide's hour-long tour through the educational facility where the Internet was forbidden but controlled computers access was available for select information. We disturbed numerous classrooms in session, with many children reading or doing stretching exercises. Short bows and thank-yous spread throughout the group. I had the eerie feeling that the country was a graveyard for the living.

Mr. Li's smirk was back and he passed it on to Kim. Chook wasn't in a smirk mood but drove us to a large recreation center. Kim and Mr. Li hurried us inside. The pungent smell of chlorine indicated a swimming pool nearby. There were empty tennis courts and an abandoned bowling alley. Mr. Li raced up the steps ahead of us and waited at the top. He smiled as we joined him at the door to a hair salon–Dad could get his haircut. So would Sean and I.

In front of us were three chairs and three hairdressers, organized at the ready for our arrival, cleared by Mr. Li. We were shown a collection of 13 pictures of North Korean men on one section of the wall, each with a slightly different style. I picked a style that I wasn't entirely sure my hair would accommodate. The women worked with speed and efficiency. When the haircuts were done, the hairdressers leaned us forward for an upper body massage and spent a special few minutes on our faces. Dad was happy and this made Mr. Li giddy. We all looked like the pictures of the men on the wall and not at all like any haircut we'd ever had. We praised the women for their skills.

Chook drove us across several streets before pulling over at a corner. The traffic girl was serious, stomping around in circles as cars approached her. Arms went up, signaling directions. Truncheons dominated as the routine endlessly repeated its beautiful ballet.

"Can we take pictures?" Dad asked.

"Of course," said Kim. "Just no video."

We took a few shots, and both Dad and Sean disobediently filmed the girl stomping around her circle. Chook became animated and spoke to Kim. This was very unusual behaviour for him. Kim looked at me and asked, "Do you think she's beautiful?"

It seemed an odd thing to ask–they were all beautiful to me. But I said, "Yes, she is really beautiful."

Kim explained: "She is Chook's daughter."

Sean revived his want of a North Korean flag, though he'd heard from Kim

"That's unlikely. No one leaves Korea with our flag." Then the increasingly mischievous Mr. Li saw his opportunity to entertain us. He'd found a store with a large flag in the window as part of a cultural display. The store was closed. Kim offered to pay a visit when it re-opened the following morning and mail the flag to Sean. Mr. Li hollered at Chook to take us to another store, a mile away. It was closed. Tapping his bottom lip with his blue pen, Li conferred with Kim and they told Chook to drive to another store. The owner was locking the door as all six of us trooped in. Sean's eyes welled up as the smiling man wrapped up the flag that had been in his window a few minutes earlier as part of his May Day display.

Our train left Pyongyang at 21:00, heading to Beijing. We were back at the hotel with enough time for one last meal in the restaurant. Lucky us.

"Did you see this?" Sean turned to me. "I got a 'Western Menu' with hamburgers, chips, even nachos and…."

"What the …?"

"Just kidding. Seeing the look on your face was worth it."

We met Kim, Mr. Li and Chook in the lobby, our last rendezvous. The British tour had left the country earlier by plane. We might have been the only Western white people in all of North Korea. Chook grabbed our luggage as we climbed into the van. The last glimpses of colorful propaganda slid away in the night as Kim Il Sung smiled down at us from a billboard.

We arrived at the station with 45 minutes until departure. After carefully loading our luggage into our roomette on the train, we descended back onto the platform to meet Kim, Mr. Li, and Chook a final time. I looked at Kim in her simple blue dress adorned with a red Kim Il Sung pin. I had asked her about it earlier and she had told us that every adult must wear one every day–and it must be straight 'or the police will catch you and take you away.' I asked her if I could have one but she said they were given to children on reaching adulthood. I hinted, I asked. The cost of giving me hers was too much to pay.

I thanked Kim for taking a week away from her family and spending it with us instead. It was her most interesting tour, she said; many people she guided were either opinionated or silent. She said she was happy to have helped us and gave me her business card. On it there was an e-mail address. Kim noted, matter-of-factly, that 40 people shared this one e-mail address at her workplace.

During our time in his country, Mr. Li had performed miracles in revolution-izing our itinerary. I thanked him with a handshake as I asked for his Kim Il Sung pin. He said nothing and neither did his face; it would be like befriending a cop and then taking his badge. Chook didn't like goodbyes, or maybe he just wanted to leave. Driving is my passion and I had asked him–through hand gestures–if I could drive his van but he'd drawn a line across his neck. I think he'd wanted to help me out and was maybe even sad that he couldn't. But lacking the words, I gave him a strong handshake and a hug.

An announcement in Korean, then Chinese, cleared the busy platform. We swiftly boarded our train to China. Kim and Mr. Li stood on the platform with sad smiles. Chook was gone: might he be sipping from his water bottle in the men's room and texting a South Korean girlfriend? Waving at Kim and Mr. Li as one minute of farewells stretched into another began to feel awkward. Surely their services were complete and we were no longer their responsibility. Nonetheless, they stood on the platform for another 10 minutes. Finally, a train's horn blew into the dark North Korean night and the wagons slowly started to move. Kim kept pace, walking and waving while Mr. Li–who seemed out of place in doing the same–fell behind and stopped. Then Kim, perhaps with her head full of our world, was lost to the night.

Our heads were full of her world.

FIFTH JOURNEY ~
Moscow-Minsk-Warsaw-Berlin-Paris-London
MOSCOW TO LONDON

In 2009, I'd turned 40, Sean was 36, and Dad—well, we'd have to cut him in half and count the rings. It was time for another train trip.

Sean arrived first one evening at Neighbours Restaurant to be greeted by George with the Greek salutation, "Yassas." I arrived minutes later at the same time George was placing a plate of calamari on the table. Dad, true to form, arrived half an hour late. The plate of calamari was stirred, but every single piece untasted and now cold. "Saving it for Dad," said Sean when George pointed to it. "Those are a North Korean treat." George asked, "Where do you three want to train next?"

Dad said, "What about Australia's Indian Pacific?"

Sean upped the ante. "Well, here's a different idea. If we travelled from Moscow to London then we'd have circumnavigated the northern hemisphere on land, by train." I seized the opportunity to seek out how difficult it would be. "I know we can get from Moscow to Belarus; always wanted to be in Minsk. Surely from there it'll be workable to get to Kyiv in the Ukraine. To Poland. Germany, France, the Chunnel to England. This can be done."

The mileposts in our personal lives were an exciting blur. I was accepting a teaching post in China. Sean and Hilary recently had a son. Sean had always said he'd like his kids to be named after rivers of the world and this little guy spent nine months in the womb being called Euphrates. Luckily, Hilary's naming rights prevailed. Riley it was.

Sean had become a father and it had made him a better person. I was inspired to be an equally good example as an uncle. Being a grandpa gave Dad a leap over his own sons' interest to nurture this new life, eclipsing his excitement over the publication of his book about his travels to Timbuktu. While trains were influencing our interpersonal relations every three years, there were lots of things yet to fix or mold or evolve in our characters. Completing something as one-off unusual as circumnavigating the planet's land mass captured our commitment; indeed, it helped persuade Hilary to give her blessing to what she clearly thought was Sean's unearned parental leave.

That left one person's approval outstanding; expected but not taken for granted. George had joined us periodically over dinner that evening and toward the end sat stirring his coffee. He said, "Dinner's on me when you return. Stories on you." Keeping with his statements over the years he said, "Come back different than you leave. Let the ties you travel across bind you as family."

A week before a train was to leave Moscow for Belarus with Sean, Dad and me aboard, I'd arrived in the Russian Federation alone, curious and full of energy. I'd taken the train from Moscow to Voronezh, the city in the south where I had taught English eight years back. My return visit opened old wounds and closed chapters – formerly broken hearts had mended. I was unimpressed with what the city had become. The innocent backwater town that I had written about in my first book, *Of Russia; A Year Inside*, no longer existed. In Voronezh, I had lived right across from the state department store, the 'РОССИЯ,' which is their spelling for 'RUSSIA.' So every night I lived there, except during power outages, I looked out at neon letters spelling out my adopted home...and perhaps that's the best possible place for me to have been in that entire country. Consequences aside. This many years later, that mood of innocence in a Russian backwater town had all changed. Big money had ruined everything and wiped out the village of kiosks, the Rossiya department store, the trams, and thus their Soviet urban landscape. The damage long done, I returned to Moscow on the overnight train and confirmed our hotel reservations near Belorusskaya Station. It was luck–we would be able to carry and pull our luggage two blocks to the station we'd be departing from the following night.

Dad and Sean's flight into Moscow's Domodedovo Airport was early. I'd arrived three hours before them in order to accommodate any change in schedule that often brings Russian airplanes down earlier than the scheduled time. My father and brother erupted from the crowd. Louder than all the others, their voices resonated with eagerness and the relief that comes with having your passport stamped at the Russian customs kiosk. As we embraced in a group hug, blocking other families waiting to reunite, Dad announced: "Now it can start. T…the final journey around the world by rail."

When I originally set out to research our route, I had desperately wanted to go to Kaliningrad because no one goes to Kaliningrad; it's the only part of Russia separated from Russia proper and sits like a wedge of pie on the Baltic Sea. The more I tried to find a route and get visa information, the more dubious and questionable the search sites became. I found a Russian agency eager to help. In the following months, our operator Daria helped shape a strategy with rail and hotels—identifying cities where Sean's hotel industry contacts could get us rooms with Wi-Fi, and cities where we'd need a driver. Still, she could find no way to get us into Kaliningrad before signing off on the itinerary a week before we left. As amazing as Daria had been in managing the difficult details of our trip, her spirit had only gotten us halfway: Moscow to Warsaw. With Poland now part of the European Union, Sean and I reasoned a credit card could get us a last-minute train booking from Warsaw to London.

┆┆┆┆┆┆┆┆┆┆┆┆┆

My fluency in Russian slowly came back. I walked across the airport, through a mob of 300 men claiming to be taxi drivers and headed straight for the taxi wicket with Dad and Sean following behind me. Two thousand rubles would get us into town, guaranteed. It was right there on a placard–the placard I'd come across seven days earlier when I arrived in Moscow on my own.

And though I could now adequately fumble words to convey a point, my words would often not be the ones a Russian might use. The value of learning "the opposite of" made things easier. If I forgot the word "strong," I would say "not weak" and so on. Rusty as they were, my Russian language skills would be needed for four of the seven countries we'd cross in the coming weeks.

We arrived at the hotel at 9 p.m. Moscow time; Dad's and Sean's bodies were 11 hours behind and none of us could rest soundly–no matter how sleep deprived we all were–until our emails had been checked and everyone back home was noti-fied that it was -20°C and snowing. At a table of computers offering free Internet, Sean and Dad faded away even while their faces glowed in the screens' reflected light.

This was the way of our brave new high-tech world; communicating with friends and family members 6,000 miles away was more compelling than talking to the ones who sat 20 feet away. But when Dad and Sean had done whatever they needed to do and notified whoever needed to be notified, we turned toward each other once again.

Sean's hotel connections allowed us a few nights in properties of prestige. But this one–perhaps because of its prestige–was being restored, all day and all night. As Dad and Sean went to deal with each other's jetlag in their shared room, I sat in the seventh-floor lobby smoking to the sounds of Bing Crosby's Silent Night. Though it was mid-January, Orthodox Christmas had been celebrated throughout the former Soviet Union only a few days before. Moscow had been cobwebbed with shiny, twinkling lights and glittering trees. Russia had apparently hijacked the West's vault of precious Christmas carols and played them day after day and week after week.

When I awoke next morning, the TV was broadcasting an apology for the construction noise that had been pounding the hotel all night. I waited for the call from the other room indicating both Dad and Sean were up, dressed and ready for a day in Moscow. Our train to Minsk left at 9 p.m. so we had a lot to pack in, despite the fact we had no plans. After 10 cigarettes and five cups of coffee in the lobby, I couldn't wait any longer. They're family, I reminded myself, and they'll appreciate a military-style wake-up call. Dad answered my SWAT-like knock on his door with the expression of someone who wasn't sure where he was but knew it was nice.

Let it be said that Dad rolls well with such inconvenient intrusions better than Sean.

"Morning, Dad! Five coffees are in my system. I suggest we move quickly."

"Sean is trying to find himself. Eleven hours jetlag and a son who snores is… This is a really nice place."

Sean arrived in the lobby soon after Dad and me, and ordered a coffee.

"Want one?" he asked.

"No, a sixth coffee would put me into an experimental state. This Russian variation of our beloved coffee bean has a hidden agenda because its strength lies not in its flavor bu–"

"Too many words, too early."

Outside our hotel was Tverskaya Street, basically a freeway running through a pedestrian shopping district. Hundreds of upscale stores, many foreign, displayed their wares: monstrous LCD screens, disco balls, twisted neon tubes, and concert-style lighting shows. Moscow had a death grip on the market economy and it was all here to see, day or night, eating up huge electrical resources to advertise a chair...or two chairs. There were restaurants and take-outs. ATMs popped up every 20 feet. If there was a space where someone might be standing in need of euros or a rapidly devaluing ruble and didn't feel like walking more than 20 feet, there was always a small door with a small window and a poster with the latest rates. This door, window, and poster often indicated the government's hand in the street-level economy: SberBank. And this in a country that until recently did not have a banking system for mortgages, extending credit or much of anything other than taking your money and telling you it was safe.

Tverskaya Street ends at the Kremlin and is one of the main spokes radiating from Moscow's core. Within the hour we were in Red Square as a light snow fell around us. We stood, amazed. Of the pinnacle moments that dot my journeys, standing in Red Square easily owns top spot, encompassing all the symbols of almighty Russia. My adopted home.

We skirted Saint Basil's, which has a tendency–if you walk slowly–to draw you into a delusional world that swirls with color and spirit. The exterior has said "Russia" for four centuries. Before postcards. The coiled domes rise above other domes and–in turn–a dome rises from within that, crested with an Orthodox cross. Even a veteran engineer would shake his head at the undertaking.

The rear of Saint Basil's offered an alarming view of nothing. Where once stood the proud and ultra-Soviet design of the monstrous Rossiya Hotel, there was a square mile of billboards covering up a construction site. Despite following the

Russian press, this caught me by surprise. Four thousand rooms and Europe's second-largest hotel was rubble. This was a sensitive area and the anchor of Red Square, namely the ambience of 850 years of wars, pilgrimages, tanks, revolutions, demonstrations, parades, ICBM convoys, dead leaders, processions, et cetera. Maybe leaving the billboards as they were might be best; it could always be imagined that something great would be built there. (In 2017, it would officially re-open as Moscow's rebuttal to New York's Central Park.)

Moscow had lately become the most expensive city in the world to live in, and GUM department store was Ground Zero for residents wishing to avoid looking Russian. Once the door of capitalism opened, foreign companies leaked in and set up shop wherever there was a large enough group of potential customers. In 1994, when I was living in Estonia, I'd called Sean to tell him that Samsonite had opened a store in Tallinn. Despite the fact that most Estonians had neither the means nor a need for luggage at the time, the Samsonite shop became the first real *store* to arrive from outside the Soviet Bloc. Now, a GUM-like availability was spreading rapidly across Russia. There was a need to look rich, a Darwinian extension of burying the ego in GAP and Benetton attire. In Russia, anything could be bought for a price. You could get a Gucci handbag ($2,000), a Breitling Aviation watch ($3,900) or a counterfeit MasterCard (priceless).

I wanted to see the Lubyanka. Its name sounds benign but the former KGB headquarters was the first tragic stop for many on their way to the Gulags. I pulled Dad and Sean from the warmth of the GUM department store and outside into the snowy backstreets.

Earlier that day, I had relearned an eight-year-old lesson from Voronezh: plugging a 110-volt appliance into a 220-volt outlet will fry your appliance. And so it was that I had melted my camera charger. Dad had his charger but forgot his camera. Sean had his camera but forgot his charger. Before its battery light flashed its final red warning, I borrowed Sean's camera to capture the Lubyanka's intimidating facade. As soon as I had lined up the shot, Yulia Tymoshenko's motorcade whisked by. Ukraine's prime minister–best recognized by her braided halo of blonde hair and opposition to the nation's president–was scheduled to meet with Russia's Vladimir Putin to resolve issues of Russia's state-run gas company Gazprom which sold gas to Ukraine and 22 countries down the line. All of this gas ran through Ukraine. Ukraine had been getting side-deals on its own gas purchases but had still amassed a stupendous debt to Russia. Gazprom's resulting decision to halt gas shipments to Ukraine strangled many downstream Eastern European countries' lifeline during this particularly bitchy winter.

Almost three weeks later, Ms. Tymoshenko would again travel to Moscow to meet with Putin and settle the dispute. As her motorcade sped by this day, pipes were starting to flow again in her homeland. The (very small) neural zone in my brain that had been following this gas problem wondered how a country that had received a whopping $16.2 billion from the International Monetary Fund had not used this cash to solve a crisis that was more important than all its other crises combined if for no other reason than warmth for millions and the saving of face. All isn't well that ends only temporarily well. Ms. Tymoshenko later faced politically motivated charges of working outside her parameters; in other words, the opposition stated she had no business conducting the successful transaction. But we did not yet know this on that day, nor could we know years after her mission to resolve the threat Russia would again shut off the gas and knowingly let people down the pipeline freeze to death.

Dusk settled over the city as we pulled up our lapels, wrapped our scarves tight and finally strolled out of the Metropol Hotel after having a drink-on-Dad to massage his reminiscence of staying there during our 1974 trip. With the setting sun came a bitter wind. Outside of Red Square, I never really cared for Moscow. I never liked the cosmopolitan slant—the three-storey neon billboards rippling with new and improved shampoo ads ignite the streets; the use of simultaneously blinking and twinkling lights to attract attention to a restaurant, shoe-repair shop or yet another chair for sale.

A New Year's celebration was taking place alongside the Kremlin. Two older men were on the stage trying to sing, dance, and play their instruments at the same time. My eye was drawn to the one who looked the spitting image of Lenin. He was trying hard to stand up. When he realized he could do so between dance steps, he clumsily pulled a bottle of liquid bliss to his lips. His companion, armed with an accordion, drew adrenaline from the crowds clapping to the beat. Never mind the off-key notes or the disregard for the beat; Russians forgive live theatre combined with alcohol because, sooner or later, everyone ends up on that stage.

Dad went off in search of the perfect Russian hat, finding one with earflaps. He blended in almost immediately. But his Russian *chapka*–and his head-covering future–would soon be doomed.

We set off on the pedestrian underground, surfacing on the opposite side of the Kremlin. Without maps or any sense of direction, we wandered the snow-covered, austere back streets of Moscow. Here, the city's fierce lights and strangling sounds fell away.

Bells started to ring from a small church, punctuating the night with their rhythmic prose. Sean and I stopped at the church entrance while Dad slipped inside silently and stood near the back wall. As the scripture was read and worshippers nodded and blessed themselves, Dad never looked back toward us. I surmised he was gripped by something that introduced his younger self to the person he'd become.

With darkness falling hours ago, we were now on the wrong side of daylight and had a train to catch soon.

Sean looked at me. "Did you bring your cell?"

"If I even open it here," I said, "it costs me like $12 for roaming. What about you?"

"No–no cell on this trip." Sean lived and breathed work through his phone and just seeing it would have been a call to a duty he couldn't shake.

I asked a passerby for the time and discovered we had less than three hours until our train's departure. The neat thing about rail travel is that you can envision running after your train as it's leaving and clutching onto the last wagon, sighing with relief and saying you made it. (Of course, the same cannot be said for air travel and this technique should also be avoided with ships.) We walked up the center of the lonely boulevard, breaking the fresh snow with our footprints. Only a few cars slushed through the streets at our sides.

"Guys," Dad said with outstretched arms, "do you know where you are?"

Sean and I smiled at each other; we had been waiting for this. As snowflakes wrapped the dark branches above in a white blanket and settled on our clothes, the distractions of the city were muted. We knew exactly where we were. And, despite the things that made Moscow un-Moscovian, it was a rush to be here.

I led the way as we crossed the street towards the bustling Belorusskaya station, deciphering the Cyrillic landscape. Inside the station was first aid, luggage storage, currency exchange, baby-changing tables, lockers, train ticket booths, information booths and Metro ticket booths. It wasn't hard to pick out our gate or train with its beautiful dark carriages labeled Moskva–Minck where we were greeted by two strikingly attractive provodnitsas at the last two carriages. The provodnitsa beside the steps of the last carriage flipped through our tickets and checked our Belarus visas, then did a full palm wave inside. Her beauty was overwhelming and breathtaking. The only provodnitsa I'd hitherto would have dared bring home to meet my parents was short a few teeth and minus an eyebrow. But I recall that a lot of beer had restored those missing teeth and offered up healthy eyebrows. It's one of the top five reasons I stopped drinking.

Dad and Sean, however, had not stopped drinking. They bought two bottles of red wine and two 355-mL cans of wine for the novelty. I joined them in arguing over which cheese to buy and then which buns to buy. Dad sometimes puts up a front and retains his position even though he has no idea where he's standing. It's usually fleeting but this cheese debate was pointless. If any one of us was qualified to buy cheese in Russia it was me, because it was one of only three things I'd eaten for a year while living here. I bought all the types of cheese Dad thought best, carried them to the carriage, and dropped the issue.

We were on board the first of many trains taking us from here to London. We would ride three trains between Moscow and Warsaw: Moscow to Minsk would be 419 miles (675kilometers); Minsk to Kyiv 352 miles (567 kilometers), and Kyiv to Warsaw 425 miles (690 kilometers). From there were three non-EU borders to cross; all three were going to be hit at three in the morning on three different trains: Warsaw to Berlin (318 miles/512 kilometers), Berlin to Paris (545 miles/878 kilometers) and Paris to London (212 miles/342 kilometers.)

At 10:35 p.m., a provodnitsa with razor-cut hair accenting her Russian beauty pulled up the stairs and we were on our way. The platform inched by as we climbed over each other to get into the hallway. "We're onboard the *025Б*–Moscow to Minsk," said Dad, unable to pronounce the "*beh*" that is *Б*. A few people stood quietly at the windows. Unlike most departures where there's laugh-

ing, talking, and at least one baby screaming through an open door, this was different. Maybe the provodnitsa's superior looks and the tranquility of the other passengers were signs that Minsk was somehow going to be different, too. As cheese and bun stores fed their happiness and Dad and Sean high-fived to declare our voyage under way, I wondered what I knew of Belarus. It is like a Baltic state but with no Baltic coast to qualify it as Baltic. It had declared independence from the Soviet Union shortly after the Baltics had, so it would seem to be geographically, politically, and historically not that far removed from my familiar Estonia.

Just how wrong can a qualified assumption be? I was so damn wrong.

Sean had bought me a small Belarus travel guide months before and I finally cracked its spine only once on board this train. Then a familiar urge hit me. I always think more clearly while smoking so I left to check on the facilities. The gorgeous provodnitsa stoked the samovar from a bucket of coal with a spade while a young girl stood against the railing staring out into the night. I slipped into the unheated, unoccupied vestibule. No one smoked with me the entire night and the wagon taking us into Belarus was the last car on the train. There was no caboose, no dining car, only the finest view I'd ever had. I stared down the track at the rapidly receding capital city of Russia and noticed the train was exceeding the 90 mph (140 km/h) speed limit. Its wake pulled dovetails of snow from the sides of the track and wove them into a fierce storm. I could have happily spent the entire night in the vestibule but -20°C will quickly turn happy into not-so happy. I rejoined Sean and Dad in our roomette, where my absence had cost me my vote in sleeping bunks–leaving me in the top bunk with Dad's backpack, a virtual Everest. I was pissed off.

"I lost the bottom bunk, eh? Just for the record, I have–in my pack–a record of the number of times I've been stuck on the top."

"You do not," Sean replied, reverting into a younger-brother grievance collector. "You've never made a list in your life. And you don't always get the top bunk."

I do. I did. I always did. And since Dad injured his shoulder at a company baseball game by sliding into all three bases at once (as the story goes), he was allowed the benefit of having the bottom bunk on all of our trains. He sat in front of me caressing his bottle of red.

"Son, would you do us a favor and see if that beautiful woman running this particular car has any cups?" he asked as interference.

"Yes, Father. I'd love to get you some cups…and the only reason is that I'll get to interface with my first member of the Belarusian proletariat. Just don't shake my Pepsi while I'm gone."

I approached the provodnitsa, an appellation she didn't deserve but nonetheless held, and asked for cups. She threw open a door across from the samovar, yelled into the room and a large man—one I guessed was not a provodnik, but a companion of all sorts—emerged and handed me two plastic cups. My animal instincts kicked in and I sensed my nostrils flaring.

Damn, she's got company.

"Spacebo." Dejected, I returned to the room while trying to figure out how to de-flare my nostrils. The only room open, and making enough noise to keep the engineer awake, was ours. Apparently, something funny had happened; maybe Sean and Dad had finally solved a Sudoku together, or perhaps I'd missed a "remember when", or maybe they were simply adjusting to train life again with the three of us cramped into a little room, hurtling off to a place we'd never been.

No. They had shaken my Pepsi. I reverted back to being the oldest-brother grievance collector.

I grudgingly pulled myself onto the top bunk with my Belarus book. Before opening it, I rifled through my mental Rolodex for any information or insight on this country. But Belarus had no file in my head, despite being comparable in size to Great Britain or Poland. I remembered only that Belarus had a bigger post-collapse handshake with Russia than any other former republic. Aside from that, I was going into a country I knew absolutely nothing about. Belarus never made headlines; it had never offered to partake in the Missile Defence Shield, never enriched plutonium, never threatened to blow foreign planes down, never reported a high school shooting, never won an Oscar, never tried to launch its own astronaut, and never threatened any adjoining country. Belarus seemed tidy. Too tidy. Squeaky-clean Estonia had its scars and skeletons *so there must be something dirty about Belarus.*

The first three lines of the Belarus guide included the words: "Belarus is the last dictatorship in Europe." This was followed by, "Belarus was listed by the US as Europe's only remaining outpost of tyranny."

Okay, Belarus, let's have a look-see in your closet.

There is no formal border crossing between Russia and Belarus. No customs and immigration, no collection of passports, no no-man's-land where the train's bathrooms are locked to discourage escapees. When we arrived in Minsk, no one knew we'd left Russia. It was that uneventful, that bland. The handshake between the two countries was indeed tight, and the plot thickened.

Dad waddled down the hall and off the train with his baggage before returning to help us.

"Go out and say hi to Yulian," he said.

"Yulian? I want to say goodbye to the provodn–"

"Yulian is our driver. And from the women I saw out there… you won't miss the provodnitsa."

It was true. Something had happened with the women in Minsk. They were supermodels, all of them; bikini, lingerie, swimsuit, runway, although I thought some were just your everyday models or had been models a decade before. The crowds were sparse on this Sunday morning but as we wove through the new Minsk railway station, everyone I saw was both attractive and possessed a fashion sense I hadn't seen before. When I looked at Yulian, he alone did not look like he wanted to be there at 7 a.m. With his mock-Gortex jacket and woolen cap, he lowered the spike on the Belarusian beauty bell curve.

We loaded Yulian's Skoda and, via my pidgin Russian and his limited English, we headed to the Hotel Belarus. The streets were wide and the buildings–though most leveled off at four or five stories–were distinct, appealing and finished with ornate workmanship. We drove by a large open rink of ice fronting a proud, square-columned building and a giant New Year's tree, prompting Yulian to say "Kalinovsky Square… skating rink."

"Guys," I said as I twisted my head back, "have I got info for you. Minsk is not all it appears to be, and that–"

"The skating rink?" Sean said.

"Yes, that skating rink is not all it appears to be."

"He made more sense when he was a teenager," Dad murmured to Sean, dismissing my attempt at low-ball irony.

The city's buildings altered quickly before us, becoming a mesh of centuries thrown together. Old facades with tiny windows, slim doors, and cracks in their plaster fronted a large lake covered with snow.

"Old Town," Yulian confirmed.

"Guys," I said, twisting my head back. "Old Town is not all it appears to be…"

Dad rolled his eyes.

Across the lake, half covered by clouds, rose the Hotel Belarus. The ample simpleness of its Soviet signature was visible from a mile away. Yulian turned off the main boulevard and headed for the hotel. Dad queried Yulian on possibly going for a drive the following day. Yulian said "Uh…it is possible," but his eyes told us he'd already booked a hangover for the following day.

We dropped our luggage inside the hotel foyer and stood waiting as Yulian sped off. Several babushka-staffed wickets were open for various purposes in the foyer and we made it clear we were going to stand there until recognized as early check-ins by the appropriate wicket. Finally, a woman flagged us over. Our passports would be held for the duration of our stay–a troubling issue, one that Russia had recently done away with. But we were not in Russia; we were essentially in the last bastion of the Soviet Union. Belarus was far more rigidly Soviet than Russia had been 15 years earlier.

"Check-in is at noon," the woman said.

"It is 7:30 a.m.," I said uselessly, for all to hear. An early arrival meant one thing for Dad… a walk. Dad loves parks. Dad looked like he needed a park. And soon. I don't much care for parks but there was nothing to do but leave our luggage in a room designated for such rule breakers, shake off the tiredness and see Minsk in its early-morning state. We agreed that finding coffee took precedence over finding a park and donned our woolly gloves and scarves. Dad unsnapped the ears from his Russian hat and we headed off to Old Town using its church spires as our compass point.

It was the most beautiful and placid cityscape I could recall seeing in my life. It rivaled Venice in the fog or Chicago with an incoming storm. Minsk's lake wasn't really a lake; it was the Svisloch River at a point where it widened to a fifth of a mile for maybe four times that length. A Monet-esque bridge crossed the narrows near the hotel and the main boulevard raced over the pinch near Old Town. The abundance of fresh snow on both ground and sidewalks made the entire area calm and white. With no one on the streets and the absence of lights shining among the office buildings, this was a picture of contrasts–a stark black and white postcard.

"So tell us," Dad said. "Belarus…?"

"Well, they still have the KGB and the rooms are bugged. There is spying, I'd say covert, but I think that's implied. Wiretaps, low water pressure, and the national pastime is ice skating. This is the last country in Europe, one of 15 in the world, with monitored and restricted Internet access. I'll let you mull those interes–"

'Belarus is one of 15?" Sean asked, his inflection turning my fact into his doubt. "North Korea, Myanmar, Saudi Arabia…those I can see. But how un-European is it to…Are you sure?"

"Do I look like the kind of brother that would twist this to make me look better?"

"No, you look the same when you're lying. You could fry a polygraph."

"We'll have to test this restricted nonsense. How can they restrict Wi-Fi through a private phone line?" I asked. "Are multilingual censors going through every email, or will they terminate my IP address KGB-style, so that it will be mangled and unrecognizable in a ditch somewhere?"

"I'll leave that to you and the authorities to deal with. Ah shit…I packed my camera in the lower left pocket of my brown bag–"

"And why are you detailing its exact whereabouts? So I can go and get it?"

"I'll buy you two coffees if one of you goes to get it," I offered. "Any kind you can imagine." It didn't work.

Coffee was currency and the task was usually not worth the caffeine. All I could find was bland coffee costing twenty-eight cents. But I knew we needed the camera and returned up the road to the hotel, explained the situation, and traversed three hallways to the luggage room.

As soon as I walked outside and squeezed through the Ladas and Peugeots in the hotel parking lot, I caught sight of a man on the corner dressed in black–including black gloves and a black hat–eyeing Dad and Sean in the distance. After I passed him by about 20 meters, I turned as if to take a picture of the hotel. The man spoke into a 1970s-era walkie-talkie and, caught off guard, quickly rotated towards the hotel. I managed to take a picture of the hotel and of him, and waited to see if he might pursue me. And though he didn't, everything just got a little spookier.

Only forty minutes in Minsk and the KGB are following us?
"Guys. Wait up…things are not as they appear."

Though Old Town's shops were closed, the cobbled alleyways, slanted staircases, worn railings, and laundry lines of a lost century were still on view. The Nazis had leveled eighty percent of Minsk yet this small part of downtown somehow survived. Stenciled into the center of the city, Old Town retained a depth, an angle, and an ingredient of the past that the rest lacked. Resilient in the face of death and war, this quarter of the city acted as a reminder of the 400,000 Belarusians killed by German invaders.

The reason Minsk has buildings blooming with personality, wedding cake moldings, and charming un-Soviet flair is straightforward. Captured German soldiers were held in the city for up to 10 years after the war, forced to rebuild broken-down Minsk. The effort didn't bring back any lost lives but it does seem appropriate and it made possible much of Belarus's rebuilding.

We crossed beneath a quiet boulevard through a wide tunnel filled with kiosks, eventually emerging outside a white church. Inside, the wooden pews were packed shoulder-to-shoulder with local elders attending an early mass. With the interior overflowing with worshippers, some of the babushkas and dedushkas spilled out to the front of the old church. Beyond the house of God, and in striking opposition to the surrounding architecture, stood a profoundly European building with Hotel D'Europe strung across the doorway in an old Parisian font. The elegant edifice screamed five stars and a genuine multi-talented coffee machine for maximum caffeine injection.

The Hotel D'Europe exceeded itself, taking elements of the quintessential European experience and splattering them across the walls, desks, uniforms, glass elevators, and chandeliers. Since we looked foreign, there was no reason not to let us in. There was a time when Soviet prestige had an armed doorman at establishments to keep out anyone without a foreign passport. We mounted the stairs, settled into cushy chairs, and ordered three distinctly different coffees. However well the waiter pretended to understand English or make coffee, three identical foamy coffees with whipped cream and straws were placed on the doilies before us. We'd barely finished toasting when I was ordering a second.

"So..." Dad looked at me, "tell us about Belarus?"

"Well, they have a tradition of saying that check-in is noon but they never let foreigners in until one. It harks back to the age of Nimbus the Great–"

"Sometimes I look at you and wonder if I was away the night you were conceived," Dad said.

"Obviously in jest. I'd be fine if you felt now was the time to tell me I'm adopted. Trust me, it'd clear up more questions than it would raise."

"You weren't adopted. You were a surprise."

"Okay, let's not get into that right now," I said, pressing the pause button on familiar bantering. "The president is Alexander Lukashenko. He was a collective chicken-farmer leader or something, but in 1994–three years after independence– he gets democratically voted in. But then he refuses to leave when his term is up a few years later. He has stripped parliament of power and everyone who opposes him is jailed, killed, or made to disappear. The opposition has a hard job. Lukashenko loves his power; it certainly beats being the top man in chicken farm- ing. He also loves playing hockey. But no one will check him, everyone passes to him, and he always scores."

"The Vancouver Canucks could use him," Sean said on behalf of his favorite hockey team.

"Yeah. So he's against foreign investment and, though we're in a hotel likely built with German money–which is weird, because the Wehrmacht probably blew up whatever was once where it now stands–foreign capitalists are severely restricted, to the point of lunacy. They are to be repelled by the bureaucracy, red tape, 18 taxes, and limitations of access, progress, et cetera."

Dad leapt in. "So they have their own economy bustling with...?"

"Tractors. That's what they're good at. And the Soviet era was their best time because, of course, tractors were an important part of the agrarian lifestyle. But with the collapse of the USSR came a stall in exports. And with this current global economic 'oops,' Belarus has gotten $2.3 billion from the IMF. They are also a major arms exporter, arms adapted from tractor parts. This is painting a pretty picture, ain't it? But Minsk is also ranked as one of the safest cities in the world."

"That's kind of an oxymoron," Sean said.

"Quite. So, back to what I've read. Lukashenko totally opposes the privatiza- tion of state enterprises. He's ringing a bell that is rung by so few now. Belarus is the only European country that is not entitled to be in the Council of Europe because of human rights abuses and rigged elections, calling them 'neither free nor fair.' Some independent people have done polls and no one says they will vote for him, yet he wins by 95 percent. The EU has frozen all of Lukashenko's assets in the EU and the US. And, at times, the EU has forbidden either Lukashenko or his ministers and officials to enter EU countries."

"You would think he'd take the hint," Sean said as he ordered three more coffees.

"Well, he seems lost in his own admiration for the way things were. He has tried to forge one unified country with Russia called 'Russia and Belarus.' To bring that to the table takes balls the size of tractor wheels...and although that union hasn't happened, none of us knew we'd crossed the border this morning."

"So that's Belarus, eh? Wow." Sean played with his straw and the foam.

"No," I said. "I'm only a quarter of the way into the book. I add to those facts: Belarus was a founding member of the CIS, the Commonwealth of Independent States, whose headquarters are here in Minsk."

Dad added, "'The world is full of people whose notion of a satisfactory future is, in fact, a return to the idealized past.' Robertson Davies. Good quote."

"I did want to pass on one of the most salient passages I've read yet," I said. "The granting of a visa cannot be taken for granted...most foreigners are businessmen or members of official organizations such as embassies or the UN. Independent travellers are few."

"It's North Korea of the West," Sean said, surprised.

"Twelve hours ago, I knew none of this," I said. "I thought it'd be a small country trying to press itself onto the world stage."

Sean added, "Instead, it's locking itself into a toilet stall backstage."

The concierge approached us from the side, unsure if he should impose. His name was Aleksi and he'd overheard us speaking English. From that he went straight into hockey, specifically the two Belarusian players in the NHL and the rules he opposed. Sean is hockey-wise and dueled with Aleksi as Dad and I sat back and watched. He promised to send Aleksi a postcard from Vancouver. On his part, Aleksi told us of the few things to see in Minsk and spoke of the country's fresh hopes. It seemed like there wasn't much to entertain a foreigner because Belarus doesn't get a lot of foreigners. He said many restaurants turn into dance clubs at 10 o'clock because of space issues. Beyond that he shrugged his shoulders.

Throughout my travels, I've made a habit of collecting oval country stickers to stick on the back of my car. Sadly, most of my cars move on pretty quickly and take those hard-earned stickers with them. But I wanted a Belarusian BY sticker for my current vehicle. Sean was still collecting flags and has an incredibly diverse collection. There is usually an unbelievable story that goes along with each acquisition. Aleksi said Belarus flags were sold everywhere, that Belarusians were patriotic even though…Aleksi knelt in closer. "Try to find a *real* Belarus flag. It is white, red, white," he said softly, stepped back and smiled. Then someone summoned him. He left, but he reappeared, placing an empty envelope on the table before fleeing.

"What is this for?" Sean asked.

"Maybe he wants a postcard," I said.

"Why would I mail a postcard inside an envelope?"

"Maybe he wants a tip," Dad offered.

"A tip for telling us how the NHL should be run?"

"I've worked in hotels for 20 years now," Sean said, "and at no time–whether I was a concierge, bellman, sales manager, or simply human–did I ever give anyone an empty envelope."

"Maybe it's got writing in lemon juice and we have to heat it up to read it," I suggested.

We finished the last round of duplicate coffees and headed outside with caution as we passed Aleksi. People were out and about and I was again struck by their charm, sense of style, and the polished way they carried themselves. This was evidenced by the scarves woven around their necks like ties and hats worn with defined tilts. I don't know much about fashion and am usually 10 years behind any trend, but the colors, the furs, the purses –every woman was wearing a complete package. Since most people living in the country earned little more than $150 US a month, this was puzzling. Belarus typically has the world's highest divorce rate and lays claim to being the "saddest" European country, implying a national low self-esteem problem that was not evident to me on Lenina Street that morning. To an eyewitness, it was filled with smiling, superficially happy people. Just maybe everybody else has got it wrong about Belarus.

Minsk's low buildings wrapped as a border alongside the curving Svisloch

River. That divided and cornered us into the half of the city that didn't hold our hotel. Minsk was low-rise and the taller Orthodox churches, office buildings, and our hotel were useful landmarks for much of the walk.

I was wearing dress shoes. Before leaving Vancouver, Dad had said, "Get boots. Lotta walking, lotta snow." I couldn't find any. Acquiring boots was now high on my Minsk agenda.

Belarusian is its own language, closer to Ukrainian than Russian. But it primarily uses Cyrillic characters, with the odd Latin one thrown in to confuse people like me with affection for new languages. Although Belarusian is recognized as the country's second language (after Russian), it is basically outlawed. And though the street names and menus seem to retain it for nostalgic reasons, speaking Belarusian in public will draw stares. Hearing it is an affront to most Belarusians, signifying that the speaker favors revolution. There was a youth movement underway to reignite the nation's cultural identity and it encouraged the fluent, free use of Belarusian but the government takes pride in crushing anything of the sort. Belarus will remain a tinderbox for the foreseeable future. Russian dogma, even that which is no longer relevant, prevails.

Aleksi had given us directions to the GUM department store, which turned out to be almost identical to Voronezh's Rosa department store where I'd spent most of what I earned while teaching English in Russia. After taking different directions in the crowded three-storey mall, I finally found the *state boot section*. Even Dad, who no one has ever asked for fashion advice, agreed that the black Belarusian-made boots were perfect. The price was 144,000 Belarusian rubles. In Russia it was 32r to 1 US dollar. In Belarus, it was 2,600r to 1 US dollar, which required an adjustment and slowed down any purchases to make sure we weren't getting abso-lutely screwed by a clever clerk who could benefit from our confusion. The printed currency's artwork isn't flowing with nationalism or pride; it's rather staid. And there are no coins. Imagine pennies, nickels, dimes, and quarters as small bills. I walked out with boots and a handful of change.

Weaving through the city's streets before our hotel check-in, we encountered a Minsk that looked more as expected–a residential area where laundry waved in the breeze between aged tenement buildings. An old car sat with its hood up awaiting a part. Color had drained from everything; the cherished character of the buildings downtown was gone. Across the street stood a brick building waiting to be occupied by someone who trusted it wouldn't implode when they closed a cupboard. Tall, blanched grass poked through the snow surrounding the property. This wasn't derelict territory awaiting a development idea; these areas are remnants of the former Soviet Union–when it had a full fuel tank and direction. The collapse of the USSR in 1991 changed the lives of 400 million people and these backstreets were also its victims.

A large, busy road ended our walk-through time. Crowds heading towards a building enveloped us. A large sign over a concrete roof spelled Rinok–Market. Aha. *Country sticker and flag*, we thought. But the Rinok was a football-field-sized food market with aisles of aging fruit, quickly butchered meat, dozens of cheeses, brown eggs, and just-out-of-the-oven baked goods. About a thousand people milled about in the building, conducting sales, querying prices, asking for that one which looks better than this one. And yet, with all that going on, it was quiet. No one shouted to be first or to be heard, no one tried to sell a product with a loud or obnoxious announcement that it was better than Mikhail's because Mikhail was a drunk. Everyone was calm, cool, and complacent. When ordering two apple pies for Dad, I felt the need to whisper. Any other market of this size would be a one-way to a migraine.

We headed back to the hotel and were in our rooms on the seventeenth floor by 2 p.m. I hadn't asked for the single room but it was given to me and I knew there would be payback for this extension of my privacy, likely top train bunks forever. The traditional customs of lodging in the Soviet Union were fully intact. There was, for example, a floor-lady who would–after looking you up and down so that she would never ever forget you–issued your room key to you. Every time upon leaving the room, I was required to return the key. Many created jobs in Soviet times delivered ceaselessly boring employment.

I parked my luggage in the room and gasped. I don't gasp often; it's mostly reserved for crossing into oncoming traffic. But rarely does a view affect me like the one afforded by the height and direction of room 1702. The hotel was situated on a bluff and rose higher than the surrounding office buildings, with layers of the city stretching out to the edge of town. Across the expanse of the snow-covered lake was a covered skating rink, where hundreds of people glided in a slow oval. Further to the side was an open-air skating rink. All of Old Town, the cathedral, the Hotel D'Europe, and GUM department store were identifiable a mile away. I don't think it would have struck me as a gasp-worthy scenic wonder were it not for the silencing effect of so much snow and the low ceiling of grey sky, breathing a supernatural charm into the scenery. I hung my cares on the skyline. It occurred to me that maybe Lukashenko wasn't locking himself in a toilet stall for purely personal reasons; maybe he knew this beauty came at a price and would vanish under capitalism, and the people of Minsk would not skate with their families in slow ovals if they had Nintendos, 500 cable channels, and broadband to keep them at home.

The door hanger said 'DO NOT DISTURB' on one side and 'DISTURB' on the other. I hung the appropriate side face out and sat on the bed, propped up a Soviet throw pillow, and returned to my Belarus guide in peace and solitude. Occasionally I got up and walked to the window, trying to impose the guidebook's static impression on the view. It was hard to believe the negative things I'd just read about off my balcony. *Out there* was a striking view similar to one seen by a troubled young American who had defected to the Soviet Union in late 1959. He was sent by train to Minsk to work in a radio and television factory. He would fall in love with a woman and begin negotiations with the US Embassy to return him and his new wife to America. After two and a half years in Minsk, the bored American defector was allowed back into to the United States and settled in Dallas. Just over a year later, this suspicious man, Lee Harvey Oswald, lined up his 6.5-millimeter Italian carbine with a four-power scope from a sixth-floor window and shot President John F. Kennedy as his motorcade passed below.

Dad knocked on my door at dusk. As I crossed the room to let him in, I could hear the floor lady scold him for not leaving his key with her. I waited by the door, ready to open it as soon as I heard Dad try to explain his way out of this. Was he speaking French to her? He was. (Dad had taken French lessons a few years back for a trip to Timbuktu, and he sounded like none of the lessons were effective.) I opened the door before Dad had the misfortune of pissing off the floor lady enough for her to alert someone with genuine authority.

"Hey. Want to grab dinner in Old Town?" he offered.

"*Oui. Apres vous.*"

"Oh…this 'key' thing—people are overly protective of their duties."

"Well," I said, "she will have your key, we will have dinner, and she will go through everything you brought."

"You think she'll go into our room while we're out?"

"Why do you think the keys stay with her? You've travelled through, what... 100 countries? You've never lost your passport or wallet, and here we are with a system that doesn't trust you leaving the hotel with your room key. She'll know more about you in two hours than do most of the people you work with."

As we exited the foyer, it became clear that Minsk at night was more sensitive and even more attractive than it had been thus far. The office buildings weren't screaming companies' names in eye-searing neon; their giant lights were dim and quietly provided information like Gastinitsya (hotel) and Telefon. The skating rinks were still busy and every light in the night had a purpose. Colored bulbs, soft and approachable, illuminated the houses and low buildings that led to Old Town. And Old Town itself had a few pale bulbs that reinforced its antiquity, beckoning you to visit the courtyard and choose a restaurant. With a light snow softening the hard edges and dimming the lights, the scene was as fine as oil on canvas. Minsk, too, had a superb fashion sense.

I hadn't noted this earlier as it was of little consequence during the day, but a mile-long block of ugly and traditional 1960s Soviet-styled tenement buildings stood behind our hotel. Someone had decided to adorn them with soft lights that shone angles of light across their weary facades, pitting them with shadowy creases. They looked like tuxedos. I had seen hundreds of these buildings in my life and never thought they could be improved upon without the use of explosives. Who had done this beautification to the city? And why? What budget supported their brilliance, intuition, and creation? And who was it for? The people of Minsk? That's not Soviet strategy. Visitors? This was January and, aside from us, there were no foreigners we could see. And if Belarus repelled foreign investment, why make Minsk so inviting and even captivating? If you don't want businessmen in town, you turn off electricity to their room at 9:30 p.m. and turn it back on six hours later. You spit in their food but you do it in front of them. You charge for elevator usage. You don't de-ice the plane. No, something told me the president was far out of line on many things but he might well feel there was more at stake than merely opening the door to Nike, Benetton, and Rolex.

No other country I've spent time in indulges in deflecting visual commercialism and product propaganda as well as Belarus. Imagine buying nameless shoes, shirts, jeans, food, books and jackets–all without the cash and credit going to a brand name that wants to put up billboards and TV commercials in return. The West no longer questions ads on bus shelters, rotating signs, jumbotrons, and–the most prevalent–the Internet, which Belarus monitors by law. We are as immune to advertising as we are persuaded by it. But Belarus was still fortified against the West's indoctrination, a socially harmful price to defend the last vestiges of the Cold War mindset. And if Belarus goes, the semi-Soviet mentality, temerity, and ideology are gone.

However, we ate at a food chain establishment, Petri Pizza in Old Town. This restaurant started in Estonia and had crossed borders, likely cornering the meat-lovers' market in the Baltics, squeezing through a crack to allow Minsk to redefine what makes its palate dance. It's surprisingly good pizza. And I've never strayed beyond the basic order: the trusted Margherita. This is world-pizza talk for dough, sauce, and cheese. Dad and I had the bench seat, our backs to the wall. Sean sat across from us, his back to everything else. There were four screens bombarding us with a Kylie Minogue concert. Every song ruined the atmosphere in a different way. We were surrounded by beautiful people, noteworthily so.

"Good seats," Dad said softly, taking in the female patrons.

"Hah," I nodded.

"What? What's so special about these seats?" Sean asked.

"Nothing that would interest you," I said, downplaying the 180 degrees of *Maxim*-worthy cover models. "Some women, and a concert on the TV ripping paint off the walls. And there are women at the bar looking this way...one's coming over. Oh God, is this a country where the women hit on men? I'm burning my passport and claiming asylum."

"I'm the night waitress. Zhadashtra has gone home but she asked me to give you this." She placed a piece of paper on the table. It was still warm to the touch and had enough handwritten digits for a phone number, but it was the bill in Belarusian rubles. "Any more drinks?"

"You're not wearing a name tag." I smiled wide. "So I'll just call you *Myod*.'

"*Ezveni*...? What would you like?"

"You ampersand me," I said.

"Another Coke and two more beers please," Dad interrupted.

"Pepsi okay?"

"There's no difference after 20 years of smoking," I said.

Sean raised an eyebrow. I shushed him. Women, usually in twos, descended from the dark staircase, unraveling their incredible bodies from the tangle of winter wear they'd likely spent hours putting on. Then, they would sit or lean somewhere for a drink. Within a short time, this modest eatery held 30 Miss Worlds and one unattached male. Lucky me. Combine this with a Petri Pizza Margherita and the situation was better than any religion's reward for martyrdom.

Dad noticed my state of awe. "So… why don't you go talk to one of them?"

"I'm actually playing catch-and-release with my eyes."

"So…."

"Listen, I also read in the guidebook that they are superstitious. When the provodnitsa did her four-finger point with her thumb down–that was because pointing with one finger means you are a Satanist. They cover mirrors here when the wrong people visit their homes. They believe in the invisible. How can you trust something you can't see with your own eyes?"

Dad gave me a Dad look.

"Pffft."

We paid the bill as Bon Jovi usurped Kylie Minogue and sent her back to her day job. But it was too late to stay; we had our coats on and two gorgeous women were waiting for our seats.

Rather than take the direct route back to the Hotel Belarus, we followed the lake's southern sidewalk. The snow started to fall fiercely but the rinks were still– at 9 o'clock on a Sunday night–full of hundreds of people skating.

The hotel foyer sported an Internet sign. I approached the woman behind the wicket and asked in Russian if I could use her government restricted and monitored Internet. She produced a card for 60 minutes online and said I could only use the Internet in the lobby. I retrieved the laptop from my room, returned to the lobby and found the only outlet in the three-acre lobby sat behind the bellman's counter. After praising his hairdo (perhaps a little too much) and shaking his hand with a rolled 50,000r note, I was authorized to use the power source. The 60-minute card had two areas to scratch to reveal the codes to be entered into the hotel's site. We were online in Belarus.

I gave Dad his time online and Sean and I sat there smiling at his enthusiasm. (It may be hard to recall, but there was a time when the Internet was a novelty and not an expectation.)

"How are you doing, dude?" Sean asked me.

"I'm great. You?"

"It's weird. I've been away for only four days but I miss Riley. Obviously, Hilary too. But when you have a new kid, you miss him. They change so much, so fast. I go away for a week on a business trip and come home to a different kid."

Riley is Sean's son, seven months old at the time. Over the previous six months, my brother had become a different person; responsibility had made a new man of him. Though the time we spent together shrank, everything in him grew: his patience, his sincerity, his confidence, and his pride, even his punctuality. He had moved to another level of life. It was good to see Sean deal with all the shit that comes with a baby's first year. Some species walk or swim away from their parents right after birth but humans are far more complex and hands-on. Sean's world had changed, much for the better.

After Dad finished his date with the Internet, Sean jumped online to convey his sentiments home.

When it was my turn, there was something specific I wanted to try. Courtesy of Reporters Without Borders, I had a world map titled *The Internet's Black Holes* showing the 15 countries with restricted Internet access. Dad and Sean had used 55 of our 60 minutes of Internet time so I had to be quick. Curious if the controversial map could exit the country and arrive in at least seven other countries, I sent it to everyone in my contact list and shut down my laptop. My task for the day was done. I just hoped I didn't get *the knock*, followed by the KGB's service to apprehend me at 3 a.m., escorting me somewhere Lonely Planet has never been.

There was a loud knock in the early morning hours. *Dad*—not the KGB. When I answered, he said my hair was defying gravity. I told him it was cheap Russian mousse. Our day had begun.

"The hotel itinerary said breakfast is included and so I went to the restaurant."

"Oh," I yawned, "and how is the Proletariat Plate?"

"I could discern the bun, but the rest...anyway, I'm going to walk over to the

Hotel D'Europe for breakfast. My treat if you make it there. Otherwise, I'll come back in a while and we'll start your days."

Dad would have welcomed us had we shown up at the Hotel D'Europe but I think he was slightly happier we didn't. It afforded him time to think, write, read, and ponder–as well as enjoy a breakfast he could recognize.

When he returned hours later, I still wasn't prepared to leave the discomfort of my bed. But he said we had only five hours until the driver picked us up for our train. I soon met Dad and Sean in our lobby.

"So," said Dad, "what do you guys want to do?"

"Coffee," I replied.

"Yep, coffee," Sean confirmed.

Within 20 minutes, we had skirted Svisloch Lake's riverside, bypassed a thousand people trying to fit into the church, and were seated in the Hotel D'Europe. Not surprisingly, I was served a coffee completely unlike the one I ordered in succinct Russian. If Lukashenko had anything to do with restricting coffee choices, he is a bad man. Although this monstrous barista machine was capable of making 2,500 types of coffee, it had intentionally been limited to one.

"That machine does a lot more than this," I said to the waiter. "A lot. You should read the manual."

"Da," he said unsmilingly and walked away.

The hunt for a Belarus BY car sticker and Sean's flag became imperative as time wound down. We looked in kiosks, checked stores and found nothing. Every time Sean and I asked the storeowners for a flag, they would produce a tiny one with the country's current colors. Sean's flag collection consists of only 36" x 72" authentic flags, and nothing smaller or on a stick would be acceptable. Each time we asked about the white-red-white flag, the owners recoiled in horror as if we were trying to overthrow the government–which was silly because we didn't even know where it was. This flag was clearly not a safe seizure. They'd furrow eyebrows with a look of alarm, confusion, and mistrust. This happened every time, with the woman in the last kiosk gasping "Contraband." (I would later discover that this particular flag flew for only three years after independence, after which Alexander Lukashenko reintroduced the current flag and made it illegal to possess the very flag that Aleksi had told us to search out.)

In one particular bookstore, I found a beautiful Russian edition of *Doctor Zhivago*. I'd hinted to Sean and Dad that a book such as this was often a sweeter reminder, and an excellent souvenir, when purchased as a travel gift. That way, it could be inscribed with a personal note about where and when it had been acquired. It cost 8,100 Belarusian rubles. Neither bought *Doctor Zhivago* for me, so I purchased it for myself. When we finally ran out of kiosks to visit and shop-keepers to panic, I found a lonely plywood kiosk extending linen as its edges into the market and taped to the back linen drape was a BY sticker. I bought it and pointed to a small flag in the corner, asking the woman if she had a standard-size one of Belarus.

"Bolshoi–big?" She stretched her arms out, intrigued.

"Da… ochin," I said.

"Konyeshna–of course." She turned around in her small space and dug through Belarus hockey jerseys and pillowcases embroidered with a coat of arms. "Aha. Vot!" Ceremoniously, she unfolded a full-size legal flag of Belarus. She passed it to Sean with a victimless smile.

Sean pulled out a few hundred bills of various denominations. The kiosk-woman refolded the flag with a sense of occasion and honor. I took a breath, put my hands behind my back and asked if she had the white-red-white flag for sale. Expecting the worst, I took a step back.

Her eyes moved around in thought. "*Niet, nye zdyec*–no, not here," she said, her voice a combination of two parts treason and one-part anxiety. Our transaction was over. But she looked like she knew that I was secretly aware of a slow revolu-tion was underway within her country. And I sensed that she was uneasy a foreigner was aware of it.

It was dusk, time for us to prepare to leave Minsk. We had a reflective dinner in Old Town at a restaurant named, appropriately enough, *Starry Gorod* (Old Town). Within two hours, we had collected our luggage and waited in the lobby for Yulian's arrival. To kill the time, I bought an Internet card and once again compli-mented the bellman on his hair before unplugging his heater and plugging in my laptop. But this time, I was denied access. I tried a dozen times, without success, and asked Dad and Sean if they could figure out the sign-on process. But no one got past the login page. I returned to the desk clerk and, instead of arguing the card didn't work, bought a new sixty-minute card. This one didn't work either. It finally dawned on me that my email had been 'detected'; because of my transgression, my computer had been locked out of any Belarusian network. I tinkered with everything that I thought might circumvent Mr. Lukashenko's umbrage at my posting the forbidden map.

Finally, the screen came alive and we each had a few minutes to see who cared about us. I had many replies from people all over the world saying they'd received the email, though the map was never included. I looked briefly for a Belarusian government email address to send it to, but Mitya–Yulian's replacement–suddenly showed up. Mitya asked for *the Antonsons* and, on being pointed to us, grabbed our luggage. His eyes indicated that Yulian had taken the night off which, in hindsight, was predictable.

Minsk's railway station was stark, modern and covered with metal and glass, in complete contrast to the city around it. At this time of night, the station bustled with trains leaving for Moscow, Vilnius, Warsaw, and the next city on our itinerary: Kyiv, Ukraine. Dad and I parked Sean on the cold platform and built a fortress of luggage around him. Leaving him there to hold the fort, we left to find sustenance. Dad wanted good red wine and enough food to get us through the night.

Either Dad truly knows good wine or he convinces himself that he does by saying no to the first two bottles presented for his approval. He always seems to go for the third. Bread, too, takes time for him to get right. In the former East, you can get a dark bun that weighs six pounds or one that is the light fragrance of freshly baked, which wins him over.

Our train to Kyiv arrived with perfect punctuality, reeking of diesel fumes and clearing dust from the platform with its airbrakes. We had a standard-issue provodnitsa and a room to ourselves. Minsk slid into the night.

"Well, did anyone think that this country on our itinerary would turn out to be what it was?" I asked. "Because it wasn't what it appeared to be."

"This was one of the most delightful travel surprises," Dad said.

"Had I not read that guidebook…well, to paraphrase T. S. Eliot, we would have had the experience but missed the meaning."

Dad held up his wine bottle in my direction. "How would you like to do Sean a favor and get him two cups?"

I sought out the provodnitsa, waited while she swept the four square feet of her roomette for five minutes, claimed the cups, and tossed them to Dad on my way to check out the smoking quarters. Again, I was completely unprepared for the vestibule view. Our engine was loud, aggressive, and struggling with the twelve carriages. The couplings shuddered as the engine danced on the rails, wrestling with the powerful torque, quite independent of the smooth ride we enjoyed in the quiet of our wagons. The pride of Belarusian Railways, the *094Б*–Minsk to Kyiv, moved down the tracks.

"Passports!" The Belarusian border guards slammed open our door, felt around in the dark for the light switch and found it. The guard carried a firearm and his hand caressed the closed holster but over various journeys we'd become accustomed to such intimidating border procedure and always kept our passports accessible. The young man didn't look us over or go through our bags. He didn't ask us anything, nor did he tell us anything. He squatted in the corridor, opened a small laptop and swiped our passports through a scanner. After handing back our passports, without a word, he left.

Silently, we passed through dark miles of nothingness outside the window— the border of Belarus and Ukraine. It was exciting, the idea of being somewhere between two countries. Forty-five minutes later, we wheezed to a stop. The metal stairs dropped with a thud, followed by the sound of heavy boots walking the corridor. There were two customs agents. Then I was sure a third climbed aboard. This usually sped things up or indicated things were about to get ugly. A man with the bearing of a wrestler appeared and asked for our passports in a soft voice. Or maybe it was a tired voice. Either way, he didn't intimidate; rather, he simply collected our passports and swiped them through an iPhone with a swipe-card peripheral. I looked down at Sean and Sean looked over at Dad. Procedures had certainly changed, as had the technology.

I'd have liked to ask him a million questions–about not checking our bags, about not verifying anything with a single question, about not specifically matching up the identity of the people inside the room with the passports given to him, and about the leap to technology. Presumably if there'd been a problem with any of us, if Interpol had raised my trouble-maker membership to the red-flag level, there wouldn't have been enough time for him to have received that information at the doorway, either by wireless or satellite. There was no pause to see any results; it was all too easy. But we'd just crossed an international boundary, one with touchy relations: Belarus, still sucking the Russian teat, and determined EU-hopeful Ukraine. The train moved on and six hours later stopped in Kyiv.

╫╫╫╫╫╫╫╫╫╫╫╫

Nicolai had waited at the station an hour for us. His head was shaved and dusted with snow. He wore a tailored leather jacket and black dress pants. He was brawny, serious, focused, and committed to our safe transport. Even if he didn't kill people when he wasn't driving them, he held that tension in his eyes. He took the heavy share of our luggage, leading us from the central station to his Mercedes minivan. He asked that we put on seatbelts, then pulled black driving gloves from the visor, slipped them on his hands, and eased us into traffic. I wanted to be Nicolai.

My first question to him had little to do with Kyiv, lots to do with Ukraine, and much to do with Belarus. I have a need to see Chernobyl, something that few people relate to. After years of research and numerous documentaries and movies; the disaster felt personal to me. The world's largest peacetime nuclear disaster site is not for everyone. Some people chase tornados or stand at the ocean's edge during a hurricane. There are two exclusion zones requiring government approval to pass. I had wanted to see Pripyat and challenge the nucleotides for just a short time. This is my tornado, except these forces are invisible…a violent 30-year-old storm you can't feel, certainly not until the first malignant lump or two.

I asked Nicolai, "Can I get to Chernobyl?" In my mind, it should be affordable with the right bribes. I could hire his taxi and head 65 miles north while tossing $50 bills at the exclusion zone guards. Nicolai dissuaded my rouge approach, and said, "It is possible to visit but the paperwork takes five days at a minimum. And should it be the whim of the processing department that you take a medical examination, you must at your own cost. You also have to sign a form saying if you get cancer, Ukraine is not to blame."

An alternative was an online service, passed on by Daria, offering a tour with lunches and various stops. The cost was $700 US. With 38 per cent of Ukrainians living below the poverty line, this seemed a farcical amount. But I could not find it cheaper. I didn't want lunch and a guide to see what they wanted me to see; I wanted to stand alone in the threshold of an apocalypse.

I refused to pay the $700. I put Chernobyl and Pripyat back on my shelf of travel dreams under 'C' and 'P' respectively.

Whatever parts of Kyiv we passed through in Nicolai's taxi, none of it made a favourable impression on me. It was the opposite of docile Minsk and, a sister to Moscow. Kyiv is tall, confining and without an obvious grid of streets, instead offering a smattering of angular streets crossing straight avenues. Highway signs directed people out of downtown. The one particular name that carried meaning was Odessa. Even though it was 300 miles south on the Black Sea, that name has forever evoked the root of travel for me.

From the main street, a road climbed up and wove around small buildings. Guards manning a booth recognized Nicolai and raised a large red gate. This was Hotel Rus, our accommodation. Nicolai removed his driving gloves, rubbed moisturizer into his palms then helped us with our luggage. He confirmed arrangements the following evening, offered a slight nod, and, to my mind's concoction, left to finish someone off or bury something. He had a macabre brow, and probably hadn't smiled since aged in the single digits.

Check-in was at 2 p.m. and it was just after 9 a.m. This meant one thing: a long walk. The bellboy issued us a chit and left with our bags. We followed the lonely side road back to the main area and here, when faced with turning right or left, both Dad and Sean voted for right. Democracy is fine for countries but it's the shits for travel decisions. Left looked far more promising to me but family-decision making kept me in tow. The first 40 stores we passed were all for decorating one's home. There were imported track lighting, imported kitchens, and imported tables with imported tablecloths.

"This is fascinating," I said. "I bet there's a dishwasher store coming up."

No one said anything as we passed a dishwasher store.

Another block farther, we happened upon a coffee place with a menu boasting every one of the 2,500 variations of coffee the capable barista machine could produce. Many of these were enjoyed with long buns filled with Edam cheese and mushrooms. It was like an edible pep talk, because we were again invigorated and ready to go another wrong way.

Sean saw something he thought might be a park; this would be a sort of excitement to him and Dad. We let Sean lead us—it was as much his fault for taking us there as it was ours for following him—into a vast snow-covered hole in the midst of being transformed into a four-storey deep parkade in the snow-covered ground left the bare sides of a large apartment building. Affixed to the side of this building, some freaky fifty feet up, was a steel walkway, encased in plywood. We cautiously followed Sean along the physical manifestation of insanity, stapled into someone else's property. This exited onto the stairwell of the adjoining building and once at the bottom, we saw just how crazy the walkway looked. Now we were in said snow-covered hole. There were workmen leaning on a crane and they didn't look like they were expecting visitors.

"How many parks have you been to with rebar and a foundation that will be worked on when lunch is over?" I asked innocently.

"It looked like it might–"

"Trees. Let's use 'many trees' as a rule-of-thumb when determining what's a park."

Either we could head back up the wall or squeeze around the fence that spelled out in perfect Cyrillic: "CONSTRUCTION–DANGER."

Beyond the fence sat old housing developments. They had been kept up and looked brand new in spite of their forty-odd year heritage. But the cars proved that this land, this close to the city, belonged to the kind of people that are high up in business, politics, or accept bribes from people in either business or politics. There were brand-new and top-end Mercedes, Skodas, Hummers, Audis, and a Corvette.

Hours and miles later, we wandered back to check in at the hotel. The lobby overflowed with a hundred people. Arabs, Africans, Germans, Brits, and Italians lounged in large, plush chairs talking to each other through translators. Checking in was seamless. Our passports weren't retained. Sean and I were sharing a room.

While Sean played catch up with CNN, I brushed my teeth and turned on the shower. If 200 PSI rips concrete, this shower had 198 pounds per square inch bruising me. It was a hand-held device stubbornly pointing outside the confines of the bathtub. In my attempts to attain control, I saturated the toilet, the floor, the lower parts of all three towels, then filled my toiletry kit with hot water and blew it off the counter. Five minutes later I exited, exhausted.

Sean turned to me. "So Barack Obama gets inaugurated tonight, eh?"

"Yeah, I'd like to be back here for that."

"Me too. Dad won't want to miss it, either. Good shower? You were saying pretty nasty things."

"No," I said while putting on my pants. "I flossed too hard. Just a bloodbath. Everything's fine. Your turn to wash up."

Dad and Sean met me in the lobby.

"You. Suck," Sean said, drawing the words out. "The shower blew the toilet seat up then filled my toiletry bag and blew it against the wall."

"I thought you were having a bath," I said.

Not trusting Dad or Sean's sense of direction, I asked the bellman *exactly* where downtown was.

"At the bottom of the hill, turn left," he said. "In six or seven minutes, you will be in the heart of downtown."

"Left…" I repeated in a loud, high pitch, indicative of feigned surprise.

"Yes, if you go right, there is not much of interest unless you are furnishing a home," he said, earning his right to be the fourth member of our democracy.

Kyiv was a concrete forest of towering neo-classical and Stalinistic buildings. Advertising in every form for every conceivable product and service was pasted, painted, or illuminated on every possible surface. Prostitutes handed out their business cards. The sheer volume of stores overwhelmed, as did the unlimited quantity and quality of everything excessive to suit excessive tastes and prove status by provoking the rich to buy a $3,000 US diamond-encrusted pen or a $5,500 really purple purse. The city wanted you to defy the nakedness of birth by adorning your body with proof of everything you had earned since. City streets hummed with Skodas as well as Bentleys. It was capitalism gone wrong–wrong because more than a third of the population lived below the poverty line. At the time, a pension cheque was €10 a month.

We escaped the heavy traffic by accessing expansive underground walkways and rose up a lonely staircase into a boulevard that seemed more like a wide park that stretched for miles. Dad walked ahead of us, perhaps reflecting the 34-year gap between our last family visit in 1974 when Dad, Mom, and I had come to Kyiv, and I was five years old. Sean, being a year old and already annoying, wasn't with us then. My mother wasn't with us now, though I imagined she would have loved to be.

We soon found ourselves approaching an exceptionally yellow university. It was so yellow that if I said to someone back home that I saw a university in Ukraine, they would ask if it was the yellow one. Dad wanted to go in.

"Dad, I taught at two universities in Russia. You can't get ten steps inside the door before armed guards intercept you…if you do make it ten steps. Terrorism is taken seriously."

Not easily dissuaded, Dad entered as students flowed out. I was a foot behind for witness verification. Dad made it two steps in before security surrounded him. I almost unleashed my Russian on them before doing the math; instead, I opted to quietly step outside and blend in with the students.

Dad emerged unimpressed with their customer service. "They yelled."

Downtown Kyiv isn't large, though the looming buildings give the impression of it being otherwise. After a while, sad to say, we stumbled upon another damn park. This one was a gulley with a hundred slippery steps down and a hundred slippery steps up. Dad stopped in a place no human had stood since the snow started falling in October. He took large breaths. For Dad to stand in the silence of a mighty cityscape shrouded in cowering, over protected foliage was, to him, bliss. Me, I don't stop. Momentum propels me forward until there's a reason to stop–be it a wall, dropped change, or police tape. I led the pack. After 30 minutes of testing us with Ironman-like challenges, the path spilt into a busy thoroughfare with bus stops, taxi buses (*marche-routkas*), and women selling dacha-grown sunflower seeds. We happened across a restaurant on the edge of downtown.

Dad came to our room to watch Obama be inaugurated as the 44th president of the United States of America. He arrived sporting a bottle of red wine, and a pile of fried chicken parts, and fried potatoes he found at a nearby street vendor.

The Inauguration felt as if it took place in our little Room 1005 in Kyiv, Ukraine. It was a curious event for the entire world. Countries that burn US flags and spit at Americans were stilled, waiting to see if beyond those captivating speeches that spoke of global unity was someone who would, once armed with superpower abilities, be able to exercise his talents for the benefit of future generations. We toasted the new American president and his country.

Time would be the barometer in measuring this historic ascension.

Morning brought sunlight and melting snow. Dad came to our room and said that the 'included breakfast' was…

"Yes? Yes?"

"Amazing. You won't believe it."

The businessmen we'd seen at the hotel lobby the night before occupied the other 50 or so chairs. And though everyone was piling plates higher and higher fearing the food would run out, empty pans were efficiently replaced by full steaming pans. It was a compliment to the hotel that it could satisfy a dozen nationalities in the same room. After all, a glass of ice water could offend someone for a thousand-year-old reason. The culinary offerings of Minsk had repelled Dad, a man who has eaten sandy camel meat washed down with a glass of fresh camel milk, with its culinary offerings. Kyiv embraced him.

Our afternoon train left us three hours to explore before Nicolai showed up for the transfer to the station. Intuitively, I knew we didn't want to piss off Nicolai. We took the familiar left and walked through downtown, accepting the invitation of a hundred steps leading up to God-knows-where. I'm glad I didn't complain because the plateau at the top of the stairway offered the grandest view we were to see in the country. The mighty Dnepr River–wide, still, and strong–sat far below us, busy with ships and cargo ports. Some industries clung to its shores farther up.

This plateau was also home to three children's rides. If I had a child, there is no way in hell they'd be allowed near these machines, such was their obvious disrepair and unsafe appearance. But in the spirit of ignorance, the three of us approached the bumper cars.

"*Nye rabota*," said the woman at the desk. "Ride is broken"

With the exception of us and three park-employed Ukrainian women, no one else was around, no children, no families, and no people. It was below zero. So why was it staffed? We headed to the second ride, one that looked like miscalculation on the part of mechanics could render you crippled. We were stopped with another "*Nye rabota.*" The woman at the third ride, seemingly built from defective parts of other rides, gave us a look that said, "Don't even bother asking." As we walked away, the three women met at a central bench, lit cigarettes, and laughed at us.

I hadn't noticed it right away but we were in another park. And there was no way out or around, only through. The three of us did have great conversations in parks; the volume of city life is low enough that not only can we hear ourselves think, we can hear what the others are saying. Sometimes we'd separate. Dad and Sean would discuss child-rearing, hotel occupancy rates, or why Sean has the same legs as the stork that brought him. And I would carry on alone, with no iPod to grace the setting with song. I'd wonder if a sniper had me in his sights or why a new ink cartridge cost three times more than my printer. Then I would slow down and Sean would give Dad and me the time to talk about writing or why I should embrace my 40th birthday. Back home in Vancouver, it would be rare to go three or four weeks without seeing one another but email has given us the opportunity to visit without all the complications of getting dressed, warming up the car and driving half an hour to troll for a parking spot. This park, an extension of the trip itself, let us fire thoughts at each other without pausing to click and send. We interrupted each other's sentences and fought for verbal dominance. But the best part of the park–the end of all discussion points and promises of 'finishing this later'–was actually reaching its end. Conversations might never end but Dad's penchant for endless ramblings could at least be contained.

To our left sat a building with huge Cyrillic letters at the top: Hotel Ukraine. Dad gasped. This was where we'd stayed in 1974. We hustled into the lobby and Dad remembered it being not unlike its current incarnation. We took a picture for Mom and headed back to our hotel.

At an underground kiosk, a proud Ukrainian flag draped over the cluttered inventory sheltering it, as would a towel. Taped to the left wall was a Ukrainian country sticker: UA. Usually our two hardest items to find hadn't even required a search.

I smoke a pipe or, more precisely, cigarette tobacco in a nice cherry-wood pipe. This alienates me from every other pipe smoker. In Russia and the satellite countries, I can find my favorite brand–and it's cheap. In China, Europe, and America, I can still find brands I like and–most often–they are cheap. Attempts at quitting have been only that—attempts. I quit, I start. Parental pressure to quit is constant and when I visit their homes, I have to leave half my clothes outside. Dad commands the English language with skill and talent, a gift to the listener. He can be persuasive and encouraging. I've been the victim of this all my life. When I drank after the point when most people decide to stop, Dad had a one-step program: don't. This seems simple, nice, and easy–but it takes a little more than that. His repeated opposition to smoking hasn't been effective. So I was filled with wonder when we came across a tobacconist and Dad encouraged me inside. He told me that if I were planning to let others nearby—like him—enjoy my pipe's aroma, I should be coiled in the scents of true pipe tobacco. Make it a tobacco that goes back a thousand years from a family recipe that is passed on only on the deathbed. He handed me Ukrainian currency, the hryvnia, and pointed to a wall of mysterious cans, tins, and pouches. They were handsome, compellingly designed, and inviting. I browsed through them, mindful of our departing train's schedule, and chose one I couldn't pronounce.

Nicolai was on time. So were we. He stepped inside the lobby while talking on his cell, removed his sunglasses, and scanned the people intensely. I thought that Nicolai probably worked six jobs and this was the only legal one. We loaded into the van, buckled our seatbelts, and headed off to the railway station where he came to an abrupt stop still having not spoken a word with us.

Nicolai, still on his cell, was tipped generously by us, and leapt back into his minivan. He donned his seatbelt, slid on his black gloves, and drove away. The station covered many long floors and had–romantically–one of the few of a dying breed: a large Arrivals and Departures board with rolling letters. We stood agape as the sound of thousands of little metal clips restructured themselves, revealing new train numbers and newly opened platforms. Ours was one of them.

Enroute to platform seven, we passed by a bakery and bought a lot of stuffed buns on faith. Across from that, we found a wine shop where Dad bought the third bottle of proffered wine (but, of course). Upon boarding our train, a young provodnik asked for our passports then said in Russian that they'd be kept in his roomette. This was an uncomfortable first; we had never before given up our passports to a train employee. But we had room number one of eight, which put us right beside him. I had smiled at him as he looked through our tickets on the platform. It would be his last smile from me.

We had 19 hours on the Kyiv–Warsaw train. Poland's border procedures were expected at 3 a.m. Other than that, and the groggy act of looking coherent, this stretch of train travel was exactly what we wanted. Many of our five train trips had days without a border or a transfer or a destination. This would be special; we'd cherish it for all it was worth. The train schedule allowed us seven or eight hours comfortably awake before sleep. If customs were electronically armed, this would be the best leg of the journey. With only Kyiv's ugly industrial buildings bidding us farewell out the train's windows, I sought cups, accepted my place on the top bunk, and headed down the corridor for a pipe.

Usually you can walk from end to end on a train, though not always. Frequently a dining car splits the wagons and–depending on the country, economic status, or custom–that may be as far as you're allowed to go walking your own section. It prevents people in cheap seats from sleeping in an empty bunk. But the wagon attached to ours was completely different. The washroom was in the vestibule–a floor plan I had never seen. And the plate was up, indicating their door was locked and I was not welcome or even able to cross into their carriage. I chalked it up to the many quirks of travelling and, blocked from continuing farther, tried to get all my coughing done at the end of the hallway before returning to our room. We were nearing where trouble coughing had been redefined by a disaster.

On April 26, 1986, reactor number four at Chernobyl's nuclear plant in northern Ukraine detonated–exploding with a radioactive blast that was a hundred times greater than Hiroshima with 400 times more fallout. This tragedy occurred at 1:23

in the morning during a misdirected and poorly understood test. The local fire department attempted to put out the fire but the 2,200-degree heat turned the water from their hoses into steam before it hit the flames. All the firefighters died from exposure to radiation. For three days, the residents of nearby Pripyat were told nothing. Children played in parks, weddings were held, and people shopped and walked through the streets. When it was discovered the accident was far greater than could have been imagined or prepared for, every resident of Pripyat was given two hours to collect his or her things. Twelve hundred busses from Kyiv carried all 55,000 residents away. They were told it would be for three or four days only.

No one has returned since.

Pripyat is the world's only ghost city of its kind and still highly radioactive. Since it's only two miles from the actual reactor, Pripyat—and its 55,000 population—is considered the nucleus of the devastation, close to the Belarus border. Belarus, though, suffered greatly as winds carried the furnace of radioactivity north across the indefensible border. Birth defects and abnormalities are common. Women from Belarus seeking online dating often lie about where they're from because of all the disturbing documentation, pictures, and video footage. Sixty per cent of the fallout landed in Belarus, creating exclusion zones where people can no longer live. When the nuclear dust settled, more than 336,000 people were evacuated from the affected areas and resettled elsewhere.

This singular event contributed greatly to the collapse of the Soviet Union. It was the costliest disaster in modern history: $18 billion US ($40 billion today) to cope with, suppress, and attempt many ways of stopping or remedying it. Half a million soldiers, engineers, miners, and volunteers did an astounding amount of work to shore up the broken reactor. The core's meltdown turned 192,000 tons of uranium, plutonium, caesium-137, iodine-131, strontium-90, krypton, xenon, and much, much more into lava that burned through concrete and threatened the water table of the Dnepr River–which would then contaminate the Black Sea. No one wanted to think beyond that. Their efforts did stop the lava, though it retains harsh radioactivity. A concrete sarcophagus was built to contain the damaged reactor. There was nothing else they could do. Clean-up crews worked 45 seconds a day, such was the exposure to radioactive elements. Remote control tractors committed suicide, driven off the roof as their wiring fried amidst the contamination.

With the loss of the Soviet Union's authority and money, Ukraine was left with a terrible secret. The sarcophagus is breaking away. One hole is "large enough to drive a car through." Birds live inside it. The cause of such a frightful reality is two-fold: the reactor building was structurally unsound after the explosion, yet the sarcophagus was built using it as support. Then there's its roof. If it collapses, the lava will fragment into a radioactive dust storm that will again follow the wind and likely affect all of Europe. If water collects on the roof, causing it to collapse, or enough rain penetrates to the lava, it could start a chain reaction leading to a nuclear explosion that would render Europe uninhabitable for more than a million years. Even if neither of these events happen, the 22,000-ton lid of the reactor blew off in the explosion. It flipped and landed inside the broken core, wedged into cracking concrete. Should the reactor core split from age and swallow the lid, the dust storm scenario again presents itself.

The enormity of the potential consequences doesn't seem to get the attention it deserves. EU countries started a fund for a second sarcophagus–one of vast engineering and labour. In sketches, it is appealing because it promises to remove the threat by fully containing the area around reactor number four by constructing the largest movable structure ever built. Research led me to believe that the contributed funds didn't amount to the total needed for the project. Ukraine, poor as it is, has not had the funds to deal with Chernobyl. The world will deal with Chernobyl again—and, again, by accident.

† † † † † † † † † † † † †

We enjoyed the look of layered homes of small provincial towns and villages our train took us through or beside. We hadn't travelled a lot in daylight on our recent trains, and before anyone had the chance to say it was neat to be able to see everything, it was dark. We talked, we ate, we drank, and I smoked. Lazy hours slipped away in our favorite fashion aboard the *Д67*–Kyiv to Warsaw. Hoping for an expedited border crossing, everything was going well until it started to go wrong.

I stepped out of our room at 9 p.m. In the hallway two women were unscrewing the plates that cover the radiator, which ran the length of the wagon and stood against the wall a foot high. Many six-foot covers were already off. Beside the two women sat a tall stack of cigarettes, in sleeves of 22 packs apiece. The second woman was jamming these packs into the radiator space. I walked down the length of the wagon, stepping around the women, and carried on to the vestibule as though I had seen nothing. I really, honestly, didn't want to see anything. In the vestibule, I saw more. A (male) provodnik I'd not yet seen carried a large transport bag–about two feet high, two feet wide and four feet long–overflowing with cigarettes. Meanwhile, the (female) provodnitsa opened the roof and an access panel in the vestibule's side with her precious and company-issued rail key–which also happens to open windows, washrooms, doors, and everything else on the train. They were speaking Ukrainian so I only caught every twelfth word if it happened to sound the same in Russian. Added up, I understood nothing–which was fine by me. After sizing me up, maybe they figured I was a traveller with little reason to ask why on earth they were sticking cigarettes into awkward hiding places.

As I nursed my LD Krasni cigarette, I did the math on the bag's contents: 2,400 packages of cigarettes. All of which were being smuggled from a country where they cost 40 cents a pack into a country where they could fetch five euros a pack. I yawned convincingly, signaling that I'd finished that 'last smoke before bed' and walked back to Dad and Sean as the women continued stuffing cigarettes into opened spaces along and down the hallway. The young provodnik stood outside his roomette wearing a concerned look–concerned, no doubt, that I'd seen what I'd seen. I met his eyes, held the stare for two seconds and turned inside my room.

Dad and Sean thought it was exciting. We felt clear of any suspicion and carried on reading our books. At 10 p.m., Sean went to the washroom right by our room. There are always two, one at either end, but provodnitsas traditionally lock the one at their end to save having to clean it. Sean came back in, closed the door and whispered there were three more of those bags in the vestibule at that end. Our carriage was becoming a dangerous place for us to be. Since the provodnik, the provodnitsa, and at least three passengers were in on this, we were now a threat to their operation. And they were a threat to our innocence. We agreed locking our door and staying in the room, maybe even going to sleep, was the safest idea.

I had to go to the bathroom. It was 11 p.m. Though the radiator plates were back on, different women were working the train. The washroom door was locked but as I went to the adjacent vestibule, the provodnitsa used her key to unlock it for a woman carrying an oversized satchel clearly filled with packages of cigarettes. The open vestibule door revealed two women sticking the long sleeves of cigarettes under the train's decking plates and wherever their applied adhesive would hold it in place.

The bitter wind and snow from an open door on our speeding train blew fiercely. I had a cigarette while contemplating what crossing the border from Ukraine to Poland might bring. Poland joined the EU in 2004. The requirements included exceptionally strong border control. Why pro-EU Ukrainians would risk black flags on their passports by smuggling cigarettes, I could not fathom. Whatever the net worth of the smuggled cigarettes, many people were involved–including railway staff. Any profits had to be split many ways. It didn't seem worth it. Narcotics, electronics, alcohol, fissile isotopes–where the duty was so high that the risk was worth the substantial reward–that would make sense. I walked through the first door towards the washroom where I found the woman standing atop the toilet seat shoving cigarettes down the inside of the roof–accessible via a removed light fixture. Cigarette packages stuffed into pantyhose littered the bathroom. Since these sleeves were elastic, she'd resourcefully tied them together and suspended the packages down the toilet plumbing. Washrooms are usually locked during border procedures, which can make them the safest places to hide on the train.

Ukrainian officials woke us at the promised 3 a.m. with harsh knocks on our roomette's door. I said that the provodnik had our passports. The agent went next door and of all the mumbling, I could only understand the word "Canadian." He returned to us holding our passports, confirmed our names, and left with our documents. Other guards walked by, waking up the other compartments. Two agents came to our door and picked through all of our luggage. We were all clean; I hadn't even bought my customs-allowed 200 cigarettes. Our saving grace was that I'd not borrowed a cigarette or bought a packet from these people. If anything like that was sitting on our table, we were involved.

The officer, a fairly large, fit man, returned and asked me to stand. He shone his flashlight in my face, returning his attention again and again to my passport. Then he stared directly into my eyes for at least a half minute. If the purpose of this exercise was to make me buckle, capitulate or blink…it didn't work, though I really had to go to the bathroom. He returned Sean's passport then slowly went through Dad's, whose pages are filled with exotic destinations from Libya to the Maldives; it is a collection piece, deserving a display case when it expires. Dad's passport was returned to him but mine was taken down the hallway while I was left there standing and trying not to blink. Ten minutes later, the man returned with two senior agents. The tallest one with the biggest hat stared at me, looked at my picture, and then at me again. He did this 20 times, it seemed, to discern that the picture and the physical manifestation before him were the same. Then he stared at me again for another 30 seconds. I didn't flinch–not even one nerve–a skill made possible by the sleepiness circulating through my body. I decided to take a risk and used my Russian to ask if the problem was with my picture.

"Da," he answered.

Well this I can work with, I thought. My passport was three years old and I had lost twenty pounds since then. I tried to explain this but the question then became "Why?" Why did I decide to lose 20 pounds? Immediately the Russian words for "I was too fat" leapt to mind but I looked at the stout man who had started this whole thing and replied, "Health and exercise." I was then asked to tell him every country I'd ever visited. Clearly they did not understand many of the 40-odd country names, in English. They had a two-minute conversation in Ukrainian before returning my passport with no hint they were convinced. Life must be hard when your employment requires you to be at an isolated post, suspicious and pissed off for the 3 a.m. arrival of the train to Warsaw. Or maybe it was EU-envy.

†††††††††††††

The provodnik leaned on the railing across from us, scowling as though we'd become a threat to the night. I was unsure if he was part of the criminal operation. I closed the door as the last of the border checks wrapped up. We began moving; Ukraine was gone. We chuckled in nervous relief.

Ten minutes later the train stopped again. Our door was thrown open. A uniformed woman demanded our passports while six or seven men passed behind her with SWAT-team efficiency. Some wore t-shirts; others were dressed with absolute authority. The woman had a loose grip on English and we were entering a country where my Russian would be of little help. I didn't know a single Polish word except *ginkoya* (thank you) and I was hoping I'd get to use it soon. She collected our passports and left amid yells and shouts from her comrades working down the corridor. A man in a t-shirt thrust into our room with a screw gun. The official lifted up our beds, our bedding, and searched around and under our luggage, but did not ask for it to be opened. He peeled back our walls. He had a full set of screwdrivers and ratchets in his back pockets. Satisfied we had no contraband, he left.

Next door was not so lucky; what I had thought were three old nuns with a 10-year-old girl had their room ripped apart. The sound was akin to a big cat in a big litter box. A shitload of cigarettes was hidden in their walls. Guards disassembled the entire radiator, and dismounted beds from the walls. The man in a t-shirt removed their ceiling tiles. Lighting fixtures were brought down.

I had to go to the bathroom.

Our passports were handed back to us without a question about my weight loss.

"*Ginkoya*," I said.

The provodnik leaned on the railing across from our compartment, sweating like he'd just compromised his short future. He crossed his arms nervously then unfolded them again. The yelling was frequent now. Whining screw guns echoed throughout the corridors for hours. Breaking wood and metal sliding across metal were evidence the agents and t-shirt-authorized men were finding every last package of cigarettes. The young provodnik looked at me. I was already accidentally looking at him. When eye contact was made, he angrily reached out, turned off our light, yelled, "Sleep!" and slammed the door. It was 120° in our closed room so I challenged the guilty provodnik by opening the door halfway. I used my Russian to say "It's hot" but he slammed the door in my face before I finished.

"He's probably in more international shit than he ever thought possible," Sean said. "He might be saving us from being involved."

"Well, now my bladder is involved."

The train shunted. I assumed that we had a schedule to keep and the hours we'd spent static had rid the train of personae non grata, but with considerable delay. We could still hear the searching sounds of bending metal and cracking boards in the hallway.

After five minutes, I told Dad and Sean I desperately needed to go to the bathroom.

I opened our roomette's door. Broken beds and parts of walls, flooring, and ceilings littered the hallway. Other roomettes were open but only the sounds of de-construction could be heard. I sped by the provodnik's open door without looking in. The bathroom break went well and as I proceeded to Phase Two (a smoke break), the provodnik stood in the vestibule smoking. He fused his eyebrows and gazed at me distantly. His sharp railway outfit looked like he'd been on a weekend drinking binge. Buttons were undone and one side was untucked. What fate

awaited him or why he was allowed into Poland, I don't know. I was tempted to ask if he was an informer but stopped myself.

It was then I realized everyone else from our coach had been removed from the train. We had spent a night in someone else's hell.

We stepped onto the platform in Poland. Dad immediately realized he had forgotten his Russian hat in our room on the train. He ran back to get it but the room had been cleared. The whole cigarette-smuggling incident accented this Russian hat debacle, as it was obvious the provodnik still somehow blamed us for the confiscation of the cigarettes so he was of no help –particularly, we suspected, because he now had himself a new hat.

Warsaw's Central train station has a labyrinth of a mall woven through it. The configuration would be confusing even with English signage but we were faced with a completely different alphabet written out in a series of aggressive accents. Although this alphabet had its roots in the same Latin of our own cherished tongue, the Slavic influence had thrown lines through the L and done curious things to the C. Without coffee, there would be no further attempts at exiting the building. A McDonald's appeared and, fearful we'd lose it if we walked 10 paces away, we dragged our luggage inside and took up eight seating areas. Sean left to change his Ukrainian hryvnia for Polish zloty and returned with a smirk.

"We're in Euros now. I knew that. I forgot, but I knew it."

And we were. Indeed, we were now inside the largest community of countries, unified in not just name only but by a common currency, the blessed Euro. I pulled out our itinerary and read "End of service" to Dad. That was Daria's way of saying, "I hope you can read Polish." Daria's duties were done and we praised her with a toast of coffees. She had navigated us through an amazing week. We were now on our own.

Since the night hadn't been the promising repose we'd planned, Dad said he'd park himself where he sat and look after the luggage.

Sean and I walked through the mall and rail station looking for an actual entrance but got lost three times. Christmas carols serenaded us, piped through ceiling speakers and therefore inescapable. People who walk briskly usually know where they are going so I motioned to a brisk-walking fellow traveller to pause long enough to give us directions. Her meager English, peppered with Polish, was accompanied by gestures pointing left, then straight, left again and a sharp right. This did little to enlighten us. She threw her coffee in the garbage and waved to follow her quickly. We had probably waylaid her plan to get to work on time but, with true Polish spirit, she wanted to help stray travellers in her city. We mounted a staircase. Beneath a 100-foot ceiling was the sign displaying the neural network of the rail system. I said "*Ginkoya*" and offered to buy her coffee but she was off to work, unbuzzed.

At the international ticket counter, the clerk told us we could book as far as Berlin only. There, we'd have to consult the Deutsche Bahn counter on the best way to proceed to London. Within minutes, Sean and I paid first-world prices for three tickets to Germany. For that, we could have bought a trainload of Ukrainian cigarettes.

It was possible, however, that although we were under the same roof, we'd never find Dad again.

"We might have to leave him here," I mumbled.

"We leave no man behind. Even if it was you. Unless the odds were stacked."

"You are a broken person."

Returning to Dad and our baggage, armed with onward bound tickets for a train two days later, we made for a taxi and our hotel.

Dad and Sean were re-living his lost hat episode and I was the only one paying attention when we stood outside our hotel, having relieved ourselves of our cumbersome luggage. Just as I was about to say we should take a right, Dad interrupted his story about how much he missed his hat, and pointed off to the left saying, "What do you say we head off up this way?"

"Sure," Sean said. I just followed, my vote to turn right but a moot sigh.

The wind's chill was up. Wandering off into an Eastern-Slavic language-dominated city where you can't understand a word, whether written or spoken, can be fun. Unlike China or Korea, Polish words at least looked semi-legible to my English trained mind. Looked, not sounded. Though I couldn't read the difference between 'go' and 'stop.' I'd briefly searched 'Polish' and gave up when I realized the sign for the city of Łódź was pronounced *Wootzh*. "Loads" would have been so much simpler.

We crossed the Wisla River and erroneously followed a sign saying "to the outskirts." As business buildings gave way to fortresses of other worlds, the embassies of smaller countries appeared as houses devoid of any threatening razor-sharp bars or guards.

"Hey, a park," Dad said innocently. I tried to stop myself from imagining what architectural marvels we'd be enjoying if only we'd turned right leaving the hotel.

There was an old man with his wares spread across the stony entrance. He had Polish books and records, broken toys, and pins. I stopped to peruse, if only to make the gentleman happy he'd had someone look at his belongings. I found Nazi buckles and a helmet. They smelled of bad luck and few would use them as conversation pieces. I spotted a small brass horseshoe and decided it would bring good fortune to the back of my car. He took the money and said a 14-syllable word in exchange. He had no use of one arm and with his other he fumbled through a rucksack that kept tipping over. Dad scooped it up for him. The old man smiled and withdrew a second brass horseshoe. Responsibility made me dig for another two euros but he refused the money. He just wanted the two small horseshoes to remain together–probably as they'd been for decades. I gave one to Sean.

The park access had slopes, icy stone walkways marked by trees on both the left and the right in equal numbers. Slippery steps wound into a valley of more icepick-required terrain.

After we'd walked two hours, Dad stopped, his breath leaving a cold trail of vapor. "Do you guys know where we are?"

"No," I said, "and neither do you."

"We're in Warsaw." he said proudly.

"That's an assumption."

"How far is the Czech border?" Sean asked, stomping his feet to keep warm.

"Not far if we marched straight, but we could be talking World War II trip-wires and land mines."

Sean's feet stopped stomping.

We retreated up the slope to post-Soviet suburbia. Whatever the unemployment rate in Poland might have been, this was where the jobless lived. Old women beat rugs while young men in undershirts and messy hair stood on balconies pretending not to freeze. The buildings were run down and the streets appeared not maintained since the tanks had rolled through. Grass tried to escape the bleakness by growing in the sidewalk cracks and not within a foot of dirt. Soon we reached the end of the uncivilized part of civilization and found ourselves walking through a forest.

"We have completely walked the outskirts of Warsaw by park. We haven't seen downtown. We haven't seen the Jewish Ghetto. We haven't seen anything significant in a city that was completely leveled in the war–in a country that deserves much respect."

"You enjoying Warsaw, kid?" Dad asked.

"Haven't had this much fun since I started recycling."

This frolic spat us onto a long stretch of abandoned road. At the end was a rusty steel overpass that contained enough metal to build a rusty aircraft carrier. My mood brightened as a tram pulled into view. I felt Warsaw for the first time, a city in its habitat. As shops, bakeries, cell phone marts, and grocery stores began to populate the sidewalks, it was evident we were nearing the cultural heritage of Warsaw proper. Dad picked up the scent of oregano and suggested that a late lunch replace dinner. None of us was predisposed to Italian food but the culinary aspirations of many restaurants chased the Italian trend. So even a Polish restaurant, its name written out in letters unpronounceable to 99 percent of the world, might offer that cherished Italian ambiance and menu.

"I can't read this," Sean said as he canvassed the menu in a little cafe. "Can either of you decipher it?"

"I think Poland outlawed vowels. Seems like a strange thing to revolt against. If anything, go after the letter K or H. They're silent more–"

"Well, spaghetti looks like the third thing down," Dad surmised. "But there's a Z and a C in it."

The waitress, lacking any English except the word 'English,' flipped over Sean's menu, then mine, then Dad's. The other side was in English.

"Decide," struggled Dad. "The waitress really wants to take our order."

"Pizza Margherita and whichever cola got in here after communism."

When it arrived, I raised my cola in tribute to two women who had been able to put up with Dad for many years. "To Mom and Janice."

It was dusk in Warsaw, and we hadn't seen its core as yet. If we dared tell that to a Polish person back home, they'd ask how it could be possible. Indeed, how can you spend nine hours walking through a city of rich culture, diverse heritage, an impossible past, and not see or experience a place that has been twisted and torn by the most powerful losers the world has ever seen?

To such questions, I could reply that Dad got us lost in Lazienki Park for much of the day.

Into the night we walked. We came across the Palace of Culture and Science as fog drifted to the midsection of the tallest building in Poland. Lights sculpted the Stalinesque facade of the city's dominant landmark. Moscow's seven Vysotki towers defined the skyline, and the eighth one was this building. More were planned but never constructed. Strolling there I felt curiously connected to the history of Poland. The busy business district sat opposite us as we made our dogleg approach to the hotel.

Sean had booked us rooms at the Sheraton. He took the single room, leaving me to bunk with Dad. We met in a spacious business center/bar near the lobby. Dad and Sean each found keyboards and sank into their circles. I walked 15 feet to a table and ordered a coffee. I asked the waitress how we would get to Warsaw's downtown core. She said that after exiting the hotel, a right turn would take us there in five minutes. Right. I knew it. Our corrupt and misguided democracy had again taken us in the wrong direction. Still staring at their monitors, they slept-walked through the conversation.

"Sean, I have a confession. I called you 'it' until you were five."

"Yeah... Oh man, Canucks lost."

I turned to my father.

"Dad, if we were built in the image of God, why do you suppose that there's a spot on our backs that we can't scratch?"

"Hmm...it's a PDF file, and it opens...but it's blank. It's like it's there, but it's not."

I like to think the lines of communication between the three of us are always open, but with static. If I couldn't get them to join me in conversation I decided to join their fascination in what appeared on the computer monitor. "Hey, Google— what historic sites should we check out if we ever return to Warsaw? You don't say? Frederick Chopin, my third-favorite composer, grew up in Warsaw? As did Marie Curie, who conducted her important radium experiments here and stuck her hand into violent *radioactivity* to see the X-Rays, coining the term." In my quick research, I also learned the city has 82 parks–Intel I kept to myself.

A 7:30 a.m. departure from a Polish train station requires a wake-up call somewhere shortly after midnight. When you shower in the early morning, you shower in silence. I lazily pulled my toothbrush across my teeth. I took the hotel's shampoo, conditioner, hand lotion, mouthwash, and shower cap. I made sure the caps and lids were on tight (that lesson was a hard one to learn) and stowed them in my toiletry bag. As I walked into the room, Dad had CNN on at twice the legal volume. A bomb had killed a lot of people somewhere and there were plumes across the massive plasma screen. It put the news that Dallas Stars had shut out the New York Islanders in last night's NHL game into perspective. Dad turned the television off. A modicum of silence returned, save for the zippers on the packs and the song of the first Polish bird of the morning.

Our train was a commuter, compartmentalized into six seats with immobile armrests. Dad and Sean had purchased English newspapers. I had a book called *Russia*, authored by a BBC journalist, which Dad had bought me the night before at an English bookstore near the hotel. Three people with their feet up on the opposite seats will take up all six seats. A problem is therefore presented when a German businessman confirms he, too, is sharing the room. The whole dynamic changes again halfway through the trip when said German businessman slumps asleep sideways, his lap partially covered with the newspaper that Dad, slumped sideways towards the German businessman, is no longer awake enough to read.

It was the only event worth noting on the journey and peaked when Dad's paper spilled apart covering the floor and the far side of the room. At least Sean had folded his newspaper before slumping over. I was left feeling stung by the injustice of not being able to sleep on any form of transit.

I alone was staring out the window as the *Berlin-Warsaw Express* shot by Germany's border. Seventy years earlier, armies had marched across the border to unify Europe under the flag of the Third Reich. Germany would eventually be at war with 53 countries. Millions of lives were lost, cities destroyed. Today, the European Union has transformed border crossings into such a mundane act that it didn't even warrant an announcement aboard the PKP Polskie Linie Kolejowe. Battles were still being fought over who gets to join—or, a decade later, leave— the EU but at least the only weapons are politicians' barbs. The historical quirkiness of a German borderline now being a line in the sand still brought a chill to me. And maybe that's a good thing. Coming generations might not get so much as a shiver of conscience.

Berlin's Hauptbahnhof is an architectural feat of such complication and wonder that there should be "awe" in the middle of its name. This wiry-glass filigreed structural achievement was the most modern crossing station in Europe at the time and would make anyone a little curious how it all fits together. The station comprises four floors, with the lower two accommodating the arrival and departure of north- and south-bound trains. The upper two levels are a mall, with shops owning the outer edges of the station's large square. The top floor houses the arriving and departing east- and west-bound trains. The entire station is crisscrossed with a maze of complex yet stunning overpasses and pedestrian catwalks. You're outside and inside at the same time. Stand on the bottom floor and you'll see trains arriving four storeys up.

All of this deserves mention because Dad, Sean, and I stood mouths agape at the sheer beauty of this sophisticated industry. We were mesmerized by a station that thrums with more than 1,000 long-distance, regional and rapid transit trains on 14 platforms. Every day.

We raced to the Deutsche Bahn office and booked three tickets to London, via Paris. The cost made a huge dent in my financial situation and possibly my pension.

"I may have to resort to prostitution," I told Sean.

"I don't want to sound cruel," he said, "but maybe try and sell drugs instead."

We stowed our luggage and talked of how best to spend our six hours in Berlin. I had been there once, Sean had been three times and Dad was a periodic visitor for business reasons. But Sean, Hilary and Dad had met there in 2001 when I was teaching in Russia. Dad had then come to visit me, rendezvousing in

Moscow before travelling to my home in Voronezh. Dad and Sean had shared Berlin and I wasn't party to the excitement they were reliving.

After crossing a huge grassy area outside the station, we joined a sidewalk that guided us east. The Reichstag building, home to the Bundestag–the German parliament–sat across from us in a profoundly dominant German design. Allegedly, a communist had burned it to a shell in 1933. This "forced" the Nazis to suspend much of the constitution in order to weed out communists. Theories abound, conspiratorial in nature, that this was a way to sap power from the German public with their permission. Call it Homeland Security or Nazi Germany's 9/11. The Reichstag building sat in ruins until it was bombed in WWII air raids, at which point it became more rubble and ruin. After reunification, the capital was to be moved back to Berlin, from Bonn, and into this gutted and rebuilt building.

A sign outside the entrance said that if the queue was at this point, it was a 30-minute wait to get in. It was time we didn't have. We contented ourselves with admiring the exterior of the dramatic edifice, armed at the corners with four large towers, each hoisting a large German flag. At the center of the building sat a semi-circle walkable rotunda wrapped in glass.

Sean patted himself down a few times and shook his head.

"I left the camera in the luggage," he said.

"No coffee in the world will make me get it," I replied.

"Film," he said. "We'll have to resort to the 20th century."

The shop beside us was a tourist zone. We made our way through the souvenir cups, spoons, shirts, plates, stuffed animals, key chains, nameplates and hats to the counter, behind which was a woman who looked like she had been over-Berlin-ified for too long. Behind her was a rack of cheap disposable cameras. We bought one. I lined up the parliament building.

"It's blurry," I said.

"Use your good eye…."

I drew back and tried to feel Berlin. It is the most historic city of the 20th century for both good and bad, but mostly bad. I didn't have a sense of place yet and there was little around us but trees. Sean pointed down a path, Dad followed and I voted a silent "yes" because they knew where we were. The short path led to a wide road–a road of such beguiling significance that it put me into the Berlin I had seen before. Unter den Linden, the main street now reunited, leads directly to Brandenburg Gate–a neoclassical monument dating back to the 18th century. It is

Berlin's most famous landmark. The Gate glowed, its columns illuminated in a shade of rich copper.

"The Luftwaffe used to land planes on this road," Sean said. Studying the Second World War had been a hobby of his. "That was during the really difficult period. Like near the very end."

Brandenburg Gate had been the prize taken by the Soviets when the city's spoils had been divided; then, they wrapped the Wall around it–keeping it in their sector and promoting it as a party symbol. John F. Kennedy and Ronald Reagan visited the Gate as presidents. Kennedy gave history "Ich bin ein Berliner" but Reagan trumped him with "Mr. Gorbachev, tear down this wall!"

As we approached Ebertstrasse to cross, a line of off-colored stones ran along a semi-circle that veered off in either direction.

"This is where the Wall was…," Sean said, reverentially. "This crosswalk is history."

Upon approach, it was clear that curbs and steel posts had been put into place so that vehicles could no longer be driven through the Gate. Sean and I exchanged a conspiratorial look. Back in 1997, when we'd visited the city together, we'd strolled through the Cold War symbol, musing about the sidewalk vendors in Pariser Platz before returning to our rental car. Sean drove us down Unter den Linden. Then he did something he isn't known to do: he blew by a policeman, speeding our little Opel Corsa through the narrow columns.

"You just drove through Brandenburg Gate," I'd said at the time. "The last civilian to do that was probably in 1945."

Now, as we walked beneath the 300-year-old monument with steel barriers blocking anything wider than a scooter, Sean and I looked at each other and smiled. There was no sense telling Dad of our recklessness.

"Where are you two trying to get to?" I asked.

"The Hotel Grand," Dad said. "It's a fine sense of Old Europe."

The Hotel Grand was impeccable, a cushion of opulence anointed with sophistication. It was a movie rich with character and characters. Bushy-moustached businessmen in their bespoke Savile Row suits checked their shiny pocket watches, sipped sherry in expensive crystal, and laughed rich, hearty laughs. A woman in a striking dress sat at a cherry-wood corner table wearing a crisp white fedora, perfectly tipped over one eye. Although a mere 30 feet separated us, so did an entire world. She had never jump-started a Ford, had a landlord pry his way in for the rent, or hung off a ladder trying to get free cable for her buddy's play-off party. No, not ever. Plus, I didn't even own a suit.

As was our practice, we were soon out of the hotel's comfort and back on the street, walking. In a city that could keep you occupied for months, our time was measured in hours, and we wanted to make the best of it.

Unter den Linden was crowned with trees. It actually qualifies as a park (oh, the glee) and was initially the hunting grounds for Friedrich Wilhelm who–in the mid-1600s–had Linden trees planted in a vast tract of land that later became Tiergarten. The trees were spindly and young, arching over a few icy walkways. Sean deviated from the path, leading us into forested corners and encroaching foliage.

"This entire park was cut down for firewood," he said. "In the last days of the Second World War, this looked like a stumpy field."

Surprisingly enough, Tiergarten became our own little oasis. Among its patchy snow cover, beneath black leafless branches, I took a long breath. Here, I finally felt a small sense of bliss. Looking down, I saw a dirty 10-euro note encased in mud. In such remoteness, a large bill seemed unlikely. I held the wet note at arm's length to dry.

"Do something good with it," Dad said, as if that isn't something he'd say.

"Why? After all, it came to me. Maybe it's a bad note, meant to be spent on bad things."

"Maybe it's a sign," Sean proposed. "Maybe good fortune is heading your way."

Hauptbahnhof station bustled with people. We'd heard our last Christmas carol the day before, chased out of limelight by the Chinese New Year. A Chinese dragon procession wound through the busy station, its sonic rhythm provided by a large drum. Fifty-odd people were a part of this deafeningly loud, two-hour parade–blocking, crossing, and weaving through crowds of people who were becoming increasingly concerned with catching trains.

I leaned against the railing, again mesmerized by the rhythm of the passing trains and travelling public. A blind man passed a few feet in front of me, tapping a ball at the end of a long, striped cane. Holding onto his arm was another blind man, tapping a ball at the end of a long, striped cane. *I was on camera; I was on some stupid German reality-prank TV show. I had to be.* I was watching a cliché: the blind actually leading the blind.

Our train arrived, pulling into the station with an elegant flair, its sleek design sculpted for speed and long-distance travel. In 14 hours we would arrive in Paris with 90 minutes to travel the less than one mile from Gare de l'Est to Gare du Nord. From there, the *Eurostar* would carry us beneath the English Channel to London in three hours' time. But first we had to see what one could expect when you spent what seemed like the equivalent of an illegal housekeeper's annual salary on a railway ticket.

We boarded Deutsche Bahn's *Berlin-Paris ICE*. Elena was our carriage attendant. She spoke five languages fluently and had the biceps for lifting heavy bags. She showed us to our room and asked us not to touch anything until she returned. I feel certain the room was engineered by a German who had been forced to work late nights, likely causing his wife to seek attention elsewhere and, as a result, turning him to drink. When given the task of fitting three recumbent passengers into a five-foot by 12-foot space, he imaginatively stacked three beds on top of each other, a combination we'd never seen. The top bunk stretched across the bulkhead. Dad and Sean had drawn straws earlier and apparently I had lost. I would be up top, under the roof and over the hallway. I heard them joke there were only two straws.

Elena returned, cautioning us that the room was sophisticated. Touching a button or moving even the smallest of levers could flip beds into the wall or start the *morning process* before the lock-guards were sufficiently in place. Apparently, upon boarding, the only thing to do was sleep. In the morning, with guidance, random parts would fold into seats and a table would reveal itself. Elena bade us goodnight. I used the eight-rung ladder to arrive at my perch, where I stared down at about four feet of floor. Until you pressed a button.

Elena knocked on our door. I sat up into the roof. Unsavory language followed. She had told me that I could step off the train for a while at Hannover; and

Hannover was fast approaching. I thanked her and climbed down the ladder, saying hi as I passed one family member, then another. Hannover turned out to be a half-cigarette city. It was my first time there and that is all the time the stop affords you. One more drag and I would have been left there.

╫╫╫╫╫╫╫╫╫╫╫╫╫╫

"What the hell is that?"

"What?"

"What is that noise?"

"Did you say something?"

"The noise. What is it?"

"I don't know."

The room was black. A sound emanating from the walls sounded as if we were in a farm populated by a variety of electronic birds.

"Maybe it's the wake-up call."

"We didn't ask for a wake-up call."

"Hold on, there's a button here...."

"NO!"

Dad disarmed the electronic farm without injury to any of us.

"It must be an emergency drill," I said, climbing down and heading out the door of our cabin.

When I returned, having found myself alone in the corridor, Dad was in the middle of attempting to raise his bed. His button pushing had led to the discovery of three seats beneath it.

"I don't think...," I said. "Maybe Elena should –"

The bed abruptly took on a life of its own. Springs that had been primed to spring, sprung. Dad's bed shot directly into Sean's, tossing Sean mere inches from the bottom edges of mine. The bed then attempted to cram itself behind the seats, but alas that part of the equation hadn't been part of the equation.

Alerted by a series of red lights at her watch station, Elena entered our cabin. Unhappy we'd violated the conditions, Elena nonetheless threw on a smile. We'd be off her train in an hour. We loitered in the hall as she conducted the symphony of the "morning process"–merging beds, sliding chairs and pulling a five-foot-wide table from thin air. Three breakfasts, designed to appeal to the tastes of most everyone, were grossly unappealing.

Claude Monet's *Gare de Saint-Lazare*, my favorite painting, has graced my wall for the better part of 15 years; it evokes the inspiration of travel, the excitement of embarking on a new adventure, the symbolism of railway culture…and the same blurred vision I have in my right eye. Gare de l'Est sat beneath a canopy not unlike, but not really like, that in Monet's painting.

When you have exactly 90 minutes in Paris and you find yourself at Minute One, there isn't a whole lot of choice. I had a friend who lived 45 minutes away, but even a kiss on her cheek would make me two seconds late for our next departure. We climbed into a cab, expecting a 20-minute transfer to Gare du Nord; in the time it took to click on my seatbelt we reached our destination.

"*Ce n'est pas loins*," I said to the driver. He told us it was three blocks. He didn't want to lose the fare, but he was honest; other drivers would have driven us around the 10th arrondissement for a half hour. This earned him a good tip, likely the equivalent to a half-hour drive around the arrondissement.

"This leaves us over an hour. Anything particular you want to do with it."

"The Moulin Rouge. I'm dressed better this time; they won't kick me out," I said.

"Okay. If you make it to London by tomorrow night, dinner's on me."

"Coffee?" Sean said with a smile. That wasn't a difficult decision. Coffee. Writers. Paris.

We spotted a small restaurant across the street. As scooters zipped by and honking taxis navigated around screeching Renaults and Peugeots, we clumsily lugged our luggage.

The café was quiet, bright, and clean and had worked hard to make its dominant theme *white*. Half the tables sat out of commission, with upended white chairs resting on them. We managed to secure the last available seating area that would allow our bags to sit with us. A skinny man with a thin moustache and a tight gray ponytail appeared. His white nametag said François.

"*Bonjour*," he said. I took the initiative and ordered for all three of us.

"*Bonjour. Trois cafés au lait et deux baguettes avec du buerre.*"

'Okay, dat's tree coffees wit milk and two breads with butter, yes?

I felt as steamed as a cappuccino's hot milk. "Every time I have been to this beautiful country, I have spoken the French I spent seven years learning in a specialized program that stripped me of a social life and wiped away any chances at understanding electronics, sex education, and check endorsements. All I had was French grammar, French literature, French math, French social sciences, and music for third trumpet. And every time I speak your limited language on French soil, the reply I get is always in limited English. And that English, just like yours, is far worse than my French."

"Dare is such a ting as French math? Is it hard?"

"There goes your tip."

"I will be sure to pass dis information on to Mr. President Sarkozy. Maybe he will take Québec back tonight. And maybe I move to Laval and send your girl-friend a free ticket to Chez François…."

I stared him down; he retreated with his hand professionally behind his back, his fingers making a sign that needed no translation.

Our cafés were delivered. Wordlessly. And though mine looked bubblier than the others, I didn't assume it was spit.

"I saw your ticket…*Eurostar*," Francois said as we brushed the breadcrumbs off our laps and prepared to leave. "You will soon leif my countree of lovers within minutes and be in the countree of prudes. England will adore you. They are awkward like you. *Vive le Québec libre!*"

Sean had been deported from the United Kingdom in 2003. It wasn't for spying or treason or getting mixed up with fundamentalist bagpipe players. He had over-stayed his welcome. He and Hilary had ended up in Scotland after long and hard travelling through Europe. Hilary has British lineage, which allowed her to work in England. Sean spent his time making airplanes out of newspapers, not realizing he needed to board one soon. As a result of being forced to leave, now every time he passes through British customs, screens turn red and armed people emerge from secret rooms. Providing Sean has an airline ticket home, as well as proof of accommodation and current employment, the situation resolves itself quickly.

This was the case when the three of us passed through corridors and catwalks that led us beside a tall bulletproof fence that signified we were now officially in Britain—even though we were about to board a train stationed at Gare du Nord.

The *Eurostar* is as comfortable as a bus and the passengers in our wagon were sparse. It was an underwhelming atmosphere for such a momentous occasion. This was our majestic last train–the final leg of a journey that took us 12 years to complete, even though we didn't know we were on it when we began. The train moved, imperceptibly at first. The canopy of Gare du Nord was pulled back. I looked for anything tall and familiar: the Eiffel Tower, the Basilique du Sacré-Coeur, the skyscrapers of La Défense. But the view was apartments and industry until it was countryside. At some point we reached 186 miles (300 kilometers) per hour, but it was not announced as it had been in 1997 when Sean and I had thrilled at the experience. I suppose the novelty had worn off for the train's emcee.

The Channel Tunnel came upon us abruptly. What had been a hazy French afternoon was now absolute darkness.

┆┆┆┆┆┆┆┆┆┆┆┆┆┆

We surfaced onto British soil and were soon pulling into London's St. Pancras station. Transiting by taxi to our hotel at Green Park via Buckingham Palace, we threw our luggage wherever it fit and walked off in search of that special completion dinner.

Westminster and Whitehall road, were buttressed by a crazy number of police vans, each holding 20 barking canine officers. Hordes of chanting protesters marched down Whitehall. At Trafalgar Square, a Muslim rally congregated around the four bronze lion statues while a man armed with a bullhorn spoke of a Free Palestine. He wasn't angry; he was informative. The only people sensing the possibility of riotous acts were those in police uniforms, not these legal provocateurs. These times, this world, is not easily understood when thought to be black and white.

At Covent Garden, it was Dad's turn to practice the persuasive art of eloquence. Despite it being a Saturday evening, despite not having a reservation, surely, he told the restaurant hostess, there must be a cozy place for three travellers returning to where they'd left from. Dad offered his coy smile and an abridged version of our five trips around the world by rail. The hostess listened, manipulating her eyebrows with studied ease to convey she understood but…but, nothing.

Dad pressed on, as is his wont. I could have told her to benefit from what I'd learned in my 40 years of life with him when his mind set on something: resistance is futile. Beneath all that charm is a man with enough fortitude and resilience to get things done, including nabbing a dinner table in one of London's most coveted districts.

Finally realizing that capitulation was her only option, the hostess led us to a table, removed the *reserved* sign and told us to enjoy our meal. It just happened to be the table where we'd sat at the start of our journeys, 12 years earlier.

"Guys..." Dad looked at each of us thoughtfully. "Do you know where you are?"

"I know where we've been," said Sean.

"We've gone around the world by train," I said.

We raised drinks and cheered to ourselves at the end of not only this particular leg from Moscow, but to trains, stations, provodnitsas, food, platforms, taxis, hotels, cities, sites, weather conditions, people, red wines, sprites, spring-activated beds, vodka, carriages, camels, contraband, conversations, friends, borders, pleasant surprises, unpleasant surprises, culture, pizza Margaritas, shaken soft drinks, immigrations, haircuts, new alphabets, ancient dialects, smugglers, travel arrangers, Daria, electronic farms, customs, inedible meals, North Korea in its entirety, horse rides, top bunks, souvenirs, and, of course, parks.

Across the table of silverware and glass, fresh buns and steaming drinks, Dad, Sean, and I looked at one another with that complex affection of fellow train passengers. We grinned, as do millions of travellers each year who move along the tracks and ties that bind countries and ideas together. We smirked in memories about sadness and hilarity, about fears and ambitions that were hallmarks of our own journeys, but also those of others who choose to board a train. We toasted railways for their gift of connections. And we smiled in recognition of the locomotive's forward motion that weaves folklore with history, countrysides with capitals, people with dreams. By any measure—tangible or intangible, personal or impersonal, or in terms of self-sufficiency, self-esteem, self-knowledge, or the math of one's age or miles wandered—we were no longer the three men who boarded *The Trans-Siberian Railway* a dozen years before.

On their final of five journeys, Sean, Brent, Dad in Minsk, Belarus.

EPILOGUE
ABOARD THE ROCKY MOUNTAINEER

This epilogue presumed that the three of us would take the famous Rocky Mountaineer through our own province of British Columbia. But Dad took Sean's son, Riley, instead. What would have been a wonderful two weeks of seeing eagles, tunnels, stunning scenery, and wildlife for all of us wasn't possible. Sean and I couldn't take the time off work. But Dad and Riley took the trip and it amounted to my Dad writing an entire book, *Train Beyond The Mountains*, which came out in April 2023. This book, *Ties That Bind* was completed in June 2023, 26 years after the first train trip in 1997. We three men grew up in different ways but being bound to these trips kept us in what otherwise may be less frequent contact and a broader family. However, due to Janice's jobs, she and Dad have lived in the Bahamas, Australia, Scotland, and Germany. And I went back to teaching in 2011 and taught in China, Iraq, and Russia for a few years. We have been scattered across the globe. As this book comes to a close, we are all living in British Columbia, some distances apart, but never have the ties that bind us come undone. Travelling has built us into different people from the same family. And George, George is still around, ready to deliver lasagna, top up a glass, and say some prophetic line of encouragement.

Acknowledgments

Many people enabled our journeys: Russia to China in 1997, Canada in 2000, the USA in 2003, North Korea in 2006, and Moscow to London in 2009. Support and encouragement from home was imperative; base-camp strategy sessions with friends and family alike strengthened the dreams and made them a reality. Once aloft, we were at the mercy of our meager arrangements but the people involved at each location were a crucial factor in our enjoyment and understanding of the areas we travelled through. And since our first trip began when the Internet was in its infancy, more people did more things to make it possible. I wish to thank those people behind the names in the book. They gave the story strength and offered it a life that could not have existed without them.

I extend my appreciation to the following for the viscosity they added to the preparation, research, direction, proofreading, edits, and/or friendships throughout the project: Richard Liew, Tezhlemsa Ravdandorj, Vera Resnikova, Nicholas Bonner and Simon Cockerell (Koryo Tours), Christine Keon Searsley, Pat Kelly, Peter Armstrong, Debbie Quayle, Brian Antonson, Laurie Santangelo, Gordon Stewart, Daria Kozlova, Chris Bright, Christopher Hitchens and Sam Harris, Ron Shaw, David Anthony Power, MrsC, Mathew Livingstone, Arijana Dojcinov, Anisa Salmi and the Lilleagro Girl, Jack Sheremetoff, Alison Roche (that red-headed girl from kindergarten), Marina Nestrugina, Ken Williams, Bruce Muirhead, Wendy Antonson (1948—2017) mother to Sean and me, Rick Antonson, Sean Antonson, and editors John Eerkes-Madrona (J-E-M) (1950—2015), Sheliza Mitha, Martha Perkins who smoothed the ride for readers with their edits, and Daniel Sanderson for his excellence and supreme ability to decern write from right now.

ABOUT THE AUTHOR

As a traveller and teacher, Brent Antonson spent years living abroad including extended stints teaching English at universities and schools in Russia and Iraq and China. He's travelled widely including driving escapades in all 50 American states. His first book *Of Russia; A Year Inside* was published in 2008. He's written lyrics to several songs that have been recorded and released. One of his movie scripts awaits production. Brent stays tethered to the region of Vancouver, Canada (49.15'N 123.6'W) where he was raised.

An Offer from the Author
Brent's Master Class

This book took 26 years to write. That included nine years of travel, three editors, and a fantastic publisher. But it wasn't easy and through this Master Class, we will explore he pitfalls and triumphs of writing, specifically to get a published book out of it. If you have a story to tell, this class will help you go from idea to publishing it, from starting the story to crafting the ending. With my experience and planksip's assistance through this birthing process, we will explore writing from your idealistic beginning to a final published book.

planksip.me/brent

Printed in the USA
CPSIA information can be obtained
at www.ICGtesting.com
LVHW080249011223
765386LV00012B/288